WASHINGTON ON FOOT

★ ★ ★ ★

TWENTY-FOUR WALKING TOURS AND

MAPS OF WASHINGTON, DC

Edited by William J. Bonstra
and Judith Meany

Published in association with
National Capital Area Chapter
American Planning Association

Smithsonian Books
Washington, DC

Edited by William J. Bonstra and Judith Meany
New images for the sixth edition provided by José Castellanos and
Coleman McLaurin
Previous edition edited by John J. Protopappas

Published by Smithsonian Books
Director: Carolyn Gleason
Senior Editor: Jaime Schwender
Editor: Julie Huggins

Copy Edited by Joanne Reams

This book may be purchased for educational, business, or sales
promotional use. For information, please write: Special Markets
Department, Smithsonian Books, PO Box 37012, MRC 513, Washington,
DC 20013

Library of Congress Cataloging-in-Publication Data

Names: Bonstra, William J., editor. | Meany, Judith, editor. | American
    Planning Association. National Capital Area Chapter.
Title: Washington on foot : twenty-four walking tours and maps of
    Washington, DC / edited by William J. Bonstra and Judith Meany.
Other titles: Twenty-four walking tours and maps of Washington, DC
Description: Sixth edition. | Washington, DC : Smithsonian Books,
    [2023] | "Published in association with National Capital Area Chapter,
    American Planning Association."
Identifiers: LCCN 2023031670 (print) | LCCN 2023031671 (ebook) |
    ISBN 9781588347367 (trade paperback) | ISBN 9781588347381 (ebk)
Subjects: LCSH: Washington (D.C.)—Tours. | Walking—Washington
    (D.C.)—Guidebooks.
Classification: LCC F192.3 .W335 2023 (print) | LCC F192.3 (ebook) |
    DDC 910.9753—dc23/eng/20230717
LC record available at https://lccn.loc.gov/2023031670
LC ebook record available at https://lccn.loc.gov/2023031671

Printed in the United States of America, not at government expense
28 27 26 25 24   1 2 3 4 5

For permission to reproduce any of the maps and illustrations,
correspond directly with the volume editors. Smithsonian Books does
not retain reproduction rights for these illustrations individually or
maintain a file of addresses for illustration purposes.

Contents

Tours

About *Washington on Foot*

William J. Bonstra and Judith Meany

There are many ways to see cities, but for anyone desiring a sense of the history and the character of an urban place, the city is best seen on foot. A mosaic on a garden wall, the framed view of a church steeple from a narrow street, or the gleam of stained glass above a doorway—these are just a few of the visual rewards of a walking tour.

Washington on Foot is a guide to the neighborhoods as well as the monuments of the nation's capital. Twenty-four walking tours will steer you through the preserved Colonial and Federal quarters, the vital commercial districts, the distinguished residential neighborhoods, and the revitalized urban-renewal areas, as well as the renowned memorials, public buildings, and museums of Washington.

Originally published in 1976 for the National Planning Conference and updated periodically, *Washington on Foot* is used by thousands of visitors and residents interested in a close-up look at the historical, cultural, and architectural aspects of the capital. Over the past forty years, more than two dozen volunteers, including urban planners, architectural historians, and other urban professionals, have contributed to this publication; names of original authors and current updaters are provided at the introduction to each tour. More information about contributors can be found on page 255.

Washington on Foot is intended to serve the public as a guide to many of the significant features of the District of Columbia. The tours are designed for use by pedestrians, bicyclists, and those choosing any number of other personal transportation options.

The Coeditors

William J. Bonstra, FAIA, LEED AP, is an architect living in the Logan Circle Historic District of Washington, DC, since 1982. He is the founder of Bonstra | Haresign Architects, a nationally recognized architecture firm where he leads the design and implementation of complex, historic, mixed-use residential and commercial projects with unique zoning and historic preservation requirements. He and his work have been recognized with over one hundred national and regional awards for contemporary design, historic renovation, and adaptive use of urban projects. He continues his academic pursuits through his teaching, lecturing, writing, and design jury participation at the University of Maryland (his alma mater), the Catholic University of America, the George Washington University, Morgan State University, and other nationally recognized architecture schools. He is a member and active participant of the

Washington, DC, chapters of the American Institute of Architects, the Urban Land Institute, and the DC Building Industry Association. He is a member of the Cosmos Club in Washington, DC.

Judith Meany, PhD, FAICP, retired in 2018 as professor of practice in the School of Architecture and Planning at the Catholic University of America, where she created and directed the master of architecture graduate program with a real estate development concentration. She continues to advise real estate developers and financial institutions, and she consults on land acquisition and disposition, environmental review, highest- and best-use development, infrastructure requirements, and financing. She received her master's degree in city and regional planning from the Catholic University of America and her doctorate from the University of Maryland. She is a member of the Washington, DC, chapters of the Urban Land Institute and the American Planning Association.

Dedication

This edition of *Washington on Foot* is dedicated to the tireless efforts of John J. Protopappas. John first assumed editorship of *Washington on Foot* in 1980. He has been a guest lecturer on urban planning at the Catholic University of America and the University of Maryland. He has written for professional journals and was coeditor of the 1980, 1992, 2004, and 2012 editions of *Washington on Foot*. He is also a decorated veteran of the Vietnam conflict. John received a bachelor's degree from Niagara University and a master's degree from the Catholic University of America.

About the NCAC-APA

The National Capital Area Chapter (NCAC) of the American Planning Association (APA) was the original sponsor of *Washington on Foot*. APA is the major organization in the country representing the interests of urban planning and planners.

Washington, DC

Washington, DC, has matured as a major national and international city. It is a city of considerable beauty and elegance. During its 230 years of history, it has developed into a center of international diplomacy and influence. Its numerous monuments, public buildings, museums, and cultural galleries are major tourist attractions. The White House, the Capitol, the Lincoln and Jefferson Memorials, and the Washington Monument are the nation's unique symbols of American democracy.

Washington is no longer thought of as a small town, even though its ten-mile square size and more than 712,000 residents do not place it among those cities that are mentioned when one refers to large cities in the United States.

The city's sphere of influence extends far beyond its geographic size and population. Washington is a capital city, a dynamic and vibrant metropolis that retains its small-town charm with unique neighborhoods. The human scale of its buildings adds to the city's ambience.

Washington is the center and driving force of a sophisticated metropolitan region of over 5.7 million people in 2022, according to the Metropolitan Washington Council of Governments (WCOG). Jobs will continue to increase from a current level of more than 700,000. Minority groups are well represented in Washington. Recent information from WCOG indicates that African Americans still constitute a majority of the city's population, though this is declining. During the decades of the 1990s to the present, the size of the Latino and Asian populations has been steadily increasing in the city and throughout the Washington region. At the same time, Washington has experienced significant changes in total population, in the makeup of its households, and in its labor force and job base. The most dramatic shifts have occurred in the city's population and household constituency, reflecting changing social patterns. Prior to the 1970s, the city's households had been predominantly families with children. But the number of children in the city has plummeted, as witnessed by the drop in school enrollments, and newer households are largely made up of singles or unrelated individuals.

Many of the new residents have relatively comfortable incomes, which permit them to enjoy the city's cultural amenities and restaurants and to purchase homes. These households have spurred much of the new residential construction and rehabilitation you will see as you visit the neighborhoods on your walking tours. These households have also fueled the escalation in the price of housing in the city.

The employment base of the city has changed from one consisting predominantly of federal government jobs to one made up largely of jobs in the private sector. Most of these jobs are in the service industry, a term generally associated with the finance, legal, health, real estate, and managerial professions. Increasingly, although the typical Washington worker is not employed by the federal government, he or she is likely to be employed by one of the businesses linked to the federal government. Also living in Washington are the thousands of journalists, lobbyists, and employees of the many trade associations headquartered in the city. The combination of residents, tourists, conventioneers, and workers gives the city high levels of daytime activity and a moderately busy nightlife at theaters, movies, hotels, nightclubs, bookstores, and restaurants.

Washington now rivals other cities famous for their entertainment and cultural offerings. This change can be partly attributed to the opening of the John F. Kennedy Center for the Performing Arts in 1971. The Kennedy Center, with its imposing architectural styling, attracts performers and productions from all over the world. It has not only expanded the cultural offerings available in the city but also led to an increase in neighborhood and regional cultural institutions. The increasing number of theaters along 14th and 7th Streets NW, the refurbished Ford's Theater on 10th Street NW, the National Theater and the restored Warner Theatre on Pennsylvania Avenue NW, and the Arena Stage in the southwest section of the city are important complements to the Kennedy Center. In fact, the city in 1990 established an arts zoning overlay along 14th and U Streets with density incentives to retain and attract additional theaters, art galleries, and other related functions to these areas. This action has resulted in attracting many bookstores, theaters, art galleries, and other arts-related functions to the areas. Art, entertainment, and cultural activities are also being developed throughout the city's downtown, particularly along 7th and E Streets.

The Smithsonian Institution's contribution to Washington's cultural resources as well as those of the nation is unsurpassed. It has one of the most impressive (and still expanding) arrays of museums and galleries in the world, a first-rate education program, and a distinguished performing arts program, all available to the public for free or for a modest fee. The core of the Smithsonian Institution is formed by the well-known museums centered on the Mall. The Mall is a large, open space linking the Capitol and the Lincoln Memorial that was designated in the earlier plans for the city but not formally landscaped until the 1930s. It is a well-used passive and active recreation area, popular with tourists and locals during the spring and summer and a showplace for museums, monuments, and memorials. And although debates are underway about the future of the Mall and the number of memorials that should be permitted, more museums and memorials are planned.

Among the most notable of the Smithsonian's museums are the Arthur M. Sackler Gallery of Asian Art and the National Museum of African Art. Both are built partially underground and offer an exceptional collection of art treasures to the public. In 2016, President Barack Obama led the opening ceremony of the National Museum of African American History and Culture with its permanent home on the National Mall. The very popular National Air and Space Museum, the National Museum of Natural History, the National Museum of American History, the Hirshhorn Museum and Sculpture Garden, and the architecturally striking National Museum of the American Indian attract millions of visitors each year from the region and throughout the nation. Near the White House sits the Renwick Gallery, and slightly more to the north are the National Portrait Gallery and the Smithsonian American Art Museum, housed in the Donald W. Reynolds Center for American Art and Portraiture. In December 2003, the Smithsonian opened the National Air and Space Museum's Steven F. Udvar-Hazy Center in Northern Virginia to display and preserve its collection of historic aviation and space artifacts. The 170-acre facility is near Dulles International Airport, about twenty-five miles from the District of Columbia. The building contains over 750,000 square feet of exhibition, conservation, restoration, theater, restaurant, and classroom space. Visitors can walk among the engines, rockets, satellites, helicopters, airliners, and other flying machines on the floor or view hanging aircraft from elevated walkways, in addition to watching restoration take place. The Steven F. Udvar-Hazy Center is open from 10:00 a.m. to 5:30 p.m. every day except December 25. Admission is free. More information can be found at www.nasm.si.edu/udvarhazy.

Visitors should not miss the National Gallery of Art, with its impressive collection of European and American paintings, sculptures, and exhibitions. You should also visit the Historical Society of Washington, DC, at Mount Vernon Square. It can be easily accessed via Metrorail or Metrobus. The museum offers various exhibitions concerning the history of the capital city and its many neighborhoods and profiling prominent individuals who have resided in the city.

Year round, more than 25 million tourists and conventioneers visit the other monuments and memorials scattered throughout the city. These visitors make a substantial contribution to the economic vitality of the city.

Washington is well endowed with public parks and memorials, many surrounded by large expanses of open space. Rock Creek Park—which includes the National Zoological Park, hiking and bicycling trails, the Carter Barron Amphitheater, and many picnic and playground sites—extends from the city's northwest boundary with Maryland into the central business area anchored at the Potomac River by the Kennedy Center. In the very heart of the Federal area are parks providing tennis courts, open spaces, walking areas, skating ponds, and other attractions. In recent years the District of Columbia has upgraded and redeveloped many of its neighborhood parks, including new buildings offering recreational activities.

Washington has been subject to almost continual planning since its inception. Untold numbers of planners, architects, developers, and other visionaries have influenced the cityscape. Three of the most prominent were L'Enfant, Downing, and the McMillan Commission.

The core of Washington was largely developed as envisioned by Pierre Charles L'Enfant in his 1791 plan for the city, as modified by the McMillan Commission. L'Enfant focused on the siting of the major federal buildings and other symbols of the national government. His plan established the formal pattern of streets, avenues, squares, and circles that we see in the city today.

A second major plan, prepared in 1851 by Andrew Jackson Downing, was limited to the Mall area. It called for a natural landscape treatment of the Mall, deviating from the formalism of L'Enfant's plan. A third plan, which reinforced and extended L'Enfant's conception, was prepared by the McMillan

Commission in 1902. This plan advanced a bold concept for development of the monumental core and formal federal areas of the city.

A casual walk along the Mall allows you to observe remnants of all of these earlier planning efforts. Exhibits of the city's history were installed throughout the city to celebrate the bicentennial of its founding (1791–1991). Many of these are on permanent display at the National Building Museum, and the DC History Center.

The original city planned by L'Enfant extended between the Potomac and Anacostia Rivers, south of Florida Avenue. This area encompasses the downtown area as well as some of the city's most desirable neighborhoods. Downtown contains department stores, hundreds of specialty shops and boutiques, restaurants, bars, theaters—and more than 80 million square feet of private and public office space. A major entertainment complex, containing a mix of housing, retail, and office space, is at the Gallery Place Metrorail station. Business services, associations, and many of the city's innumerable lawyers and consultants occupy most of the private office buildings in the downtown area. Washington's low skyline, most noticeable in the downtown area, resulted from the congressionally mandated 1910 Height of Buildings Act, which limits the maximum height to 90–130 feet, depending upon location, street width, and zoning district. Only the north side of Pennsylvania Avenue, between 10th and 15th Streets NW, exceeds those limits, with some buildings reaching a height of 160 feet, owing to a special provision in the zoning regulations.

For over 150 years, downtown Washington was the commercial and social center of the city and the surrounding region. Although this role was challenged somewhat from the 1950s to the 1970s as suburban retail centers emerged, downtown still offers the greatest variety of goods and services to be found anywhere in the Washington metropolitan area. During the past three decades, plans and programs were initiated to revitalize downtown. Some were very successful while others languished. Much of the development evident in downtown today resulted from ideas formed during the last thirty years. Metrorail, the "old" and "new" convention centers, and the refurbished Pennsylvania Avenue and Union Station are notable examples.

The Washington Metrorail system ("Metro") opened in 1976. Together, Metrorail and Metrobus serve a population of approximately 4 million within a 1,500-square-mile jurisdiction. It was designed by Harry Weese and Associates and has won a number of architecture, design, and construction awards. The 128-mile system was completed in 2001 (later expanded) and includes ninety-eight stations; forty stations are in Washington, DC. The Metro system has stimulated substantial changes in land use and mobility patterns throughout the metropolitan area. Some estimates indicate that at least $25 billion in new development has occurred close to Metrorail stations. You will see evidence of this as you visit various neighborhoods in this publication. In addition, the combination of Metrorail and Metrobus trips has removed over four hundred thousand cars from the local road system.

The "old" Washington Convention Center, approximately ten acres, dramatically affected its immediate environs as well as the convention business in the city. Today, CityCenter occupies this area, with office and residential buildings along with luxury retail environments attracting shoppers from all over the world. Within the immediate vicinity of CityCenter and the Washington Convention Center, large, convention-type hotels—the Ramada Renaissance, the Hyatt Regency, and the Crowne Plaza—were built. The city's Chinatown is located immediately to the east of the center, and several new restaurants, bars, and variety stores have opened in this area over the last few years. One of the longest Chinese arches in the United States was built along H Street NW, in the heart of Chinatown, in 1986.

Under the leadership of the now-defunct Pennsylvania Avenue Development Corporation, Pennsylvania Avenue underwent a major upgrading and has evolved into a showplace for the city. Several new office buildings with street-level retail shops are outstanding examples, including the Ronald Reagan Building and International Trade Center, the largest government building in the city, and a refurbished John Wilson Municipal Building, the home of the mayor and Council of the District of Columbia. The new office structures, with their attractive retail components, along with residential buildings, landscaped public spaces, and urban parks, have given this thoroughfare the distinction of being the "Main Street" of the United States. The redevelopment of Pennsylvania Avenue will be completed under the auspices of the National Capital Planning Commission (NCPC). NCPC is the central planning agency for the federal government in the national capital region. It has been responsible for coordination of all federal planning activities in the region since 1952. Before the passage of the Home Rule Act in 1973, NCPC also served as the local planning agency for the District of Columbia. The city and its residents are justifiably proud of this achievement. Pennsylvania Avenue is now a major tourist attraction and should be on any list of "must-see" areas in Washington, DC.

Union Station, designed by Daniel Burnham, was built as a train station in 1908. It underwent a complete renovation in 1980 and has become a dazzling transportation, shopping, and restaurant site. The vaulted building contains over two hundred thousand square feet of retail, theater, restaurant, and entertainment space and one hundred thousand square feet of office space. It is a well-established multimodal transfer point for trips within the northeastern and southeastern corridors as a hub for Amtrak, the Maryland Commuter Rail system, and the Virginia Railway Express. A Metro station and several local bus routes serve the facility. Interstate bus service is available within a five-minute walk to the north of the station.

During your visit to Union Station, take time to view the surrounding area, which has been noticeably influenced by the revitalization of the station itself. You should note particularly the Postal Square project to the west of the station, which has added the Smithsonian's National Postal Museum and a substantial amount of retail and office space to the area. The Thurgood Marshall Federal Courts Building to the east is significant because of its architectural style, which reinterprets that of Union Station. Several buildings occupied by the United States Senate are also visible from the main entrance to Union Station on Massachusetts Avenue. Several office buildings and new and renovated hotels of all types have been built in the area as well.

From August to May, Washington's resident population includes more than a hundred thousand students who attend the city's twenty universities and specialty schools. The city has six major universities: George Washington University, Georgetown University, American University, the Catholic University of America, Howard University, and the University of the District of Columbia. Each campus has its own ambience, ranging from the Gothic architecture of several buildings on the campuses of Georgetown and Catholic Universities, to the city campus flair of Howard and George Washington Universities, to the highly contemporary facade of the University of the District of Columbia.

Washington's two great cathedrals are the Washington National Cathedral, in the northwest section of the city, with magnificent landscaping and city vistas, and the National Shrine of the Immaculate Conception on the campus of the Catholic University of America in the northeast. Their architecture and surroundings remain a vibrant part of the life of the entire region.

Outside the boundaries of the original city are more than fifty neighborhoods, largely developed during the nineteenth and twentieth centuries. A few of the more notable ones are described in this book. Others are significant because of their historic locations along discontinued streetcar routes or the prominent persons who resided within their boundaries. A visit to any one of these areas will leave you with indelible images of a strong and lively neighborhood.

Many of Washington's neighborhoods are undergoing substantial housing redevelopment and other changes. However, some remain as they have been for generations. Most significant in all of these neighborhoods are the tree-lined streets, the varied architectural styles, and the diversity of the residential communities. Overall, contemporary buildings coexist with and strengthen historic contexts.

Washington has one of the country's most ambitious tree-planting programs. It was initiated in 1815, one year after the burning of the US Capitol. Many of the streets in the neighborhoods you will visit have trees that are more than 150 years old. Spend some time observing the interesting tree canopies for which Washington neighborhoods are famous. In 2002 the city received a $50 million grant from a private foundation for tree preservation.

Two prominent organizations that have had a great influence on the scale and urban design of many of the city's neighborhoods are the Commission of Fine Arts and the city's Historic Preservation Review Board (HPRB) and its predecessor organization, the Joint Committee on Landmarks. The Commission of Fine Arts was created in 1910 to carry forward the concepts of the McMillan Commission. The HPRB is a more contemporary preservation organization, charged with identifying and protecting historic resources in Washington and advising the city on preservation programs. More than five hundred buildings, sites, and streets have been designated as historic landmarks. In addition, several of the neighborhoods you will visit are within one of the designated neighborhood historic districts in the city. These include Capitol Hill, LeDroit Park, Old Anacostia, Georgetown, Kalorama, Dupont Circle, Logan Circle and Greater Fourteenth Street, and Mount Pleasant.

Before ending your tour of Washington, take time to attend one of the many free classical and pop concerts or seek out the city's vigorous network of neighborhood art museums and galleries or sample its chic restaurants and visit its varied neighborhood theaters. Whatever you decide to do while visiting the city and metropolitan area, enjoy yourself. The following pages we hope will help you in your discovery of Washington, DC, as a memorable American experience.

How to Use This Guide

Select any of the twenty-four tours listed here by the name of the area covered. For each, you'll find the walking distance and the time it takes to walk the route (not including visits to museums and historic houses). Public transit information to the starting point is provided (courtesy of the Washington Metropolitan Area Transit Authority). A map shows the route and locates the major sights by numbers keyed to the descriptive text. Sketches scattered throughout the book highlight some important sights. Please note that for several of the sites, the guide provides specific opening and tour times. These details may change over time; please confirm this information when planning your visit.

Taking the Right Bus

The Washington Metropolitan Area Transit Authority (Metro) Information Service will tell you which Metrobus to take to any destination. Call (202) 637-7000 to obtain a bus timetable. This information is also available at Metrorail station kiosks and at www.wmata.com. Fares are paid through Smartrip cards.

Route numbers and letters accompanying each tour in this guide refer to bus services available weekdays. These routes go to the beginning point of each tour or pass near it.

Using the Metro

The Metro is a pleasant and quick way to travel to and from the tour areas in the guide, particularly those in central Washington. Six Metro lines serve the Washington area. The Red Line provides service between Glenmont, Maryland, and Shady Grove, Maryland, passing through downtown Washington. The Blue Line links Franconia-Springfield in Virginia and the Downtown Largo station in Prince George's County, Maryland. The Yellow Line provides service from Greenbelt, Maryland, to Huntington Station in Fairfax County, Virginia. Both the Blue and Yellow lines have stops at Ronald Reagan Washington National Airport (DCA) and can be used for transport from there. The Orange Line's terminals are at Vienna/Fairfax-GMU in Virginia and at New Carrollton, Maryland. The Silver Line runs from Ashburn, Virginia, to downtown Largo. It has a stop at Dulles International Airport (IAD). The Blue, Orange, and Silver Lines share tracks between Rosslyn and Stadium-Armory. The Green Line extends from Branch Avenue to Greenbelt; both segments are in Prince George's County. The Metro spans 103 miles, serving the outlying suburbs. Be sure to check the maps in each Metrorail station and car for information on extensions and new stations.

Three of the lines intersect at the Metro Center station in downtown Washington, facilitating transfers between the Red Line (upper level) and the Blue, Orange, and Silver Lines (lower level). The Red, Yellow, and Green Lines intersect at Gallery Place. The Yellow and Green Lines also intersect with the Blue, Orange, and Silver Lines at L'Enfant Plaza.

The name of the Metro station and the color of the line serving the beginning point of each walking tour are indicated in this guide. The "M" symbol on most tour maps identifies the locations of the station entrances. Hours of operation can be found on the WMATA website.

The two-tier fare system is based on time and distance traveled. Fares during rush hours are typically higher than fares during nonrush hours. Rush hour fares are typically in effect on weekdays in the morning from 5:00 a.m. to 9:30 a.m. and in the afternoon/evening from 3:00 p.m. to 7:00 p.m. Rush hour fares typically do not apply on federal holidays. Smartrip cards can be bought in any value online or in the Metro station at card machines and are good until used. Exit gates automatically deduct the fare and display the remaining value, if any, on the screen. Money can be added to the Smartrip card in any station or online. Check the charts in each station for the exact fare between stations on your route. The station attendant at the kiosk of each station can answer any questions. For more information visit www.wmata.com

On Not Getting Lost on Washington Streets

The city's quadrants (NW, SW, NE, SE) must be explained. The north–south axis through the Capitol, represented by North and South Capitol Streets, divides the eastern and western sections of the city. The east–west axis through the Capitol, represented by East Capitol Street and the center line of the Mall, separates the northern and southern sections. All streets within each of the quadrants bear the quadrant designation, and the quadrant describes its direction on the compass from the Capitol.

Street names generally ascend in alphabetical or numerical order; names of states are used for the diagonal avenues. Measuring north or south from the center line of the Mall, the parallel streets are designated by letters (A, B, C, and so on). Two-syllable names follow the letters from A to about W (such as Adams, Bryant, Channing). Beyond that, three-syllable names continue the pattern from A to about W (Albemarle, Brandywine, Chesapeake). Beyond that point, along the north–south line approximating 16th Street, the streets are named after trees and flowers, also in alphabetical order (Aspen, Butternut, Cedar). Running east and west from the line representing North and South Capitol Streets, the streets are numbered 1st, 2nd, 3rd, and 4th to somewhere in the 50s.

Numbering of addresses is also orderly. For example, between 1st Street and 2nd Street (on lettered and named streets), the house numbers are between 100 and 199; between 40th Street and 41st Street, the house numbers are between 4000 and 4099. To illustrate, nine blocks from A Street would be K Street: hence, 1000 15th Street would be the intersection of K and 15th Streets.

L'Enfant's City

Capitol Hill—West

(Capitol complex; residential restoration area)

Paul Douglass, updated by Christopher J. Howard

Distance: 2 ¾ miles
Time: 1 ¼ hours
Bus: 32, 36, 96, D6, X8, and the DC Circulator
Metro: Union Station (Red Line)

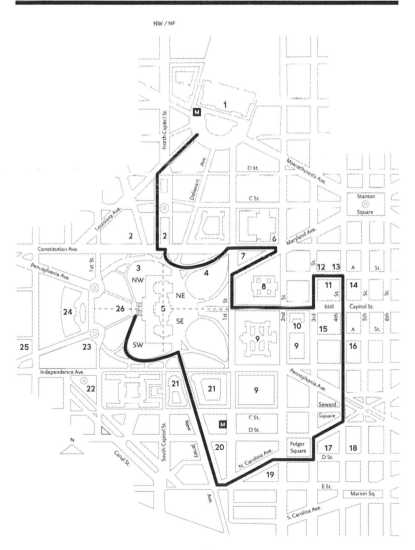

■ **1** Looking at a map of Washington, DC, you will see the result of a planned design by Pierre Charles L'Enfant, which consists of an overlapping matrix of gridded streets, diagonal boulevards, and squares at the primary intersections. While the diagonal boulevards are askew, the buildings behave according to the orthogonal grid, with the exception of one prominent monumental building that is rotated at an angle within the city's core. It is here, at this unique building in Union Station, that the tour begins. Union Station is oriented to face the US Capitol building as a monumental gateway into the city. At the time of its inception, in 1908, most people would have entered the city through the triumphal arches, then would have radiated out into the city by a multi-pronged street network. Architect Daniel H. Burnham designed **Union Station** to ensure that the two then-separate train terminals would be consolidated into one station. The design itself speaks to the aspiration of a young, industrious country making its presence known on the world stage. Through a uniquely American version of classical architecture, the building alludes to ancient civilizations past, with reference to Roman basilicas, baths, and triumphal arches.

More particular aspects of the design include an iconographic stage set of allegorical statues on the front facade, perched on top of pedestalled projecting columns and representing "The Progress of Railroading." From far left to the right: Prometheus for fire, Thales for electricity, Themis for Justice, Apollo for Inspiration, Ceres for agriculture, and Archimedes for Mechanics. Beyond the building and in front of it sits a dynamic monumental fountain, sculpted in 1912 by Lorado Taft, representing the discovery of America by Europeans in the form of Christopher Columbus.

Today, the Union Station complex serves as a busy transportation hub, offering citywide, suburban, and interstate train services and access to local tour buses. It also includes a multilevel shopping center with specialty retail shops, an elongated food court, and many well-established restaurants and bars. Just to the east of Union Station is the new Thurgood Marshall Federal Courts building. To the North of Union Station is a new office building complex. Interstate bus service is available two blocks to the north via the Greyhound

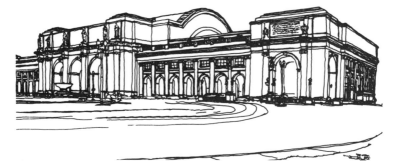

Union Station

and Peter Pan bus services. Immediately to the west of Union Station (2 Massachusetts Avenue NW) sits the former City Post Office Building, also designed by architect D. H. Burnham and completed in 1914. The building now houses the National Postal Museum, which features a stamp shop for serious philatelists, and traces the history of the US Postal Service. The National Postal Museum is open 10:30 a.m.–5:30 p.m. every day except December 25. Admission is free. More information can be found at www.postalmuseum.si.edu or by calling 202-633-5555.

■ **2** This Capitol Hill **park** is one of the favorites of many congressional aides, particularly the younger set, who brown-bag their lunches. If you are here in the spring and summer you can see why. The many red oak trees and a sparkling water fountain are irresistible. To the west juts a concrete **monolith honoring Sen. Robert A. Taft** of Ohio. Designed by Douglass W. Orr in 1959, this memorial houses twenty-seven bells that chime every quarter-hour.

■ **3** The **Capitol Grotto** (1879) is one of the best features of the Capitol grounds, designed by landscape architect Frederick Law Olmsted and originally con ceived to tap fresh spring water.

■ **4** Also designed by Frederick Law Olmsted, the **Trolley Waiting Station** (about 1876) was originally served by horse-drawn trolley cars. Another waiting station is located at the southeast corner of the US Capitol.

■ **5** Asked by President George Washington to design a plan for the federal city, Maj. Pierre Charles L'Enfant, French engineer and architect, chose to position the **US Capitol** in one of two significant locations in the future city (the other was reserved for the president's house). Jenkins Hill, in L'Enfant's estimate, was like "a pedestal waiting for a monument." President Washington laid the cornerstone for the Capitol in 1793. After being partly destroyed by British troops in 1814, the Capitol was restored with the addition of a wooden dome. In 1857, two wings were added (providing expanded space for the Senate and the House of Representatives), and an iron dome replaced the wooden one in 1865. Atop the dome stands the Statue of Freedom. According to its sculptor, Thomas Crawford, the statue represents "Armed Liberty," her right hand grasping a sheathed sword while the other holds the wreath and shield. The classical aesthetic of the Capitol was chosen very intentionally by George Washington and Thomas Jefferson, among others, to be the appropriate language to represent the ideals of our democracy. The classical forms and details seen in the columns are part of a language that is able to connect with the past, be enduring and timeless, offer nobility, and resonate with the notion of individuals being part of a larger whole. The complex yet simple repose of the design succeeds at its intention on many grounds, but is most prominently expressed by the dome. The dome was intended to be the first of its kind in the new nation and to act, as it does today, as the head of the composition and the axis mundi of the city and the nation.

The Capitol is open to the public for guided tours only. Free tour tickets must be obtained beginning at 8:50 a.m. at the Capitol Guide Service kiosk located along the curving sidewalk near 1st Street SW and Independence Avenue. The Capitol Visitor Center is open 8:30 a.m.–4:30 p.m., Monday through Saturday, except Thanksgiving, December 25, New Year's Day, and Inauguration Day. Tours are conducted 8:50 a.m.–3:20 p.m., Monday through Saturday. More information can be found at www.visitthecapitol.gov or by calling 202-226-8000.

US Capitol

■ **6** The **Sewall-Belmont House**, at 144 Constitution Avenue NE, was saved from demolition in 1974 by a special act of Congress and was subsequently entered into the National Register of Historic Places. Otherwise, the site would have been used for the Senate office building that now abuts the house. In 1800 Robert Sewall, descended from an illustrious Maryland family, built this three-story townhouse, which is characteristic of the Federal period in style. His Capitol Hill home was leased to Albert Gallatin, secretary of the treasury (1801–13). In 1929 the National Women's Party purchased the house from Sen. Porter Dale. Some of the unusual furnishings include desks once owned by Henry Clay and Susan B. Anthony. The Sewall-Belmont House and Museum is open noon–5:30 p.m., Wednesday through Sunday except Thanksgiving, December 25, and New Year's Day. Admission is free. More information can be found at www.sewallbelmont.org or by calling 202-546-1210.

■ **7** The **Hiram W. Johnson House** at 122 Maryland Avenue NE is also representative of the Federal period and is listed in the National Register of Historic Places.

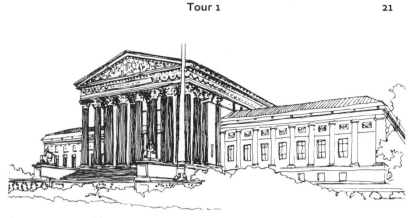

Supreme Court Building

■ **8** Evocative of the Roman contribution to civilization of the science of law, the marble-covered Roman temple front of the **Supreme Court Building**, designed by Cass Gilbert and completed in 1935, sits with an elegant simplicity to the east of, and in deference to, the US Capitol building. A spacious, one-hundred-foot-wide oval plaza lies at the foot of the main steps of the building. On the west front are powerful allegorical figures, sculpted by James Earle Fraser, representing the Contemplation of Justice, on the left, and the Guardian or Authority of Law on the right. On the east front is a group of marble figures sculpted by Herman A. MacNeil, representing Confucius, Solon, and Moses. The building was renovated in 2008 to include a visitors center.

■ **9** Quite apart from the reserved countenance of the Supreme Court, the **Library of Congress**, designed by John L. Smithmeyer and Paul J. Pelz in 1897, employs the theatrical energy of the Beaux-Arts aesthetic, even making some very implicit allusions to the Paris Opera house. The building was received with great fanfare and accolades as a great architectural achievement. Created by an act of Congress in 1800, the Library of Congress housed its materials in the Capitol until 1896, when the Army Corps of Engineers built its main building (the Jefferson Building). The library serves not only the members of Congress but also government agencies and the general public. Outstanding collections of rare Chinese, Russian, and Japanese books are among its many treasures. A visit to the main reading room is a must. Public tours of the Jefferson Building are offered Monday through Saturday at 10:30 a.m., 11:30 a.m., 1:30 p.m., 2:30 p.m., and 3:30 p.m. (except Saturdays). On federal holidays, the first tour begins at 9:30 a.m. Directly behind the Adams Building is a library annex. The **James Madison Memorial Library**, another annex on Independence Avenue between 1st and 2nd Streets, was opened in 1980. The Library of Congress's Jefferson Building is open 8:30 a.m.–4:30 p.m., Monday through Saturday. The Madison Building is open 8:30 a.m.–9:30 p.m., Monday through Friday, and on Saturday, 8:30 a.m.–5:00 p.m. Admission is free. More information can be found at www.loc.gov or by calling 202-707-9779.

■ **10** In something of a counterintuitive offering, the **Folger Shakespeare Library**, designed by Paul Cret in 1932, is not as theatrical on the outside as one might expect. The exterior facade is highly sophisticated yet spare, with the nuanced employment of bas relief carvings of Shakespearean theme. The aesthetic is also unique in its context of highly formal and classical neighbors, as seen in the Supreme Court and Library of Congress. The library is an ambiguous mix of neoclassicism and art deco, as seen notably with the use of aluminum paneling. Inside is where the theatrical comes out to play, with an aesthetic pivot to Elizabethan England, as revealed by the wood-paneled finishes and decor that one might see at the Globe Theatre in London. The library is certainly a must for Shakespeare followers; especially noteworthy is the reproduction of an Elizabethan theater, which is in active use all year. The Folger Shakespeare Library is open 10:00 a.m.–5:00 p.m., Monday through Friday, except on all federal holidays. Admission is free. More information can be found at www.folger.edu or by calling 202-544-4600.

■ **11** **Frederick Douglass's first Washington residence** was at 316 A Street NE. According to a Capitol Hill Restoration Society plaque, Douglass was the "precursor to the Civil Rights Movement . . . [and] resided in this building from 1871 to 1877."

■ **12** When it opened in this residential area in 1964, the **Museum of African Art** (318 A Street NE) was the first museum to house artifacts of African cultures and thereby promote the study of African heritage. The museum's collection has been moved to the Smithsonian's National Museum of African Art, located on the Mall at 950 Independence Avenue SW. The National Museum of African Art is open 10:00 a.m.–5:30 p.m. daily except December 25. Admission is free. More information can be found at http://africa.si.edu or by calling 202-633-4600.

■ **13** The **townhouse on the corner of 4th and A Streets NE** is a converted store built around 1869. Compare this with the townhouse at 1100 Independence Avenue SE, located on the corner of Independence Avenue and 11th Street, which is in the same style but unrestored. (At this juncture, hardy walkers can test their stamina by detouring onto East Capitol Street into Tour 2. This tour will lead you back into Tour 1 at Pennsylvania Avenue and 4th Street.)

■ **14** The **Brumidi House**, at 324–326 A Street SE, was built about 1850. It was purportedly the home of Constantino Brumidi, an Italian artist, who at the age of sixty painted in eleven months the Apotheosis of Washington over 4,664 square feet in the Capitol dome. He was also responsible for the rotunda frescoes and other Capitol decorations.

■ **15** **Saint Mark's Episcopal Church** (1888), located at 3rd and A Streets SE, is listed in the National Register of Historic Places. President Lyndon B. Johnson was a frequent visitor.

■ **16** The **townhouse at 120 4th Street SE** (built about 1876) is typical of the 1870s, with its flat facade, elaborate cornices, and lintels.

■ **17** The **Ebenezer United Methodist Church,** on 4th and D Streets SE, originally known as the Little Ebenezer Church, was constructed in 1838 and rebuilt in 1897. From March 1864 to May 1865, the church served as the first schoolhouse for Blacks in Washington. The church is also the oldest Black church on Capitol Hill, with a predominantly African American congregation.

■ **18** This vacant square is the site of the **old Providence Hospital.** It is now under the jurisdiction of the Architect of the Capitol as part of the "Capitol Grounds."

■ **19** This stretch of **North Carolina Avenue** is a fine example of the L'Enfant plan for the Federal City: the superimposition of bold, diagonal avenues over a standard grid pattern. The small, adjoining, triangular parks, particularly at E Street, have been the scene of many touch football games.

■ **20** This stretch of **New Jersey Avenue** frames a magnificent sight. The transition between residential and federal buildings, along with the view of the Capitol dome, is startling. Consequently, New Jersey Avenue residents have taken great pride in restoring their homes. The "Master Plan for Future Development of the Capitol Grounds and Related Areas" was completed in 1981 and remains largely unchanged. According to the "transition zone" classification, New Jersey Avenue will be able to retain its historic, residential character in the face of congressional growth.

■ **21** The **House Office Buildings** along Independence Avenue are, from west to east, the Sam Rayburn Building, the Nicholas Longworth Building, and the Joseph Cannon Building. You may want to stop by and visit your representative.

■ **22** The **Bartholdi** Fountain (between Canal, also known as Washington Avenue, and 1st Streets on Independence Avenue) was designed by Frédéric Auguste Bartholdi in 1876.

■ **23** The **US Botanic Garden** (Independence Avenue, Maryland Avenue, and 1st Street SW) was moved to its present location in 1933. The **Conservatory** was constructed during 1931–33. A multimillion-dollar renovation of the Conservatory was reopened in December 2001. The Conservatory houses permanent collections of plants from subtropical, tropical, and arid regions. Special exhibits showcase orchids and medicinal, economically significant, endangered, and primitive plants. It is definitely worth a visit. The US Botanic Garden is open 10:00 a.m.–5:00 p.m. daily, including all weekends and holidays. The National Garden is open 10:00 a.m.–5:00 p.m. daily. Bartholdi Park is open dawn to dusk daily, including all weekends and holidays. Admission is free. More information can be found at www.usbg.gov or by calling 202-225-8333.

■ **24**   The **Ulysses S. Grant Memorial** (1922) is the largest and most expensive statuary grouping in Washington. The **Capitol Reflecting Pool** was designed by Skidmore, Owings & Merrill. Completed in 1970, the pool is directly over Interstate Highway 395, which underlies the Mall.

■ **25**   The **National Museum of the American Indian** was completed in 2004. The first national museum dedicated to the preservation, study, and exhibition of the life, languages, literature, history, and arts of Native Americans, its exhibits showcase art, culture, and artifacts. The museum is open 10 a.m.– 5:30 p.m. daily except December 25. Admission is free. More information can be found at www.nmai.si.edu or by calling 202-633-1000.

■ **26**   The tour ends at the steps of the west side of the US Capitol. The **view across the Mall** to the Washington Monument is memorable. In the words of Pierre L'Enfant, the site of the US Capitol is truly like "a pedestal waiting for a monument."

Capitol Hill—East

(Historic residential restoration area)

Updated by Paul Douglass and Christopher J. Howard

Distance: 2 ¾ miles
Time: 1 ¼ hours
Bus: 32, 36, 90, 92, 96, D2, and X8
Metro: Eastern Market (Blue, Orange, and Silver Lines)

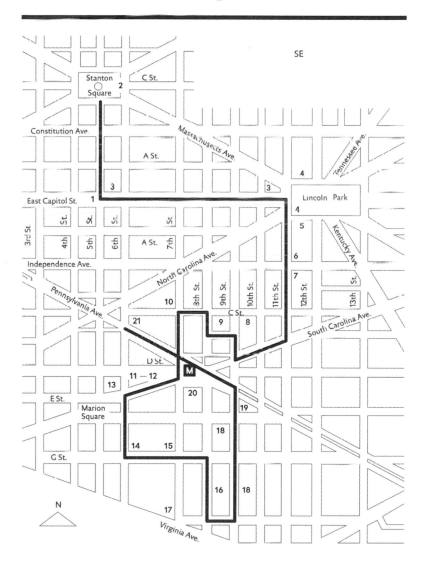

■ **1** The tour begins at 5th and East Capitol Streets SE. **East Capitol Street** is considered the "grand street" of the Capitol Hill community. It divides the northeast quadrant from the southeast quadrant of the city. The smaller scale of structures on adjacent streets north and south of East Capitol Street provides a sharp contrast. In 1974 Michael Franch prepared a report for the Joint Committee on Landmarks for the National Capital in which he found that "the general area of elite residence [for the years 1888, 1889, 1909, and 1918] was a diamond-shaped district between the Capitol and Lincoln Park, Stanton Park and Seward Square." As had been suspected, the heaviest concentration of elite residences was along East Capitol Street. The diversity of housing types and styles is tremendous. Everything from manor houses, Federal townhouses, and brick row houses to more contemporary housing exists in the Capitol Hill area; it is a designated historic district. A community group, the Capitol Hill Restoration Society, has done much to encourage and to maintain the integrity of the Capitol Hill Historic District.

■ **2** Looking north along 5th street from East Capitol Street is a **view** that is terminated by an equestrian statue of Maj. Gen. Nathanael Greene, in Stanton Square. Understood to be George Washington's most talented and dependable general during the Revolutionary War, he occupies one of the many formal squares in Washington, DC, that are formed by the intersections of diagonal boulevards. Stanton Square in particular is one of the more active and lived-in squares with a little bit of everything, including a playground.

■ **3** The **townhouses at 512 and 514 East Capitol Street NE** (1879) are representative of the 1870s, with flat facades and elaborate cornices and lintels. Some of the townhouses, for instance those in the **1000 block of East Capitol Street NE** (1899), have balconies and/or roof decks.

512 and 514 East Capitol Street NE

4 **Lincoln Park** and the **Emancipation Statue** were constructed in memory of Abraham Lincoln. The monument was paid for by small donations from emancipated slaves. The statues represent the first depictions of both Lincoln—the first martyred president—and a Black man, in monument form. A more recent statue (dedicated in July 1974) at the east end of the park is in honor of Mary McLeod Bethune, a Black educator and president and founder of Bethune-Cookman College in Daytona Beach, Florida. Hilliard Robinson, landscape architect, in conjunction with the National Park Service, designed the seven acre park. The homes surrounding the park are predominantly from 1890–95. Pay particular attention to the townhouse at 1125 East Capitol Street NE (1892) near the northwest corner of Lincoln Park. Two landmark buildings worth going the extra block are the Holy Comforter Saint Cyprian Catholic Church and the Car Barn, just East of Lincoln Park.

5 The **granite row houses** with balconies (1111–19 East Capitol Street SE) were built in 1892.

6 **Philadelphia Row** (124–154 11th Street SE) was built by James W. Gessford about 1866. He built sixteen row houses in the style of Philadelphia to soothe his wife's homesickness for her native city.

7 This group of fifteen row houses (200–226 11th Street SE) was built by Charles Gessford in 1891, some twenty-five years after Philadelphia Row.

8 Constructed in 1967, the **Thomas Simmons House** (314–16 9th Street SE) offers something of a curiosity to the historically rich neighbor with a

Philadelphia Row

contemporary and contrasting design that intentionally ignores agreed-on sensibilities and instead reflects something one might find in a more suburban context. Compelling perhaps for this reason are the clarity and authenticity of the enduring neighborhood character of Capitol Hill.

■ **9** This set of **contemporary row houses** (801–19 C Street SE) was constructed in the mid-1960s.

■ **10** A walk through many of the alleys in the area will lead directly to **Eastern Market** on 7th and C Streets. The open-market activity will mesmerize even the most hardened tourist. Designed by Adolf Cluss and constructed in 1873, in an eclectic mix of Italianate, Romanesque, and Georgian classicism, this market is the heart of the Capitol Hill community. Proof of admiration for this building was made evident when the building was destroyed by fire in 2007. The market was promptly rebuilt through the determination and passionate efforts of the local community and city leadership. It is truly a city treasure. Be sure to sample the cannoli at the bakery. Vendors offer fresh produce, flowers, and crafts; artists selling prints and other works of art surround more boutiques and shops lining 7th Street into Pennsylvania Avenue (weekends are especially busy). The market is open 7:00 a.m.–7:00 p.m., Tuesday through Friday, 7:00 a.m.– 6:00 p.m. on Saturday, and 9:00 a.m.–5:00 p.m. on Sunday. More information can be found at www.easternmarket-dc.org or by calling 202-698-5253.

Eastern Market

■ **11** The **Maples House**, now named the Friendship House Settlement, was built in 1795–1806 during the Federal period by architect-builder William Lovering and is understood to be the oldest building in the Capitol Hill neighborhood. Francis Scott Key was one of its many distinguished owners. It has gone through many restorations. The front entrance of the Maples House originally opened onto South Carolina Avenue, but today it goes by the 619 D Street SE address.

■ **12** This stretch of **South Carolina Avenue** provides a spacious and charming residential atmosphere that is typical of the Capitol Hill community.

■ **13** The **Carberry House**, at 423 6th Street SE, was built about 1813, reputedly of bricks that were used as ballast for navy ships, and has been designated a historic site/structure by the Joint Committee on Landmarks. This stretch of 6th Street to G Street SE comprises some of the oldest houses on Capitol Hill, many built in the 1840s and 1850s.

■ **14** **Christ Church** (1806, Benjamin II. Latrobe). In the past, this church at 620 G Street SE served many individuals from the Navy Yard and Marine Barracks. It is believed to have been visited by Presidents Thomas Jefferson, James Madison, and James Monroe.

■ **15** The house at 636 G Street SE is the **birthplace of John Philip Sousa**, conductor, composer, and bandmaster of the US Marine Corps. The brightly painted residence was built in 1844.

■ **16** The **Marine Commandant's House** and the **Marine Barracks complex** occupy the entire square formed by 8th, 9th, G, and I Streets SE. Constructed in 1801–4 after George Hadfield's designs, the commandant's house is set apart by its physical scale from the nearby homes. The Marine Barracks surround an interior courtyard and parade ground, precisely manicured in the traditional military style. The Marine Corps Band and the ceremonial units are housed at the barracks. Along 8th Street, from Pennsylvania Avenue to the Southeast Freeway (also known as Barracks Row), commercial rejuvenation is very much in evidence.

■ **17** The **Ellen Wilson Townhomes** on Capitol Hill occupy a portion of land that was previously developed with the Ellen Wilson public housing complex. The Ellen Wilson complex was built in 1941 on a 5.3-acre site. The site was bisected by the construction of the Southeast Freeway into two parcels: to the south, the parcel contained several remaining public housing structures, and to the north, the parcel was vacant. The northern parcel was reclaimed during the mid-1990s and used for construction of the Ellen Wilson Townhomes on Capitol Hill, a mixed-income complex of units that face away from the freeway. The complex is located between 6th and 7th and G Streets and Virginia Avenue SE. In the immediate vicinity are several examples of former public school buildings that have converted to upscale residences or other uses.

■ **18** Note the abrupt contrast of housing styles between the **contemporary and the older housing** in the 700 and 500 blocks on 9th Street.

■ **19** Constructed in 1865–66, the **Old Naval Hospital** on Pennsylvania Avenue between 9th and 10th Streets retains what may be the original cast-iron fence. Over the last few years, it has been occupied by various government agencies and community organizations. It is currently vacant and in need of rehabilitation.

■ **20** The square at Pennsylvania Avenue, between 7th and 8th Streets, is the entrance to the **Eastern Market Metro station**. Note the many buildings in the immediate vicinity of the square that have been upgraded, typical of this area of the city.

■ **21** The tour ends at the corner of Pennsylvania Avenue and 6th Street at the **National Permanent Building** (formerly named the Eastern Liberty Federal Building), built in 1975 and occupied in 1976. Designed by the architectural firm of Mills Petticord (now merged with HOK), the building features a metal mansard roof housing ninety solar collector panels designed to provide domestic hot water.

The Mall—East

(Major axis of monumental core, Smithsonian museums, art galleries)

Carol Truppi, updated by Christopher J. Howard

Distance: 2 miles
Time: 1 hour minimum
Bus: 32, 36, P6, and the DC Circulator
Metro: Smithsonian (Blue, Orange, and Silver Lines)

■ **1** The tour begins at the building popularly known as the **Castle** (1855, James Renwick), on Jefferson Drive between 9th and 11th Streets SW. In addition to two orientation theaters, the **Great Hall** contains a visitors center and café.

■ **2** Walk outside to the center of the **Mall**. You are midway on the major axis of the monumental core of the capital city as planned by L'Enfant. (The Mall was extended beyond the Washington Monument to the Lincoln Memorial in the twentieth century after the tidal flats and marshes west of the monument were filled in.) The greensward was planned by L'Enfant as a broad avenue, four hundred feet wide, lined with grand residences. The Mall as it exists today

Smithsonian Institution Building (the Castle)

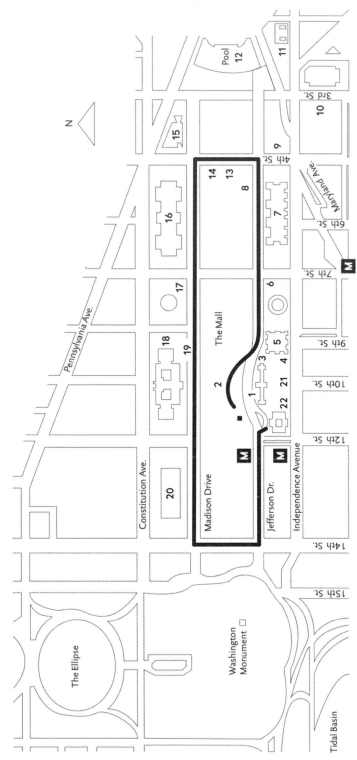

N

The Ellipse

Pennsylvania Ave.

Constitution Ave.

Madison Drive

The Mall

Jefferson Dr.

Independence Avenue

Washington
Monument □

Tidal Basin

Pool 12

3rd St.

Maryland Ave.

6th St.

7th St.

9th St.

10th St.

12th St.

14th St.

15th St.

4th St.

20

18

19

16

17

15

14

13

8

9

2

1

3

4

5

6

7

21

22

10

11

M

M

M

represents a sensitive compromise between the monumental plans of L'Enfant and those of the McMillan Commission (executed without the broad central avenue L'Enfant had proposed), softened at the edges with humanistic touches suggestive of Downing (exemplified by the present-day ice rink, carousel, and Constitution Gardens, as well as numerous sports activities and the annual Festival of American Folklife).

■ **3** Behind the Smithsonian Building is the **Enid A. Haupt Garden,** a four-acre Victorian-style garden that opened in 1987 as part of the redesigned Castle quadrangle. Protection of this welcome respite resulted in the designs for the National Museum of African Art, Arthur M. Sackler Gallery, and S. Dillon Ripley Center, which are almost entirely underground. Enid A. Haupt received the Liberty Hyde Bailey award from the American Horticultural Society for her extensive philanthropic contributions to horticulture.

■ **4** Directly east of the Smithsonian Building is an **urn commemorating Andrew Jackson Downing.** His plan for the Mall created the first landscaped American public park. In the 1930s, many of the mature trees planted in conformity with his plan were removed from the center of the Mall as it was "restored" to L'Enfant's more formal concept by the McMillan Commission.

■ **5** The **Arts and Industries Building** (1881, Cluss and Schulze, after plans by Montgomery Meigs), at Jefferson Drive and 9th Street SW, was originally the US National Museum and housed exhibits from the 1876 Centennial Exhibition held in Philadelphia. The Kathrine Dulin Folger Rose Garden at the front entrance includes the numerous varieties of roses planted by the Smithsonian. The Mary Livingston Ripley Garden (1978, Hugh Newell Jacobsen) at the eastern border of the building is a place of informality and intimacy where a parking lot was once proposed. Six gardens have been installed and, although never part of the master plans for the National Mall, they do introduce seasonal interest that humanizes this monumental landscape without taking away from the classical formality of the plan. The gardens are small pockets of the picturesque whole envisioned by Andrew Jackson Downing.

■ **6** Continue east along Jefferson Drive to 7th Street SW to the **Joseph H. Hirshhorn Museum and Sculpture Garden** (1974, Gordon Bunshaft of Skidmore, Owings & Merrill). Note the sunken outdoor sculpture garden north of Jefferson Drive, as well as the cylindrical building, which contains paintings and sculptures from the late 1800s to the present. The Hirshhorn Museum and Sculpture Garden is open daily, 10:00 a.m.–5:30 p.m., except December 25. Admission is free. More information can be found at http://hirshhorn.si.edu or by calling 202-633-2796.

■ **7** Continue on Jefferson Drive across 7th Street to the **National Air and Space Museum** (1976, Gyo Obata of Helmuth, Obata and Kassabaum). Since its

National Air and Space Museum

official opening on July 4, 1976, this has become the most popular Smithsonian museum. The National Air and Space Museum is open 10:00 a.m.–5:30 p.m. every day except December 25. Admission is free. More information can be found at airandspace.si.edu or by calling 202-633-2214.

■ **8 The elms on the north side of Jefferson Drive** are part of a continuous band of trees on both sides of the Mall that emphasize the east–west axis. In winter, this allée of deciduous trees can appear cold and barren. Downing's argument that the Mall should be attractive above all in the winter, when Congress is in session, has lost out to questionable arguments that evergreens are not tolerant of urban conditions, are messy, or present security problems.

■ **9** Across 4th Street from the National Air and Space Museum is the **National Museum of the American Indian**, which is a centerpiece for Indian arts, history, and material culture. In consultation, collaboration, and cooperation with Native people and assistance from the architecture firm of Venturi, Scott Brown and Associates, the Smithsonian, and the National Museum of the American Indian, a guide called *The Way of the People* was compiled that documents the technical aspects of the architectural program and the philosophical approach in which the building respects and honors Native American cultures. The National Museum of the American Indian is open 10 a.m.–5:30 p.m. daily, except December 25. Admission is free. More information can be found at www.nmai.si.edu or by calling 202-633-1000.

■ **10** At the corner of 4th Street and Jefferson Drive you can view the **Hubert Humphrey Federal Office Building**, located at 3rd Street and Independence Avenue SW. It was designed by Marcel Breuer, who also designed the Housing and Urban Development Building (1968). The core of the building contains a ten-story exhaust shaft for Interstate Highway 395, which tunnels beneath the Mall.

Hubert Humphrey Federal Office Building

One block to the west is the **Dwight D. Eisenhower Memorial**, which opened in 2020 and honors the thirty-fourth president of the United States. Architect Frank Gehry was selected to design the memorial, which includes sculptures that show Eisenhower throughout his life, against a stainless steel tapestry-like backdrop.

■ 11 The **US Botanic Garden**, to the north of the Humphrey Building, is one of the oldest botanic gardens in North America. The first greenhouse was constructed in 1842, and a complete renovation and reconstruction of the 1933 conservatory reopened in December 2001. Its exterior is largely unchanged, but an updated and modernized building system provides plumbing, electrical, and other architectural measures to support a living plant museum. New exhibits interpret the role of plants in supporting the earth's ecosystem and enriching human life. The Palm House reconstruction rises over eighty feet. The US Botanic Garden Conservatory is open 10:00 a.m.–5:00 p.m. daily, including all weekends and holidays. Admission is free. More information can be found at www.usbg.gov or by calling 202-225-8333.

■ 12 Walk north on 4th Street. On your right are the **Ulysses S. Grant Memorial** and the **Capitol Reflecting Pool** (see Tour 1, Capitol Hill, no. 24), at 1st Street between Maryland and Pennsylvania Avenues.

■ 13 As you look **toward the Washington Monument**, it is interesting to realize that this impressive, open, grassy mall was not completed until 1975, when traffic and parking on the interior streets were replaced by pedestrian and bicycle paths. Between 1791 and 1972, the Mall had been the location of a cow pasture and slaughtering site, swamps, a Civil War hospital, a railroad station with numerous tracks, a trash-filled and stagnant canal, and "temporary" government buildings that existed from World War I to 1972. The railroad station was demolished after the opening of Union Station.

■ **14** This is a good site from which to note how the position of the **Smithsonian Institution Building** (the Castle) is out of lockstep with its fellow museums. The twentieth-century McMillan plan for the Mall proposed a wider Mall and assumed that this oddity, the Castle, would be removed for a more rationally comprehensive scheme. Thankfully, in what is probably consensus opinion, that plan was not executed. Instead, the Mall is left with the quirky, romantic origin story of the Smithsonian Institution. The warm, rusty colors that glow in the evening sun, the irregular dimensions, and the vertical and horizontal projections are a welcome change from the surrounding lackluster white sepulchres. Even its failure to stand back of the line prescribed by the turn-of-the-century planners appeals to our hidden rebelliousness. For more information about the Smithsonian, visit www.si.edu.

■ **15** This striking building is the widely acclaimed **East Building of the National Gallery of Art** (I. M. Pei), which opened in 1978. Pei's building is an unabashedly modern solution to an awkward site. Yet its pink Tennessee marble echoes the material, if not the form, of the adjacent main building of the National Gallery of Art, to which it is connected by an underground passageway running under 4th Street. The East Building repeats its triangular theme throughout: in the ceiling designs and in the finely crafted walls whose sharp edges show wear from the admiring hands of many visitors. The museumgoer enters the building under a low ceiling and is then awestruck by a sunlit, four-story atrium around which the many galleries are grouped.

■ **16** Turn west on Madison and arrive at the **National Gallery of Art, Main Building** (1941, John Russell Pope). One of the most exquisite, sophisticated, and prominent museums on the National Mall, the National Gallery appropriately holds the richest collection of art in the city. The buildings' dignified, sprawling repose speaks to the protection of treasures within, while beckoning entry with grand stairs and a monumental entry portico. Speaking the classical

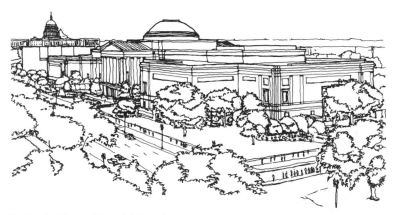

National Gallery of Art, Main Building

language of Washington, DC, the iconic dome alludes to both the Jefferson Memorial and the Capitol. Inside is the rewarding experience of going from one unique space to the next. The central domed rotunda facilitates movement in two opposing directions down gallery corridors that branch out into discrete gallery spaces, all lit with pleasant diffuse natural light from above, and ultimately terminating in delightful atrium spaces. The National Gallery of Art is open 10:00 a.m.–5:00 p.m., Monday through Saturday, and 11:00 a.m.–6:00 p.m. on Sunday. The gallery is closed on December 25 and January 1. Admission is free. More information can be found at www.nga.gov or by calling 202-737-4215.

17 Continue west to the **National Gallery of Art Sculpture Garden** between 7th and 9th Streets SW. Originally designed in 1974 by Skidmore, Owings & Merrill, this area includes a **pool and ice-skating rink**. This joint project of the National Park Service and the National Gallery of Art was redesigned and updated in 1999. The retention of the public fountain and skating rink (Olin Partnership with National Gallery staff) is a tribute to the success of the original design and the need for a year-round public space on the National Mall.

18 The **Smithsonian Pollinator Garden**, alongside the National Museum of Natural History, is a slender but rich park known for supporting plant species that attract eastern US butterflies. Plant labels provide the common and botanical names of the plants, region of origin, and life cycle they support. Habitats include the wetland, meadow, woods edge, and urban garden.

19 In front of the **National Museum of Natural History** (1911, Hornblower and Marshall; 1965 wings, Mills, Petticord and Mills), between 9th and 12th Streets, you will see a few evergreens planted in conformity with Downing's 1851 Mall plan. The holly tree amid the elms, slightly to the southeast of the building's steps, was scheduled for removal during the leveling process but was saved in the 1930s by Smithsonian Secretary Alexander Wetmore, an ornithologist, because it was the nesting place of his pet mockingbird. The museum is the home of the famous Hope Diamond, an exhibit on dinosaurs, and an insect zoo. The National Museum of Natural History is open 10:00 a.m.–5:30 p.m, Monday through Friday, with extended hours on certain holidays. Admission is free. More information can be found at www.mnh.si.edu or by calling 202-633-1000.

20 The **National Museum of American History** (1964, McKim, Mead and White), was originally called the National Museum of History and Technology, a name that helps to explain the curiously spare manner in which it was designed. The architects, while one of the most successful and prolific classical architecture firms of the time, presented a design that straddles the line of more modernist and technology-focused design, with some timeless principles of classical design. As the museum of American history, popular exhibits include the original Star-Spangled Banner, Horatio Greenough's monumental sculpture of George Washington, and the First Ladies' gowns. The National Museum of American History is open 10:00 a.m.–5:30 p.m., every day except December 25. Admission is free. More information can be found at american-history.si.edu or by calling 202-633-1000.

■ **21** The **National Museum of African American History and Culture** (2016, Freelon Group / Adjaye Associates / Davis Brody Bond), at 14th Street and Constitution Avenue NW, is the most recent museum on the National Mall and arguably the most noteworthy. After a drawn-out process, initiated as early as 1915, it is one of only a few museums dedicated to a singular cultural identity, in committing to the heritage of Black Americans, similar to the Native American Museum, which predates its arrival. The other unique quality of this museum can be plainly observed on its exterior. Composed of three upward-sloping tiers faced with darker bronze-colored ironworks, the building sets itself apart from the otherwise harmonious collection of the more traditional surrounding museums. This singularly curious expression alludes to the African Yoruban crown as well as to the rich tradition of African American metallurgy in the South. The museum houses a wide range of provocative collections and exhibits that attempt to cover the complex history of African Americans in the United States. The museum is one of the most popular and often visited and, for that reason, can be more difficult to access. As of 2023, timed-entry tickets are required, though a small number of same-day passes are available. To make reservations or find more information you can visit nmaahc.si.edu/.

■ **22** Walk across the Mall to the **National Museum of Asian Art**. The building above ground is **Freer Gallery of Art** (1923, Charles A. Platt), at 12th Street and Jefferson Drive SW. Built around a delightful interior court, the museum contains a small but choice collection of Asian art and the world's largest collection of James Abbott McNeill Whistler's works (including the famous Peacock Room). Connected to the Freer Gallery and built underground is the **Arthur M. Sackler Gallery**, also offering Asian art. The National Museum of Asian Art is open 10:00 a.m.–5:30 p.m., daily except December 25. Admission is free. More information can be found at asia.si.edu or by calling 202-633-4880.

■ **23** The tour ends at the **National Museum of African Art** and the **S. Dillon Ripley Center**. Built mostly underground, they offer exceptional collections of art treasures to the public. They are open 10:00 a.m.–5:30 p.m., daily except December 25. Admission is free. More information can be found at http://africa.si.edu or by calling 202-633-4600; and www.si.edu/Museums /ripleycenter or by calling 202-633-1000, respectively.

The Mall—West

(National memorials)

Carol Truppi, updated by Christopher J. Howard

Distance: 2 ¾ miles
Time: 2 hours
Bus: DC Circulator
Metro: Federal Triangle or Smithsonian (Blue, Orange, and Silver Lines)

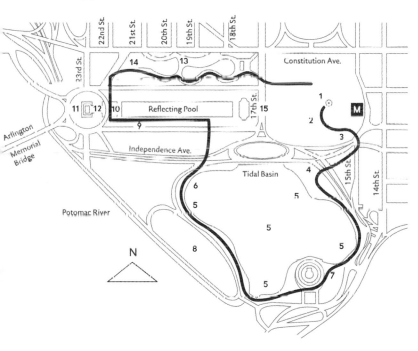

This tour includes the Washington, Jefferson, and Lincoln Memorials.

■ **1** The tour begins at the **Washington Monument** (1884, Robert Mills). Pierre L'Enfant chose this location for an equestrian statue that had been proposed by Congress, and George Washington approved the site. Because Congress failed to act decisively on the proposal, a group of private citizens, organized in 1833 as the Washington National Monument Society, offered a prize for the best design for a monument. Robert Mills's design for a six-hundred-foot obelisk rising from a colonnaded base won; the society accepted the design minus the colonnaded base.

Construction began in 1848, but funds ran out in 1855. Construction began again in 1876 after Congress had authorized the monument's completion at government expense. It was finally completed in 1885 by the US Army Corps of Engineers. If you look about one-quarter of the way up, you will see a distinct break in the color of the stone, marking the pause between construction phases.

L'Enfant's plan called for the monument to Washington to be located at the intersection of a north–south axis drawn south from the White House and an east–west axis drawn due west from the Capitol. The ground at that point, however, was at the time low and marshy, and when the monument was started early in the nineteenth century, it was placed on more solid ground 360 feet east and 120 feet south of the planned position. Down the hill to the northwest you will see the "Jefferson Pier," a stone monument placed there in 1810 to mark the true intersection of L'Enfant's proposed north–south and east–west axes. It was later removed but replaced in 1889. The Senate Park Commission planners sought to rectify the off-center position of the Washington Monument along the north–south axis by creating an elaborate sunken garden with a large circular pool to the west, but it was never built because engineers asserted that the monument's stability would be threatened. The planners also sought to rectify the off-center position of the monument along the east–west axis by slanting the Mall one degree south of its true east–west direction. At the time of this writing, the National Capital Planning Commission endorsed the design for stone walls that would ring the Washington Monument in concentric ovals. The walls and other landscaping would replace the concrete Jersey barriers that were installed as a temporary security measure after September 11, 2001. The monument is open every day from 9:00 a.m. to 5:00 pm except July 4 and December 25. It is also closed one day each month for maintenance; please call 202-485-9880 or visit www.nps.gov/wamo for updated information.

■ **2** Walk to the west of the Washington Monument and **look west toward the Lincoln Memorial**. All of the land toward the Potomac River was reclaimed from marsh and tidal land between the 1880s and the 1920s. Until then, the Potomac occasionally flooded right up to the south lawn of the White House. The McMillan Commission proposed extending the Mall from the Washington Monument to the proposed site for a Lincoln Memorial. The planners connected the two monuments with a reflecting pool and aligned the extension along the Senate Park Commission's new slanted east–west axis.

■ **3** Go south toward the Jefferson Memorial. The **Sylvan Theater**, at 15th Street and Independence Avenue, southeast of the Washington Monument, is the site of open-air summer musical, dramatic, and dance productions. Shakespearean plays are favorites.

■ **4** Continue south across Independence Avenue and walk west to East Basin Drive, near 17th Street, to the **Floral Library**. This outdoor garden is planted with flowering annuals, which are well identified. The tulips in the spring are spectacular.

■ 5 The site of the **Tidal Basin** (1897, William Johnson Twining), bordered by Independence Avenue and East Basin Drive, was originally part of the Potomac River. In 1882 the Tidal Basin was created as part of a plan to improve navigation on the Potomac and to reclaim some land for parks. The basin serves to flush the Washington Channel, as gates between the basin and channel are opened at low tide to release the Potomac waters that have filled the basin at high tide. The **cherry trees** surrounding the basin are among three thousand given by Japan in 1912. The Cherry Blossom Festival—held each year in late March to early April—celebrates their short but enchanting blooming period.

■ 6 Between the Jefferson Memorial and the Lincoln Memorial you will find the **Martin Luther King Jr. Memorial**. This crescent-shaped memorial honors Martin Luther King Jr.'s national and international contributions to world peace through nonviolent social change. By placing King's memorial in line with the axis of the Jefferson and Lincoln Memorials, the designers, ROMA Design Group, have aligned it with the larger democratic ideals that form the context for King's legacy. This line also offers historical significance, beginning at the Lincoln Memorial where King gave his famous "I Have a Dream" speech; the site's address is 1964 Independence Avenue SW, a reference to the Civil Rights Act of 1964. More information is available at www.mlkmemorial .org or by calling 888-484-3373.

■ 7 Continue along the Tidal Basin to the **Jefferson Memorial** (1943, John Russell Pope, architect, Rudulph Evans, sculptor). The McMillan Commission recommended a memorial in this location that, with the White House, forms the main North–South crossing axis with the Mall. Directly south of the White House, one would have originally been able to see the memorial. Franklin Roosevelt, an admirer of Thomas Jefferson, advocated for the memorial to be dedicated to him as an illustrious figure in our nation and a representation of republican and democratic ideals. This theme can be appreciated in the rotunda form of the memorial as a rhetorical reference to not only Thomas Jefferson's University of Virginia rotunda, but also to the Pantheon in Rome as a recapitulation of venerating not gods, but our nation's ideals. Further evidence can be found in the pediment carving depicting the drafting committee of the Declaration of Independence. The picturesque grounds, designed by Frederick Law Olmsted, evoke a romantic character, as if it were an unscathed ancient structure in the countryside waiting to be discovered. More information can be found at nps.gov/thje.

■ 8 Continue around the Tidal Basin to the **Franklin Delano Roosevelt Memorial** (Lawrence Halprin). The entrance and visitor center are off Ohio

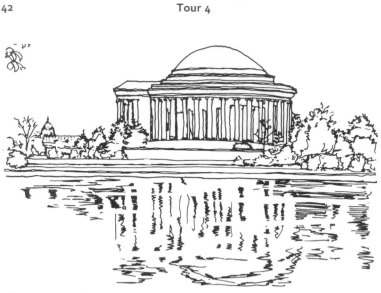

Jefferson Memorial

Drive. However, you can also enter the memorial at the point closest to the Jefferson Memorial or at the middle. Designated in 1959, it was not dedicated until 1997. This monument to the twelve-year presidency of FDR is a park with fountains, water features, and landscaping that create an attractive public space in which to view the memorial's statues, quotations, and history. Walk northwest across West Potomac Park to Independence Avenue.

■ **9** The **Korean War Veterans Memorial** is at Independence Avenue and the Lincoln Memorial. It was built by the Korean War Veterans Memorial Advisory at a cost of $18 million in donated funds and designed by Cooper Lecky. It is on a 2.2-acre site adjacent to the Lincoln Memorial Reflecting Pool. It features a sculptured column of nineteen-foot soldiers, created by sculptor Frank Gaylord, arrayed for combat with the American flag. A 164-foot mural is inscribed "Freedom Is Not Free" and is etched with 2,500 photographic images of nurses, chaplains, crew chiefs, mechanics, and other support personnel to symbolize the vast effort that sustained the military operation.

■ **10** The site of the **Lincoln Memorial** (1922, Henry Bacon, architect; Daniel Chester French, sculptor) had been debated since 1867. Many early propos- als stressed commemorating Abraham Lincoln as a war hero rather than as a humanitarian. Alternatives considered were a Lincoln Highway between Gettysburg and Washington and sites near Union Station and the Capitol. In 1911 the decision was made to locate the memorial here on the continua- tion of the axis of the Capitol and Washington Monument, as called for in the McMillan Plan, despite objections that the land was swampy and inaccessible. Following a design derived from a Greek temple, the columns are tilted slightly inward to prevent the optical illusion of a bulging top. Many motifs represent-

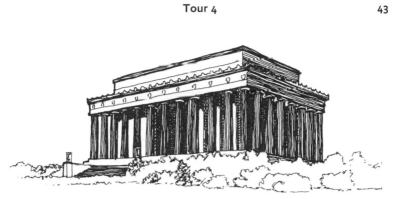

Lincoln Memorial

ing Lincoln and America are incorporated into the monument, including the thirty-six columns that symbolize the thirty-six states that made up the Union while Lincoln was president. Although some people questioned a design based on a Greek temple to commemorate someone who was born in a log cabin and who proudly acknowledged that heritage, Daniel French said, "The Greeks alone were best able to express in their building . . . the highest attributes and the greatest beauty known to man." The Gettysburg Address and Lincoln's second inaugural speech are inscribed on the walls, and a portion of Martin Luther King Jr.'s "I Have a Dream" speech of 1963 is on the steps. The memorial pays homage to Lincoln's "simplicity, his grandeur, and his power."

■ **11** Walk around the Lincoln Memorial to the rear, or west side, for the **view across the Potomac**. The **Arlington Memorial Bridge** (McKim, Mead and White, architects; Leo Friedlander, sculptor) is considered one of the finest bridges in the country. Designed with the intent of symbolically reuniting the North and South, it was recommended by the McMillan Commission and built in the 1920s. The bridge, which contains an operable (though rarely used) draw span cleverly concealed in the center section, provides access to the **Arlington National Cemetery**. About halfway up the hill, straight ahead of the bridge, is the **grave of John F. Kennedy**, where the eternal flame can be seen at night. Farther up the hill is **Arlington House** (the Custis-Lee Mansion), home of Robert E. Lee.

■ **12** Walk around the Lincoln Memorial to the entrance and look toward the Capitol. The truly spectacular view is one of the most photographed in Washington. It is here that the current design policy of maintaining a formal treatment at the center of the Mall versus a more people-oriented treatment at its edges is most apparent. The **Reflecting Pool** is designed to mirror, and to link in a formal and inspiring setting, the monuments at either end. When an artificial ice-skating facility was proposed for the pool in the 1960s, it was turned down by the National Park Service as not in keeping with the dignity of the Mall. Such a facility has been installed in the area between the National

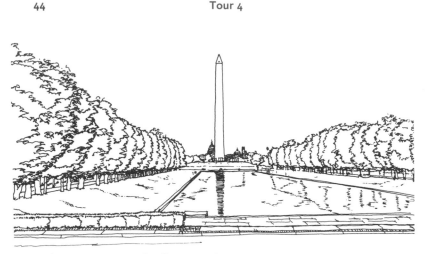

Washington Monument / Reflecting Pool

Gallery of Art and the National Museum of Natural History (see Tour 3, The Mall—East, no. 17).

■ **13** To the north (formerly the site of the "Main Navy" temporary buildings from World War I that outlasted World War II) is the site of **Constitution Gardens** (Skidmore, Owings & Merrill). Originally planned as a vibrant, day-and nighttime attraction (modeled on the Tivoli Gardens in Copenhagen), the proposed concessionary activities were almost entirely eliminated in order to reduce initial costs. Since their opening in 1976, the gardens have failed to attract the crowds expected. An irregularly shaped lake forms the center of the park. Note the total absence of evergreens, which makes the landscape barren in winter (see Tour 3, The Mall—East, no. 8).

■ **14** The **Vietnam Veterans Memorial**, dedicated in 1982, is one of Washington's most unusual monuments, both in its design and in the manner of its creation. Initiated by private citizens who had fought in Vietnam, it was built without public funds, and its winning design—by a young Chinese American student at Yale University, Maya Lin—was the product of an open architectural competition. The monument forms an open, V-shaped slash in the ground, the ends of which point to the Washington Monument on one side and the Lincoln Memorial on the other. On its polished black marble panels are inscribed, chronologically in order of their deaths, the names of the more than fifty thousand Americans killed during the US involvement in Vietnam. The monument has attracted great numbers of visitors, who move reverently past the panels, leaving small tokens of remembrance—flowers, pictures, flags—for those lost in the war. The final judgment on the memorial has yet to be written; indeed, a flagpole and a representational sculpture of these servicemen have been added to meet the criticisms of those who assert that the monument is too funereal and not sufficiently celebratory in character. Yet it can be said that the memorial is a moving work of art that rises above the controversial character of the Vietnam conflict.

■ **15** As you return to the Washington Monument, you will pass by the **National World War II Memorial** (2004, design team included Friedrich St. Florian, Leo A. Daly, Hartman-Cox, Oehme, van Sweden, and Raymond Kaskey working with the American Battle Monuments Commission and the National Capital Planning Commission). It replaces the Rainbow Pool. For many people, the memorial has altered the historic integrity of the National Mall as envisioned by Pierre L'Enfant and the McMillan Plan, including the vista between the Lincoln Memorial and the Washington Monument. Pressure from Congress and special interest groups has led to a movement to create protective legislation and agency directives for the Mall that can help to retain the integrity of this nationally significant landscape.

H Street Corridor

(Revitalized corridor, DC Streetcar)

Jim Voelzke and Andy Merlo

Distance: 1.1 miles
Time: 1¼ hours
Bus: X2, X8, X9, and the DC Streetcar
Metro: Union Station (Red Line)

The H Street Corridor is part of the original city plan laid out by Pierre
L'Enfant in 1791. Development of the street languished until immediately
after the Civil War, when the Columbia Railway Company established a
horse-drawn streetcar operation linking the neighborhood with downtown.
A large wave of speculative development followed, so that by 1900 a sizeable
working-class community was established, attracted by nearby employers like
the Government Printing Office and, after 1907, Union Station and its associated roundhouse and coach yard. As neighborhood development increased,
H Street itself became more commercialized.

By the 1920s, automobile showrooms had become a dominant feature on
the street. While H Street NE never had the concentration of showrooms that
14th Street NW did, it contained showrooms of citywide and even national significance. Ourisman Chevrolet opened on H Street in 1920; by 1930 it was one
of the largest automobile dealers in the United States. Other dealers included

3rd and H Streets NE

Steuart Motors Inc. (Ford) and Mott Motors (Hupmobile). Other notable establishments included Sanitary Grocery Company (Safeway after 1928), People's Drug Company, and Woolworth's 5&10.

The corridor was always multiethnic, and the first wave of German American residents was soon joined with ethnic Jewish, Irish, Southern European, and Lebanese immigrants. African Americans began settling here during Reconstruction, and by 1950 H Street had become a center of African American culture within the city, rivaling "Black Broadway" on U Street NW. With the assassination of Martin Luther King Jr. on April 5, 1968, riots tore through the neighborhood, ransacking and setting fire to many of the shops along H Street, including Black-owned businesses. The neighborhood entered a period of decline for several decades, even as other neighborhoods affected by the 1968 riots revived. Small, independent businesses began a revival of the corridor in the early 2000s. Since 2010, large-scale mixed-use development and a thriving arts scene has attracted affluent residents and upscale retailers such as Whole Foods Market.

1 The growth and decline of the **streetcar service** has mirrored the larger economic and urban development trends of the H Street Corridor throughout its history. Horse-drawn streetcar service spurred initial development of the corridor soon after the end of the Civil War. Later, in 1942, streetcar service was replaced by what is now the X2 bus route, which presaged the decline of the neighborhood during the late twentieth century. More recently, the revival of streetcar service in 2016 alongside the still-extant X2 route has coincided with renewed real estate and economic development along the corridor. The Columbia Railway Company was chartered by Congress on May 24, 1870, and began operations later that year, using horses for motive power. The route ran from the Treasury Building to what is now the Starburst Plaza, where H Street, 15th Street, Florida Avenue, Maryland Avenue, Benning Road, and Bladensburg Road intersect. The streetcar company erected a car barn and stable at the southeast corner of 15th Street and Benning Road for equipment servicing. It later replaced these facilities with a large Richardsonian Romanesque car barn in 1895. The company commenced an extension eastward along Benning Road in 1898 and began electric operation in 1899 after a brief experiment with a cable-driven system in the mid-1890s. Streetcars were replaced by buses in 1942, while the former car barn continued to service bus equipment until it was demolished in 1971.

Streetcar service returned to the corridor in 2016 with the completion of a modern system running from Union Station to Benning Road and 26th Street NE, where the city has erected a modern car barn and training facility. There are plans to extend streetcar service further east along Benning Road to the Benning Road Metrorail station, as well as more long-range plans to extend the service westward toward downtown and the original 1870 terminus.

■ **2** Anchoring the western edge of the H Street Corridor, **Senate Square** fills the city block formed by H and Eye Streets and 2nd and 3rd Streets NE. The project incorporates the historic Little Sisters of the Poor Convent and Home for Aged Men and Women, an Italianate masonry building built in 1870–72, with an annex designed in 1894 by Robert I. Fleming. The complex later housed the city's Children's Museum before it was renovated into condominiums in 2007. Completing the block are two residential towers designed by Esocoff and Associates. Lush private green areas thread through the block, linking the historic and new buildings. Senate Square was the first major development project of the H Street NE renaissance; it opened at the beginning of the 2008 financial crisis and subsequently went bankrupt when unit sales collapsed. The two towers were converted to rentals, and the project stabilized.

■ **3** The DC Department of Housing and Community Development erected this pair of five-story office buildings at **609–645 H Street NE** in 1987 in an early effort to revive the H Street Corridor after the 1968 riots. The simple, unadorned (and inexpensive) facades of the two buildings, with ribbon glazing on the office floors and simple brick spandrels at the floors in roofs, reflect the governmental nature of the developer and the unfashionable reputation of the neighborhood during the late 1980s. Fortunately, the architect carved back the mass of both buildings at the office lobby entries to enliven otherwise repetitive facades.

The two five-story office buildings were once connected by a one-story hyphen (a connecting structure) meant for retail stores and a small automobile forecourt. This was approximately the site of the former Ourisman Chevrolet at 621 H Street NE. Real estate developer Jair Lynch purchased the entire property in 2011 and redeveloped the one-story hyphen at **625 H Street NE** (Hord Coplan Macht) in 2016 as the Anthology, a nine-story, mixed-use residential building.

■ **4** The **Apollo DC** takes its name from the former Apollo Theatre once located at 624 H Street NE. The theater was erected in 1913 as a nine-hundred-seat cinema showing silent films. It was purchased by local theater magnate Harry Crandall in 1922. Eight years later in 1930, Warner Bros. Theaters of Washington announced grand plans to replace the building with a 2,500-seat cinema. These plans promptly went nowhere because of the Great Depression. The theater was purchased by Ourisman Chevrolet in 1949 and replaced by a five-story automobile service center in 1955, expanding the footprint of the dealership across the street.

Insight Property Group redeveloped the site in 2016 as the Apollo (SK+I Architects), an eight-story, mixed-use apartment building with a Whole Foods Market on the ground floor. The LEED Gold–rated building contains several references to the site's former use as a cinema, such as the recreated APOLLO mosaic in the floor of the residential lobby. MV+A Architects consulted on the retail design of the ground floor and designed the grocery interior within.

Apollo DC

■ **5** After the British burned Washington on August 24, 1814, public buildings in the city were reconstructed with fireproof brick or stone masonry. Homes continued to be constructed of wood through the 1870s, however. This twin duplex example at **727–729 10th Street NE** (before 1874, architect unknown) was constructed just off H Street to take advantage of the newly inaugurated streetcar service into downtown. The balloon framing technique used in houses such as this allowed for quick construction by relatively unskilled labor, as well as the freedom to easily construct exterior embellishments like the parlor windows on the ground floor of each house. Note the carved wood cornice with decorative corbels, likely factory-made with powered machinery to a standardized pattern. By 1880, Washington had finally updated fire safety and building regulations to mandate the use of masonry exterior walls on residential dwellings.

■ **6** This **Bank of America** branch at 722 H Street NE, designed by Appleton P. Clarke Jr. in 1912, was originally the Home Savings Bank, which merged with the American Security and Trust Company several years later in 1918. An addition, also designed by Clarke, was added to the bank in 1935 and doubled the size of the building. Appleton P. Clarke Jr. was a prominent architect in Washington, primarily designing houses and apartment buildings. Many of his designs were in the styles of Romanesque revival, Colonial revival, Georgian revival, and Greek revival—like the Bank of America building. The bank's grand design features a pediment with two columns on each side, so the entry way is wide and prominent. At the very bottom of the heavily detailed cornice around the facade is a meandering pattern in the stone that is reflective of the Greek revival style. The parts of the facade that are not stone are in a stone-colored brick to give a grander appearance instead of red brick, which would have been a more economical choice at the time.

■ **7** Currently a branch of **PNC Bank**, this bank served the H Street Corridor originally as the Northeast Saving Bank and was designed by B. Stanley Simmons in 1921. On March 6, 1933, during the Great Depression, President Franklin Roosevelt declared a national bank moratorium, which caused Northeast Savings Bank to be closed. The bank was then placed under conservatorship and combined with other local institutions to form Hamilton National Bank, which subsequently evolved into the National Bank of Washington from 1954 to 1990.

Architect B. Stanley Simmons designed several other Beaux-Arts style buildings in DC that included other banks and apartments buildings, like the historic Wyoming apartments located in Adams Morgan. The architectural style of the bank was popular at the time, and the use of stone was meant to symbolize permanence and stability. The pilasters flank each side of the front facade, and the wider width between the two central columns at the entrance highlights the open, grand interior of the bank. The plan of the bank that was used was the inverted "T," a popular bank plan at the time. Large windows span the side of the building, allowing plenty of light to make the interior space feel light, airy, and grand.

■ **8** The **Avec on H** at 901 H Street NE spans 8th through 10th Streets on the south side of H Street. This imposing, mixed-use development, completed in 2020 by Rappaport and WC Smith and designed by Torti Gallas + Partners and Antunovich Associates, is composed of nine distinct facade types, which serve to break down the two-block-long building into a scale more in keeping with the established development pattern along the street. The interior lobby and leasing areas look out to the street through exterior storefront windows, a reference to the commercial history of the site and the H Street Corridor.

This site was previously developed as a park by the District of Columbia following the 1968 riots, before becoming the site of the H Street Connection shopping center, a one-story retail shopping center developed by Gary D. Rappaport and J. Gerald Lustine in 1987.

■ **9** The **Douglas Memorial Church** congregation has been a fixture on this corner since 1878, when John A. Douglas constructed a small brick chapel on this site for the Memorial Methodist Episcopal congregation. The congregation soon renamed themselves in honor of the builder and his wife Sidney. The current modified Romanesque structure at 800 11th Street NE was completed in 1898 to designs by architect Joseph C. Johnson. The pressed red brick structure exhibits typical Romanesque features including round-arched openings with exuberant, oversized voussoirs and lively brick corbeling at the cornice lines, all within a blocky, compact form. The Romanesque style achieved renewed popularity in the United States in the 1880s under the influence of architect H. H. Richardson. High-style Richardsonian Romanesque buildings are almost always made of rough-cut ashlar stone to emphasize the massive, heavy nature of the style. This example successfully executes the typical Richardsonian Romanesque style in less expensive, local pressed red brick. Pressed brick was popular from the end of the Civil War until the early twentieth century and has a smooth surface, sharp edges, and notably thin mortar joints. The brick is made of a fine, dry clay pressed into molds under great pressure by hydraulic or screw presses and can still be seen on a number of buildings in the city. Note the historical marker provided by Cultural Tourism DC—Marker Number 14—on the sidewalk in front of the building.

The Douglas Memorial Church was originally a white congregation, but it faced declining membership in the 1940s in response to the changing racial composition in the surrounding neighborhood. The congregation was down to only a handful of members in 1958, when the governing Baltimore Conference assigned Black pastor Forrest C. Stith in a last-ditch effort to turn things around. Within three years the congregation rebounded to over two hundred members under his leadership. He was later installed as a bishop and continues to teach and lecture since his retirement in 1996. As of this writing he serves as retired bishop-in-residence at Asbury United Methodist Church in Washington and as president of the National African American Methodist Heritage Center.

■ **10** In April 1968, riots in response to the assassination of the Rev. Dr. Martin Luther King Jr. affected at least 110 US cities, including Washington. Looting and arson affected the city for four days, especially in segregated African American commercial corridors like H Street NE. Almost two dozen mixed-use buildings existed on this site before the riots, and their destruction along with others up and down the corridor only deepened the disinvestment and inequality of the neighborhood in the following decades. Following the riots, the land either remained vacant for decades or was redeveloped with inexpensive, single-story strip retail with surface parking, like the example here at **1207 H Street NE**, constructed in the late 1990s. Large mixed-use developments gradually replaced the vacant lots and cheaply built retail buildings, and this property is the only remaining example of suburban-style strip retail on H Street as of this writing.

■ **11** The art moderne **Atlas Performing Arts Center** at 1333 H Street NE opened on August 31, 1938, with Mickey Rooney in *Love Finds Andy Hardy*, and the distinctive modernist facade made it an immediate landmark along the H Street Corridor. The theater could seat almost one thousand customers in the single-level auditorium. During its heyday, the theater mixed movies and live entertainment for nearly four decades. The theater eventually closed because of a marked decline in patronage after the 1968 riots. After languishing vacant for over thirty-three years, the building reopened in 2006 as a nonprofit performing arts center.

Architect John J. Zink was born in Baltimore in 1886 and graduated from the Maryland Institute in 1904. After that, he collaborated with noted theater archi-

The Atlas Performing Arts Center

tect Thomas W. Lamb on the Baltimore Hippodrome, Garden, and Maryland Theaters before working with William H. Hodges and Wyatt & Nolting. While working for Lamb, Zink attended Columbia to study architecture. In 1920, Zink formed a partnership with Ewald G. Blanke and W. O. Sparklin after working with Lamb. He had a successful career as a theater designer, and his firm is said to have built more than two hundred movie theaters along the East Coast, including thirty in the Baltimore-Washington area. Zink joined the AIA in 1921 and placed second in the Harding Inaugural Court of Honor Competition.

■ **12** Located at 1336 H Street NE, the **Aldea** features street-level retail space and large, coliving residential apartments above, crowned by a rooftop deck with panoramic views. Organized in a T-shape layout, the residential floors contain three coliving apartments, each with five bedrooms, open kitchen, dining area, and living room. Generous floor-to-ceiling windows allow sunlight to fill the common area and frame urban views of the Federal City to the south. Residents step outside into a walkable urban community that's a short distance to the heart of the city located near DC's only streetcar, other public transportation, and amenities.

The Aldea is closely linked to its context, contributing to the commercial life of the street, while providing high-quality and affordable coliving resi dences to a youthful community that wants to live close to the action of the city. The Aldea engages with the energy of the street, providing a characterful presence with a flash of color that would be at once distinctive and in keeping with the local community setting.

■ **13** Pierre L'Enfant laid out his famous plan for Washington in 1791 with a grid that divided the city into rectangular blocks, all interrupted by diagonal avenues radiating out from important points of interest in adherence to fashionable French Baroque concepts. The L'Enfant Plan was destined from the start to become one of the most important works of city planning in eighteenth-century North America, but it communicated nothing on what was to happen to the interiors of the blocks themselves, or squares as they're officially called in the District of Columbia.

Real estate speculators soon subdivided these squares into smaller lots and cut alleyways through the interiors to provide access. Alleys such as Linden Court NE proliferated in the second half of the nineteenth century, typically housing working-class African American residents, even as the homes on the blocks facing the main thoroughfares housed middle- or upper-class white residents. The twentieth century saw a series of zoning reforms and community efforts aimed at erasing alley dwellings from the city's landscape, if not the alleys themselves. These efforts culminated in the urban renewal of the Southwest Waterfront starting in 1949, which razed the entire neighborhood and saw it rebuilt according to midcentury modernist principals—and without a single alley dwelling.

By the mid-twentieth century new alley dwellings had long been outlawed, and more and more existing buildings were converted to one of the few allowable uses, like auto repair, light manufacturing, or warehousing. Alley dwellings never disappeared entirely, however, and in recent years interest in them has grown. In recognition of this fact, the city radically reformed the zoning code in 2016 to allow alley dwellings once again, and a resurgence of this housing type has begun. **1305–1321 Linden Court** typifies this history. The unremarkable group of brick dwellings was constructed in 1892, with the western portion later housing an automobile repair facility before being recently renovated back into private residences, but this time at a decidedly higher price point.

■ **14** By the 1920s, automobile ownership enjoyed widespread popularity, and auto showrooms began to appear on commercial corridors throughout the country. Evidence suggests that brothers William and Charles Oshinsky erected this structure at **1365 H Street NE** (1927, Upman and Adams) as a speculative venture to capitalize on this trend. In 1929–30, it was occupied by a branch of Mott Motors, Inc., a Hupmobile dealer. Later tenants in the 1930s and 1940s included Nash RJ Motor Co. and Duke & Otey Motors, Inc., dealers of Plymouth vehicles.

The building later became the Plymouth Theater, a four-hundred-seat cinema for segregated Black audiences from 1943 to 1952, then housed a furniture showroom, a commercial printer, and a soul food restaurant before again becoming a theater called the H Street Playhouse from 2001 to 2014. This time around, integrated audiences came to attend live performances.

■ **15** This two-bay, wood-frame vernacular row house at **1379 H Street NE** is representative of the earliest wave of development on the H Street Corridor.

Soon after the horse-drawn streetcar connected the neighborhood to down-town in 1870, working-class wood dwellings began to appear on the street. Balloon-frame wood technology became ubiquitous by the time of the Civil War and dramatically reduced the cost and complexity of wood structures like this one, compared to brick and masonry dwellings. Flat roofs, made possible by the recent invention of built-up tar roofing, reduced costs even further. Nonetheless, it features fashionable Italianate brackets supporting a simple cornice. It is likely that the house originally featured wood clapboards and Italianate detailing around door and window openings, which have been lost or obscured with the later application of aluminum siding.

■ **16** H Street NE terminates on the east end at the so-called **Starburst Plaza**. This is the extreme northeastern edge of the planned L'Enfant city. Beyond this point the planned city gave way to rural farms and old turnpikes connecting to early Maryland settlements. Bladensburg Road, at the northern side of the intersection, is one of the routes that predates the city of Washington, DC. It runs from this point to Bladensburg, Maryland, to the Eastern Branch of the Potomac River, now known as the Anacostia. Bladensburg was an important tidewater port before the river silted up because of land clearing and agricultural development in the nineteenth century. To the east, "Captain" William Benning bought a bridge crossing the Anacostia River and created a namesake toll road that became an important route connecting the District and Upper Marlboro, Maryland, another important early port and county seat, which lost economic importance once its connection to the Chesapeake Bay silted up. Somewhat incongruously, tiny Upper Marlboro (population 652) is still the county seat of Prince George's County, Maryland (population 967,201).

The District was developing quickly in the mid-to-late 1800s, and space for cemeteries was getting sparse, particularly for Black residents of the city. Still rural space immediately north of the Starburst Intersection was bought and designated as Graceland Cemetery in 1870. By 1894 H Street had developed so much that the cemetery was closed, and the interred remains were moved to cemeteries in Maryland. Over the years, the intersection also hosted the termini of streetcars from the Columbia Railway and later Washington Railway and Electric Company and passenger rail lines from the Washington, Baltimore, and Annapolis Electric Railway. To the north one can see the haphazard way the District developed outside of the bounds of the L'Enfant Plan. As rural and industrial sites north of the city were sold off piecemeal, new neighborhoods were planned distinctly separate from the overall grid pattern of the L'Enfant city. The grid of the Trinidad neighborhood north of Florida Avenue shifts dramatically from the grid established by L'Enfant to the south. Recently the intersection was renovated to host Starburst Plaza, which features the "Cornerstones of History" mural, featuring Duke Ellington, Bessie Smith, Rev. Dr. Martin Luther King Jr., and Rosa Parks.

Union Market District

(Revitalized industrial marketplace, food hall, retail, Gallaudet University)

Megan Davey

Distance: 1½ miles
Time: 50 minutes
Bus: 90 and 92
Metro: NoMa-Gallaudet U New York Ave (Red Line)

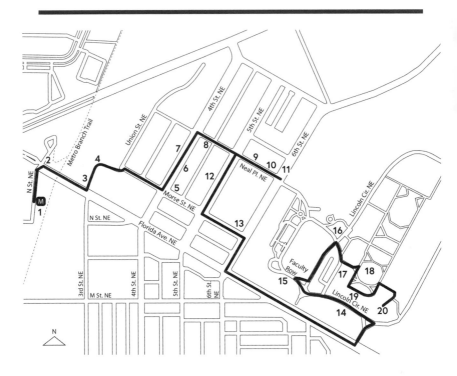

For most of its existence, Union Market District, the subject of this walking tour, was the city's primary location for industrial wholesale since the 1930s. In the 2010s, the area underwent a revitalization like no other with a myriad of restaurants, retail, and residential spaces infilling the existing warehouse hub. This neighborhood is now sought out by locals and tourists alike for being a center of culture, cuisine, art, and creativity.

Located on Florida Avenue, Gallaudet University sits next to the Union Market District. The university has been fundamental in educating both the deaf and hard of hearing for over 150 years. Founded in 1864 as the National Deaf-Mute College, the campus was laid out by the landscape architecture firm Olmsted, Vaux & Co. beginning with a plan in 1866. The initial buildings were designed by Frederick Withers. On this secluded campus, Withers's Victorian Gothic-style buildings are truly a hidden gem in Washington and will conclude this walking tour in a special way.

■ **1** The tour begins at **NoMa-Gallaudet U New York Ave Station**, which opened in 2004 as the Metro's eighty-fourth station. Its construction helped create the needed accessibility to both the NoMa neighborhood and Union Market District. A twenty-seven-foot-tall aluminum sculpture of a leaf can be seen from the 2nd Street NE entrance. Created by Barbara Grygutis, the design was inspired by the official tree of Washington, the scarlet oak, and is representative of the dense tree canopies that exist in the city.

■ **2** Continue along 2nd Street and pass the entry to **Metro Branch Trail,** accessible by pedestrian ramp at the Florida Avenue intersection. The 5.5-mile trail passes through numerous vibrant and historic neighborhoods in Northeast Washington, as well as connecting to the Union Station and the greater downtown. Although the Metro Branch Trail is not part of this walking tour, it is worth a return trip for the feel of local Northeast DC with pocket parks, ever-changing murals, and sounds of the red line Metro. For more information on the murals go to DC Wall Festival's website at https://dcwallsfestival.com/.

■ **3** Turn right on Florida Avenue and proceed beyond the underpass where **Gantry Park** can be found (open to the public in 2021). The park serves as a pedestrian gateway into the newly developed portion of the Union Market District and contains beautiful landscaping and views of the Metro.

■ **4** The design of the **Highline** (320 Florida Avenue NE) was inspired by its location in the Union Market area, DC's longtime wholesale market complex, which is now undergoing redevelopment. The brick base and the suspended metal canopy above the first floor recall the historic warehouses that accommodated rows of delivery trucks, while the massing of the upper levels evokes stacked shipping containers. Eric Colbert & Associates was also instrumental in coordinating the park on the west side of the site, which will provide a link between the Union Market community and the Metro station to the south.

■ **5** Walk back to Gentry Park and look at the **gantry sculpture** positioned at the end of the park, made by artist Don Hoover. It has become a new landmark for the Union Market District—representing a deconstructed version of the rail gantries used to load and unload heavy items in rail yards. The sculpture creates a framed view of the trains and Metro cars that pass by the site daily.

■ **6** Further down Morse Street, turn left onto 4th Street NE for the first view of the historical warehouses. Five blocks of industrial, two-story brick buildings were all formerly part of **Union Terminal Market**. Local architect E. L. Bullock used repetition of his classical design to give all five blocks an architectural rhythm

Union Terminal Market

and sense of cohesion. Each building has Doric columns, twenty-foot bays, six-over-six metal framed windows, and bas-relief carvings above each window. These industrial warehouse buildings first opened in 1931, selling meats, eggs, fish, produce, and other wares. Now the buildings are home to wholesalers, restaurants, and retail shops.

■ **7** Midway along the historical industrial warehouse strip on **4th Street NE** are the remains of Union Terminal Market's original sign, sitting on top of the second floor of the buildings.

■ **8** Although originally completed as part of Union Terminal Market in the 1950s, **La Cosecha** (2019, Gensler) on the left side of 4th Street NE is now a contemporary marketplace celebrating centuries of Latin American heritage. As a culinary embassy, La Cosecha is designed for community and conversation through food, drink, and shopping. The market also partners with Latin American embassies for seasonal experiences and is open Monday through Sunday, 8:00 a.m.–10:00 p.m. Visit unionmarketdc.com/retailer/la-cosecha/ for more information.

■ **9** Turn right on **Neal Place NE** to see how the integration of street art with industrial architecture has redefined the character of the market and solidified it as a place for creativity and experimentation. One can feel the creative and rejuvenated spirit of Union Market even though the original two-story buildings from the 1930s flank both sides of the street.

■ **10 Union Market** on Neal Place NE was originally constructed in 1967 for the purpose of replacing the Union Terminal Market buildings (passed earlier on the tour), in the 1960s. In 2012, developer EDENS reopened Union Market with more than forty local food vendors. It gained wild popularity and now averages 15,000 visitors per weekend and has hosted numerous community events. This building was the cornerstone of inspiring redevelopment and life into the surrounding neighborhood in the last few decades.

Union Market

11 Hi-Lawn, Union Market's rooftop, is accessible from the building's corner at Neal Place and 6th Street NE. With plenty of picnic tables, music, and greenspace for play, it is a popular neighborhood hangout space. To see the weekly activities at Hi-Lawn visit unionmarketdc.com/retailer/hi-lawn/. The rooftop also features 360° views of the bustling union market district below, as well as views of Gallaudet University to the east. Additionally, in 2019, this rooftop was temporarily constructed into a seven-hundred-seat stadium for the World Team Tennis season—a noteworthy moment in the building's history.

12 Those interested in street art will want to visit the side of the Union Market building facing 6th Street—a canvas for **building-size murals**, which are updated every few months. Two of the most famous murals located on the building were displayed in 2017. The first mural was by Yoko Ono, with the words, "Relax. Your Heart Is Stronger Than What You Think." The second mural was done by graffiti artist Mr. Brainwash, who spray-painted "Never Give Up" above a mass of colorful hearts.

13 Walk along the **5th Street NE arcade** to explore many exciting shops and restaurants. The arcade was originally used as a continuous loading area for goods entering the market back in the 1930s. Be sure to look down 5th Street NE toward Morse Street NE for a view of the Capitol Building in the distance.

14 The corner of Morse Street NE and 6th Street NE is the home of DC's first **Little Tavern**. The one-story building was part of a chain of hamburger restaurants in the DC region founded in the 1920s. The building will be restored as a historic landmark and used as a commercial space, in tandem with the ground-floor commercial space of Morse Street Apartments, designed by SK+I Architecture in 2021.

■ 15 Gallaudet University's **Thomas Hopkins Gallaudet and Alice Cogswell Statue** is an important landmark upon arriving on the campus grounds from Florida Avenue NE (ID required to enter the university). Thomas Hopkins Gallaudet established the first permanent school for deaf children in the United States, and young Alice was one of Gallaudet's first students. Sculptor Daniel Chester French designed the statue to depict the special bond between teacher and student that revolutionized deaf education around the world.

■ 16 The **Edward Miner Gallaudet Residence**, also known as House One, is a thirty-five-room Victorian Gothic mansion built in 1869 for Gallaudet University's founder and first president, Edward Miner Gallaudet. It can be found at the end of Faculty Row and is where Gallaudet, his successors, and their families have all resided.

■ 17 The **Peikoff Alumni House**, affectionately known as "Ole Jim," was built in 1881 to serve as the campus's gymnasium. It was considered one of the finest in the nation and contained what is possibly the first indoor swimming pool in the country. The building is a rare and charming example of Queen Anne–style architecture, and it is the only remaining physical education facility built in Washington, DC, in the nineteenth century.

Peikoff Alumni House

■ 18 **College Hall**, now a National Historic Landmark, was completed in 1877 as the main academic building and dormitory for male students. Architect Frederick Clarke Withers, English-born and trained by the Olmsted and Vaux firm, designed the college's buildings for twenty years. Withers brought an entirely new design vocabulary to Gallaudet, creating one of the most coherent clusters of High Victorian Gothic style buildings in Washington.

19 At the center of the green stands the **Edward Miner Gallaudet statue** (1969, Pietro Lazzari, Italian artist) erected in honor of the founder and first president of Gallaudet College.

20 Chapel Hall was built in 1870 and designed by the same architect of College Hall, Frederick C. Withers. The building remains as a picturesque landmark for the Gallaudet campus. This High Victorian gothic building has served as a chapel, auditorium, and dining hall. Now, serving as the home of the National Deaf Life Museum, Chapel Hall features exhibits on deaf history, culture, and language. To visit the museum one can schedule an appointment at koalendar .com/e/museum-visit.

Chapel Hall

21 Building 103, formerly known as Dawes house, was a boys' dormitory built in 1895. The architect, Olof Hanson, was the first deaf architect to design a building for Gallaudet University. Hanson made sure to design for ample natural sunlight, critical to the deaf community's need for visual clarity.

Independence Avenue and L'Enfant Plaza

(Federal office buildings, large commercial urban redevelopment project)

John J. Protopappas and Stephanie L. Protopappas, updated by Laura Hagood

Distance: ¾ mile
Time: 1¼ hours
Bus: 52 and 74
Metro: Federal Center/Southwest (Blue, Orange, and Silver Lines)

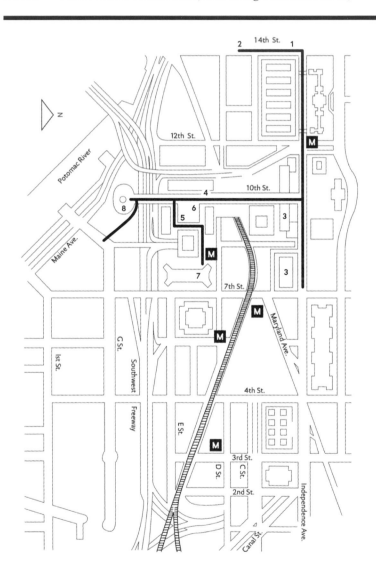

The Independence Avenue/L'Enfant Plaza area is the northern edge of Washington's Southwest quadrant. During the first half of the nineteenth century, it was a very desirable residential area. Only a few commercial structures (including the most famous of the city's slave pens) were in evidence. After the Baltimore and Potomac Railroad laid tracks along Maryland and Virginia Avenues in 1873, the western end of the area between B Street (Independence Avenue) and the waterfront became a vast railroad yard, and the desirability of nearby areas as residential neighborhoods diminished.

Prior to 1900 the only government agencies with a strong interest in the area were the Department of Agriculture, with buildings along B Street, and the Bureau of Engraving and Printing, on 14th Street (making use of the railroad for freight service). Federal interest in the northern fringes of the quadrant increased during the first decades of the twentieth century, with the erection of some additional buildings for Agriculture and Engraving and Printing offices, but in general the area retained much of its nineteenth-century appearance because government departments preferred to rent space in existing structures.

During World War I, the federal bureaucracy mushroomed, and it became all too apparent that the federal government could no longer make do with offices scattered all over the city. The Independence Avenue/L'Enfant Plaza area was included in the kite-shaped monumental core proposed by the Senate Park Commission in 1902, but its use was undefined and little action was taken. By the 1920s, a new building program had become a necessity. Most of the attention was focused on the Federal Triangle between Pennsylvania Avenue NW and the Mall. But by the 1930s, the newly created National Capital Park and Planning Commission (today the National Capital Planning Commission [NCPC]) was drawing up plans for similar developments in other parts of the city. One of the areas proposed was the Southwest Rectangle, bounded by B Street (later given the more pretentious name of Independence Avenue), 14th Street, the current right of way of the Southwest Freeway, and 2nd Street.

Nothing further was done until the 1950s, when plans for the redevelopment of the entire quadrant were drawn up. Although an area roughly the same as the old Southwest Rectangle was set aside for development as government offices, no plan specified the location of any of the proposed buildings or their spatial relationship to one another. The awkward positioning of many of the offices in the redeveloped federal area is a result of this omission from the recent plans.

This tour begins at the westernmost entrance to the Smithsonian Metro station, located at 12th and Independence Avenue SW at the northeast corner of the **Department of Agriculture (South Building)**. The concentration of buildings, which constitutes the headquarters of the Department of Agriculture, covers three city blocks. Several of these buildings were completed during the 1930s as part of the Southwest Rectangle project. As you exit the Metro station, walk west for one block along C Street SW to 14th Street SW. Tour sites no. 1 and no. 2 are located on the west side of 14th Street.

■ **1** The **US Holocaust Memorial Museum** is south of the Sidney R. Yates Federal Building, at 14th Street SW and Raoul Wallenberg Place SW. It was dedicated on April 22, 1993. Planning for the museum started during the presidency of Jimmy Carter. In November 1978, President Carter established the President's Commission on the Holocaust and charged it with issuing a report on the state of Holocaust remembrance and education in the United States. In September 1979, the President's Commission presented its recommendation, to "establish a living memorial to honor the victims and survivors of the Holocaust and to ensure that the lessons of the Holocaust will be taught in perpetuity."

Pei Cobb Freed & Partners designed the museum, a multistoried complex that provides classrooms, theaters, auditoriums, meeting spaces, a variety of interactive learning activities, permanent exhibitions, and a Hall of Remembrance. The exterior design engages with its neighboring buildings. Victorian red brick connects it the Yates Building, whereas its limestone points to its neighbor, the Bureau of Engraving and Printing. Past the familiar limestone, however, visitors find themselves in a concrete building, where design choices suggesting deception, duality, and concealment evoke the Holocaust's murderous toll.

The US Holocaust Memorial Museum is open daily, 10 a.m.–4:00 p.m. with extended summer hours. The museum is closed on Yom Kippur and December 25. Admission is free. More information can be found at www .ushmm.org or by calling 202-488-0400.

■ **2** The **Bureau of Engraving and Printing Building** is where millions of dollars in paper money, as well as stamps and other official documents, are printed every day (coins are not manufactured here, as they are under the purview of the US Mint). This impressive building was constructed in 1914, displaying a neoclassical style with Indiana limestone and a granite trim exterior, concealing a steel superstructure and fireproof concrete. Monumental stone columns march along the building's 505-foot facade, making for an imposing architectural statement for this important function. As of this writing, public tours were no longer on offer, but it is worth checking bep.gov/visitor-centers for current information. Go back to Independence Avenue and head east to 10th Street/L'Enfant Promenade.

■ **3** The **James Forrestal Building (FOB No. 5)**, at Independence Avenue and 10th Street (1970, Curtis & Davis), was designed for the Department of Defense—and for a time dubbed "Little Pentagon." Since 1977, it has housed the Department of Energy. It is the only federal office building to have both a name and a number. As for James Forrestal, 1892–1949, he was the last cabinet-level US secretary of the navy and the first US secretary of defense.

Completed in 1969, the complex consists of three structures: the 660-foot-long main building fronting on Independence Avenue, a taller office annex behind, and a separate cafeteria building. The large horizontal building originally was conceived as two of the General Services Administration's "universal office buildings," one on each side of 10th Street. However, the Department of Defense convinced Congress that the specialized nature of the department's activities required that the majority of its facilities on this site be contained in a single structure. Congress then approved the concept of a single building spanning 10th Street. Ultimately it was agreed that the first floor of the horizontal building would be lifted thirty feet above street level to avoid blocking the 10th Street vista of the Smithsonian Castle tower. It was felt that the sense of space created by the horizontal opening between the plaza and the first floor more than compensated for the loss of the narrow view up 10th Street. That said, it also had the disadvantage of closing the Southwest neighborhood off from the National Mall and downtown

The feeling of unity between the Forrestal Building and the developing 10th Street Mall/L'Enfant Plaza complex to the south was reinforced by the use of coordinated paving materials on all three projects. The presence of the surface railroad on Maryland Avenue required that the two building complexes be on different levels. Now pass underneath the Forrestal Building and continue down L'Enfant Promenade/10th Street.

■ **4** The **10th Street/L'Enfant Promenade (or Mall)** and L'Enfant Plaza (1965, 10th Street Mall, Wright & Gane, architects; 1965, L'Enfant Plaza, North and South Buildings and Plaza, I. M. Pei & Associates; 1970–73, L'Enfant Plaza Hotel, Vlastimil Koubek). Early in 1954, Webb & Knapp, New York developers, proposed a renewal plan for the entire Southwest quadrant, including 10th Street and L'Enfant Plaza. The plan originally called for widening 10th Street and developing it as a 1,200-foot-long mall. This mall was to be flanked with public and semipublic office buildings.

L'Enfant Plaza, originally planned to be farther east of 10th Street, was to be an enclosed square surrounded by private office buildings. It was also expected to develop as a cultural and entertainment/convention center, with a hotel, performance hall, theater, and outdoor cafes. The mall itself was to terminate in a semicircular reflecting pool and waterfront park on the Washington Channel, balancing another large fountain treatment in the Smithsonian yard.

By the time construction began, however, significant changes had been made in the plan. In 1960 urban designer Willo von Moltke proposed the development of the 10th Street axis as a waterfront overlook. I. M. Pei & Associates drew up a master plan for the mall and plaza that brought the plaza west to

L'Enfant Plaza and 10th Street Mall

its present location. After public hearings, this master plan was incorporated into the official renewal plan approved by the NCPC. By then Webb & Knapp had withdrawn, and the project had been taken over by the L'Enfant Plaza Corporation, a group of New York and Washington financiers.

■ **5** Walk up the west side of the 10th Street/L'Enfant Promenade to **L'Enfant Plaza**. Note that the mall bridges the railroad tracks that cut through the site. The Pei proposal had included a major focal sculpture for the plaza, but this too was eliminated. The paving for both the mall and L'Enfant Plaza is Hastings block inlaid with red granite. No effort has been made to differentiate visually between public and private property. The center strip down the mall was intended to be a cascade of water flowing toward Independence Avenue, but it leaked and was drained.

Though L'Enfant Plaza was generally celebrated as a success in 1968, it has since been widely criticized as confusing and uninviting. By the 2000s, the area was ripe for reinvention. Developer JBG retained architect SmithGroup to reenvision L'Enfant Plaza starting in 2009. Its biggest improvement became the addition of the International Spy Museum in 2019. Across 10th Street/L'Enfant Promenade from L'Enfant Plaza, you will see the **Postal Service Building**.

The buildings to the north and south of the plaza are office towers; the one to the east is a hotel. Slotted underneath a street-level glass atrium, an underground shopping mall has little to recommend it, though it does offer a welcome stop to grab a bite to eat. On nice days, tables and chairs are available on the plaza itself.

■ **6** Dropped into the middle of L'Enfant Plaza, the 120,000-square-foot **International Spy Museum** is the result of a collaboration between developer JBG, British firm Roger Stirk Harbour + Partners, and DC-based firm Hickok Cole. It brought a welcome splash of bright red to an arguably dreary vista. Its playful evocation of the business of espionage, "hidden in plain sight," conceals a robust set of exhibits, including interactive panels popular with younger guests. Check spymuseum.org for hours and ticket prices and be sure to allow a couple hours for a meaningful visit. Reservations are recommended.

■ **7 Robert C. Weaver Federal Building/Department of Housing and Urban Development (HUD)** (1968, Marcel Breuer and Herbert Beckhard), 451 7th Street SW. Walk behind the hotel on L'Enfant Plaza and take the staircase on the northern corner down to the HUD Building. This structure located immediately behind the hotel represents a midcentury modern example of brutalism, a style that describes buildings made of raw concrete (*béton brut* in French). Walk north to D Street and then around the HUD Building, along 7th Street. This route provides several appealing vantage points on the building. Robert Weaver was the agency's first secretary, as well as the first African American cabinet member.

Marcel Breuer, one of midcentury modernism's leading practitioners, became involved with curvilinear structures while designing a building for UNESCO and a research lab for IBM at La Gaude, France. At the time, Breuer's French patrons favored such buildings because they permit a maximum amount of natural light in a maximum number of offices (thereby reducing the amount of electricity required), while keeping the distance between offices to a minimum. Breuer selected a curvilinear shape for the HUD Building partly because it would yield the best window-distance ratio in a large structure on a restricted site and partly because its lines would be sympathetic to the curves of the Southwest Freeway adjacent to it. The building is a double Y, with each wing touching the property lines only at the corners. Though the HUD Building is widely accepted as a prime example of brutalism, whether it is successful or not has been the subject of animated debate. Former HUD Secretary Jack Kemp once called it "ten floors of basement." The plaza's "flying saucers" have also attracted much comment, while HUD employees claim that they do not provide useful cover.

Notice the surrounding federal office buildings, including the recently renovated Constitution Center on 7th Street. This confusing juxtaposition of buildings results from the lack of a single design plan for the section of the redevelopment area designated for office use. Each building was developed without direct coordination with its neighbors, and this lacuna is especially visible from this vantage point.

■ **8** Now continue down 7th Street, crossing over the Southwest Freeway, and make a right on G Street. Head up the pedestrian walkway to the **Benjamin Banneker Circle and Fountain,** where the tour terminates. Benjamin Banneker (1731–1806), an African American scientist, astronomer, and almanac author, and largely self-taught, is best known for his important contribution to the survey that determined the District of Columbia's boundaries.

This overlook provided a **panoramic view** of the Washington Channel prior to 2017, but the neighborhood's latest development, the District Wharf, now offers an uninterrupted wall of large buildings instead, not all of them architecturally distinguished. The park, restored in 2021, is still worth a look on its own merit. It is the work of Dan Kiley, one of the twentieth century's most important American landscape architects, and a worthy tribute of its namesake.

Once you have completed the tour, the District Wharf, just across Maine Avenue, will likely beckon with a wide range of restaurants, retail, and family-friendly amenities. Alternatively, you will see 10th Street/L'Enfant Promenade extend behind you, back toward the International Spy Museum and the Forrestal Building, leading you to Independence Avenue for a complete loop.

Southwest and the Wharf

(Established residential areas, regional theater, and waterfront)

Laura Hagood, previous text written by Stephanie L. Protopappas, and Charity Vanderbilt Davidson

Distance: 2 miles
Time: 1½ miles
Bus: 52, 74, P6, and the DC Circulator
Metro: L'Enfant Plaza (Blue, Orange, and Silver Lines), exiting at 7th Street

When the Federal City was laid out in 1791–92, it was expected that the Southwest quadrant would develop as a mixed residential/commercial center. Not surprisingly, a few wealthy citizens built stately homes in the area, and a real estate syndicate constructed several rows of substantial brick dwellings for speculative purposes. This investment never quite came to fruition, and Washington's elite soon moved on to nearby Capitol Hill or Northwest. However, the neighborhood's location—where the Anacostia and Potomac Rivers meet—meant that it would only increase in importance over time.

Its bustling waterfront eventually attracted industrial activities, such as warehouses, ice houses, and coal yards, and some of its low-skilled workers settled nearby. Over time, modest but enterprising families built a vibrant community, bringing together free African Americans, Jews, and white immigrants—even migrants from Virginia—in common pursuit of American prosperity. Some settled in the neighborhoods' alleys, which over time became overcrowded and insalubrious. The most notorious was Dixon's Court.

By the 1930s, much of this unpretentious neighborhood just blocks from the Capitol had deteriorated, in the eyes of some, to the point of blight—making it an "embarrassment" in the heart of the nation's capital. At midcentury, ambitious white architects and planners, as well as private real estate developers and congressional committees, called for tearing it all down and starting over. They argued that improved housing would somehow solve the neighborhood's social problems. These claims on behalf of urban renewal disregarded how racism and economic injustice systematically denied low-income families, particularly Black people, a safe, healthy, and comfortable life.

Early in 1952, two plans were offered for the redevelopment of 427 acres in the Southwest quadrant. The first, prepared by Elbert Peets for the National Capital Planning Commission, had called for the rehabilitation of many of the residential structures, but this option was rejected as socially and financially impossible. The second plan, commissioned by the District of Columbia

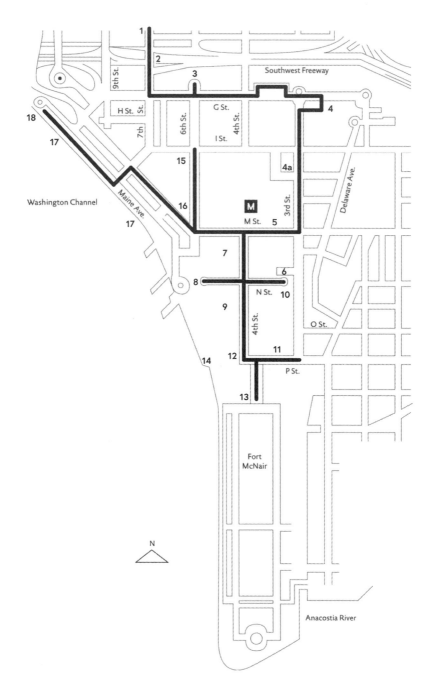

9th St.

Southwest Freeway

H St. St.

7th

18

17

6th St.

3rd St.

G St.

I St.

4th St.

Delaware Ave.

4

4a

15

Washington Channel

Maine Ave.

16

M

M St.

5

17

7

8

9

6

N St.

10

4th St.

O St.

11

14

12

P St.

13

Fort
McNair

N

Anacostia River

Redevelopment Land Agency (RLA), was prepared by the Saint Louis planning firm of Harland Bartholomew and Associates and by two Washington architects, Chloethiel Woodard Smith and Louis Justement. Their plan called for the demolition of nearly all existing structures and the erection of approximately five thousand new dwelling units. Both plans called for razing the retail commercial streets in favor of a central shopping mall to serve the entire Southwest, and a waterfront completely changed from industrial to recreational uses.

In 1953 Webb & Knapp prepared a third plan for 440 acres that had been set aside for private development. I. M. Pei and Chicago architect Harry Weese headed up the firm's architectural and planning staff. The section south of the freeway was to be residential, with high-rise apartment towers interspersed among clusters of townhouses. This proposal for mixed building types was innovative for its time, as developers had previously segregated high-rise and low-rise structures. With the intent of maximizing their and their investors' profit, Webb & Knapp also replaced low-cost housing initially intended for displaced former residents with market-rate homes.

In exchange for formulating the plan, Webb & Knapp was given a choice of areas to develop. The firm chose what is today L'Enfant Plaza (see Tour 7, Independence Avenue and L'Enfant Plaza) and the residential section north of M Street dubbed Town Center. The basic concepts of the Webb & Knapp plan (sometimes also referred to as the Zeckendorf-Pei plan) were finally adopted by the NCPC in 1956, but many of the details were altered. Webb & Knapp began work on its portion of the project but was forced to withdraw later for financial reasons.

The Peets plan of 1952 had tried to work with the original street plan, but subsequent development plans called for substantial changes, such as the creation of "super blocks" that closed many streets. One of the recurring themes in the redevelopment area is the variety of ways in which different developers have used the old street spaces. That said, the massive Southeast–Southwest Freeway, a six-lane highway bordering the neighborhood, was entirely new.

No fewer than 23,500 individuals, most of them Black, were ultimately displaced. The cost to the lives of low-income Southwest residents was appalling, and very few ever returned, as the new, limited mixed-income housing was beyond their means. The social networks that had helped them get by were shredded. The dispersal of low-income Southwesters to other parts of the city, particularly Southeast, reshaped these receiving communities, often deepening their poverty.

Most of the structures you will see on this tour are now well over fifty years old, and many have been well maintained. Modernist architecture has benefited from a recent reappraisal, and even the American brutalist style has its proponents today. Until the 2010s, this had been a sleepy community, tucked behind the National Mall and its adjacent federal office buildings. Most recently, with the complete redevelopment of the Southwest waterfront, the addition of a state-of-the-art library, and a spectacular reworked Arena Stage, the area has become increasingly vibrant and inviting, but Southwest's complicated legacy remains far from forgotten.

■ **1** Once you step out of the Metro, go right, down 7th Street; take another right at D Street. The tour starts with the Robert C. Weaver Building, named after the first secretary of housing and urban development and first African American Cabinet member. Owned and operated by the **Department of Housing and Urban Development**, the building was erected in 1968 by the General Services Administration as part of President Lyndon Johnson's "Great Society" initiative. A striking example of American brutalist architecture, this building, designed by Marcel Breuer, is ten stories high, perched on stilts, giving the street corner a haunting post–World War II appeal.

■ **2** Continue south on D Street, crossing over the **Southwest Freeway (I-395)**, a divider between the business and residential regions of Southwest. Take a left onto G Street, walking down the tree-covered sidewalks.

■ **3** While still on G Street, pass a small **park** on the left, a nice spot to stop and admire the architecture. The townhouses (1966–69, Walter Peter) grouped around **common greens** are maintained and owned by the homeowners. This quaint neighborhood is the beginning of Southwest's more mellow side. Continue down G Street. Take a right at the circle; proceed through the parking lot onto 3rd Street.

This parking lot may look familiar, as it is no different from many suburban townhome developments. But, venture in between the buildings, and you will find carefully tended courtyards and gardens that are surprisingly pleasant and welcoming.

■ **4** **Capitol Park apartments and townhouses** are bounded by 3rd and I Streets, Delaware Avenue, and the Southwest waterfront (1959, Satterlee and Smith; 1963, Smith and Associates). Built on the site of Dixon's Court, one of Washington's largest and most infamous inhabited alleys, Capitol Park was the first new project erected in the Southwest. It was given an American Institute of Architects Merit Award in 1960. The apartment tower at 800 4th Street SW was the first building (402 units) of a group that was ultimately intended to contain 1,600 units. Although built in stages, the complex was designed as a unified whole. The accompanying townhouses are Federal Housing Administration Honor Award winners. The development is best known for its parklike atmosphere. The feeling of openness that pervades Capitol Park, with its use of glass, contrasts sharply with the feeling of containment present in later area projects.

■ **4a** At 3rd and I Streets, the Southwest Public Library (2021, Perkins+Will) and its adjacent park are among the neighborhood's most impressive recent additions. Designed by Perkins+Will, this "pavilion in a park" achieved LEED-Platinum recognition by incorporating a wide range of sustainable features, such as environmentally sound and regionally sourced materials and water and energy conservation strategies. It further reflects recent trends in library design, such as natural light, abundant meeting spaces, and ubiquitous technology. The generous use of timber, both inside and out, is also a nod to its neighbor a few blocks away, Arena Stage, as you will see later on the tour. If you happen to be nearby after dusk, be sure to take in its spectacular lighting. This library is just one of many neighborhood branches recently redesigned by top-notch architects, such as David Adjaye, Phil Freelon, and Mecanoo.

Continue straight down 3rd Street. Take a right at M Street.

■ **5** On your right, at the 1100 block of 4th Street and M Street, you will see the Southwest Waterfront Metro station. Surrounding it is **Waterfront Station,** developed by Foulger-Pratt, part of the nation's first ecodistrict designed to promote sustainability, green building, and walkability. A textbook example of transit-oriented development, Waterfront Station is a mixed-use project that incorporates street-level retail and restaurants, office buildings, public plazas, and the newly restored 4th Street (which had been Southwest's commercial heart). This practical transportation, shopping, and employment hub serves the neighborhood well, but its design bona fides now pale in comparison to the nearby District Wharf.

■ **6** Take a left down 4th Street, where you will see **Carrollsburg Square,** bounded by M, N, 4th, and 3rd Streets (1965, Keyes, Lethbridge and Condon, architects, Eric Paepcke, landscape architect). The winner of a Redevelopment Land Agency (RLA) design competition, Carrollsburg Square has a central pedestrian area over an underground garage, but the plaza has been divided into smaller residential courts. Each court has been given its own character by means of variations in landscape materials and architectural detail. Carrollsburg Square was intended as a transition between Tiber Island and the public housing

Tiber Island

immediately to the east. Take a few minutes to explore the courtyards and spaces between buildings in this development.

■ **7** Opposite Carrollsburg on 4th Street is Tiber Island, bounded by M, N, and 4th Streets and the waterfront (1965, Keyes, Lethbridge and Condon). It was the winner of the first RLA design competition and of a 1961 American Institute of Architects Honor Award.

It consists of four eight-story apartment towers (368 units) and eighty-five two-to-three-story townhouses. It is especially interesting because of the spatial relationships between its high-rise and low-rise elements and the way in which the District of Columbia's zoning code was interpreted to permit the design's implementation. Like Carrollsburg Square, Tiber Island features a central pedestrian area over an underground garage. This vast concrete plaza is behind the apartment building that faces 4th Street and represents a striking contrast to the intimate and welcoming spaces in Carrollsburg Square.

■ **8** The **Thomas Law House**, also known as the Honeymoon House, is located at 1252 6th Street SW, in the southeast corner of Tiber Island. Walk along the apartments until the road ends, and it will be on your right. Law was a major promoter of Washington development. His Federal-style house, built between 1794 and 1796, is among Washington's oldest extant structures and is listed in the National Register of Historic Places. One of a small handful of houses preserved during urban renewal, it was rehabilitated in 1965 to serve as a community center for residents of Tiber Island and Carrollsburg Square. Head back toward 4th Street.

■ **9** The next development on 4th Street on the western side is **Harbour Square**, bounded by 4th, N, and O Streets and the waterfront (1966, Chloethiel Woodard Smith & Associates Architects). This complex not only includes high-rise apartments and townhouses, designed for a range of income levels, but also cleverly incorporates three of the late eighteenth- to early nineteenth-century structures that survived the extensive demolition. A larger-than-life personality, Chloethiel Woodard Smith (1910–92) was only the sixth woman architect to be accepted to the American Institute of Architecture College of Fellows, the field's highest honor. At her practice's peak in the early 1970s, her firm was the largest run by a woman in the country (though she despised being called a "woman architect").

Pass under the cantilevered entrance to the Harbour Square apartment building to take in the **Water Garden** at the center of this complex. It includes sculptured forms, platforms, walkways, and seating. Plantings include flowering water plants and willow trees. It is inoperative during the colder months of the year. This water garden faces out toward the Waterfront Park and the waterfront itself, making it an especially attractive dwelling.

The **Edward Simon Lewis House**, at 456 N Street SW, was built circa 1815 and is typical of early nineteenth-century brick houses in Washington.

Originally intended as a single-family house, the structure was converted into apartments. During the 1930s, its tenants included journalists Lewis J. Heath and Ernie Pyle. After rehabilitation in 1964–66, the house was included in Harbour Square as a single-family townhouse.

The **Duncanson-Cranch House,** 468–70 N Street SW, like Wheat Row (below), was built in 1794 by the real estate syndicate of James Greenleaf (a former American consul in Amsterdam), Robert Morris (a Philadelphia financier), and John Nicholson (also from Philadelphia). It comprises two townhouses in Harbour Square, built to look like one unit.

Wheat Row, at 1315–21 4th Street SW, is an important example of the conservative, vernacular domestic architecture constructed during the Federal period. Built in 1794, it is believed to be the first speculative housing built in the city by the Greenleaf syndicate. It was rehabilitated in 1964–66 and included in Harbour Square as four townhouses. Now return to 4th Street.

Wheat Row in Harbour Square

10 River Park Mutual Homes Cooperative, bounded by 4th, O, N, and 3rd Streets (1962, Charles M. Goodman Associates), was the first owner-occupied development in the new Southwest and was racially integrated intentionally during an era when nearly all housing was segregated by custom in DC. Renowned modernist architect Charles Goodman partnered with Reynolds Metals Company to create this development's distinctive aluminum building features.

This cooperative includes 134 townhouses and 384 adjacent apartments. The apartment building was designed to serve as a barrier between the development's barrel-vaulted townhouses and the public housing across Delaware

Avenue. This wall-like quality can best be experienced by walking north between the apartment building and the townhouses. The former street spaces in the complex have been landscaped and terminate in culs-de-sac. Stay on 4th Street and continue walking south.

■ **11 Channel Square**, 325 P Street SW (1968, Herry Weese and Associates), consists of attractive tan townhouses and an apartment tower, designed as middle-income housing under Section 221(d)(3) of the Housing Act of 1949. This section of the act subsidized the developer's interest rate, and in turn rents have been kept well below existing market rates.

■ **12 Riverside, Edgewater,** and **1401–15 4th Street** (formerly the J. Finley House and Chalk House) are bounded by 4th, O, and P Streets and the waterfront (1966, Morris Lapidus Associates). These apartments and townhouses were originally a single development. Riverside and Edgewater have been converted to condominiums; the 1401–15 4th Street properties are now townhouses. This complex won the third RLA design competition. At the bottom of 4th Street, you will find Fort McNair.

■ **13 Fort Lesley J. McNair** (1903, McKim, Mead and White), located at the strategic confluence of the Anacostia and Potomac Rivers, was established in 1794 as the Washington Arsenal to defend the City of Washington. A feature of the L'Enfant plan, Fort McNair has been known by a variety of names: Washington Arsenal, US Arsenal at Greenleaf Point, and Washington Barracks. The first fortifications were erected in 1791 and the first arsenal buildings in 1803–4. It was one of the earliest employers in Washington. All the original buildings were destroyed by an explosion during the British occupation of Washington in August 1814. The arsenal buildings were rebuilt and served as a distribution center for arms. In 1903 the New York architectural firm of McKim, Mead and White was retained to design a building for the new **National War College** and to develop a master plan for the entire installation. Most of the firm's plan, which called for a long mall, flanked by white-columned officers' houses, with the War College as the focal point at the end, was implemented. Since September 11, 2001, the college and Fort McNair have been closed to the public.

■ **14** Follow the tree-lined road that leads out to the waterfront, where you will find the *Titanic* **Memorial**, recognizing the sacrifices of the men who gave their lives to save women and children fleeing from the sinking ocean liner. Erected by the Women's *Titanic* Memorial Association, the statue was designed by Gertrude Vanderbilt Whitney. This section of the waterfront is now the quietest and most peaceful portion of the riverside walk.

■ **15** Next visit **Waterside Park** (1967–68, Sasaki, Dawson, Demay Associates). From the *Titanic* Memorial proceed north along the seawall, then veer right into the park, continuing to follow the tree line to M Street, which turns into 6th Street.

Arena Stage

■ 16 Arena Stage (founded in 1950), now part of the Mead Center for American Theater, is located at 6th and M Streets. Arena Stage's company was a pioneer of American theater-in-the-round and the first company outside of New York to win a Tony Award. It is now a beloved DC mainstay. Renovated in 2010 by Canadian architect Bing Thom, its signature structure encompasses two hundred thousand square feet. The roof, which points straight to the Washington Monument, is held high by wooden beams, each supporting four hundred thousand pounds of weight. The complex's three theaters are encased by a glass wall facade, making this the first application of heavy-timber-and-glass hybrid construction in the United Harry Weese and Associates), whose fan-shaped design emphasizes the thrust stage, seats 514 people. Excellent acoustics allow any audience member to feel like a part of the action. The recent renovations have enabled Arena Stage to expand its program to include experimental plays, children's theater, and teaching.

The **Fichandler Stage** was originally designed by Harry Weese and Associates as an iconic in-the-round theater design. Seating a total of 683, its classic steep rows allow every audience member unobstructed views. The building's thirty-five-thousand-square-foot glass curtain guarantees no outside noise influence, giving the stage an intimate ambience.

The versatile new **Arlene and Robert Kogod Cradle** appeals to audiences with its wooden basket-weave walls. Its oval shape enhances the space's warmth. Seating a mere two hundred people, this theater is predominantly used for new and developing plays, encouraging experimentation and innovation.

Now head back to the waterfront entering the District Wharf.

■ **17** As you conclude the tour, amble through the **District Wharf**, Southwest's most recent development. The mile-long project comprises high-rise residential and office buildings, appealing storefronts, and the waterfront. With 2 million square feet of urban space, it is the largest planned unit development in the District of Columbia thus far. Restaurants, bars, and shops may entice you, and an abundance of free amenities such as a firepit, swings, and a kid-friendly splash park offer plenty of variety along the way. Phase I was completed in 2017, and Phase II, which is marked by more ambitious architecture, delivered in 2022. Firms represented in Phase II include SHoP Architects, WDG, ODA, Rafael Vinoly, Morris Adjmi Architects, and Hollwich Kushner. PN Hoffman's and Madison Marquette developed the site, and Perkins Eastman served as the site's master planner.

It is worth noting in this era of global warming and rising sea levels that the District Wharf makes extensive use of sustainable technology and features, such as cisterns, green roofs, biodiverse plantings, and permeable pavement. One hundred percent of stormwater is managed onsite.

Before redevelopment began in the 1950s, this was a working waterfront. Its aged commercial establishments, dilapidated warehouses, railroad yards, municipal services, and wooden piers were in varying stages of disrepair. Renewal plans, as in other cities, focused on transforming the city's industrial backyard into public amenities. Here the NCPC called for low-scale buildings with well-landscaped open areas. The waterfront was largely developed in the late 1960s as envisioned. The few buildings that were built were kept low so that the view could be enjoyed by residents throughout the area. By the early 2000s, the waterfront was a quiet promenade, appealingly low-key to some, but a waste of a perfectly good river view to others. The developers of the District Wharf have placed tall buildings along the water, blocking the old views, but the project has been well received, and reservations at its best restaurants are still hot tickets as of this writing.

Historic panels along the way memorialize the waterfront's historical function, as well as the heart-breaking Pearl Affair, a daring but ultimately unsuccessful attempt to free as many as seventy-seven enslaved Washingtonians. It was the largest attempted escape of its kind. The 1848 event prompted whites to riot for three days, and most of the enslaved, though physically unharmed, were sold South, away from their families. Continue walking down the waterfront until it dead ends at the Maine Avenue Fish Market.

■ **18** The last stop on the tour, the **Maine Avenue Fish Market**, is one of the area's most popular local spots. Originally it was a dock where area fishermen sold their daily catch to the public. Today the market's wharf is home to a series of permanently docked flatboats that have been converted into retail seafood shops that sell products brought in by refrigerated trucks. The market, with its vintage style, attracts patrons from throughout the Washington metropolitan area. It has become well known for its supply of Maryland blue crabs and a wide variety of fresh and prepared seafood.

Foggy Bottom

(Historic residential neighborhood, Watergate complex, Kennedy Center, George Washington University, State Department, Constitution Avenue)

John J. Protopappas, updated by Denise Vogt and Frank Leone

Distance:	2 ¾ miles
Time:	2 hours
Bus:	31, 32, 36, 42, 43, and the DC Circulator
Metro:	Farragut West (Blue, Orange, and Silver Lines)

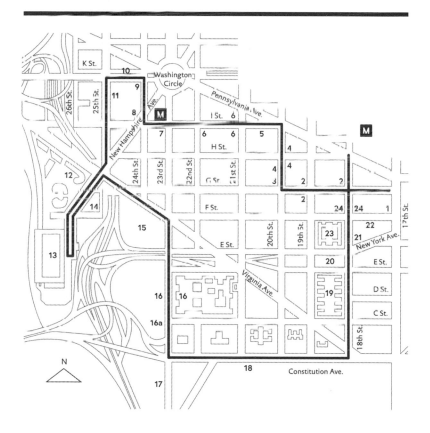

Foggy Bottom presents one of the most complex tapestries of urban growth and change to be found in Washington, DC.

Native Americans occupied the area as far back as five thousand years ago, and recent construction unearthed an important burial site from about 600 CE. In the mid-seventeenth century, most of Foggy Bottom was part of a land grant known as the Widow's Mite. In 1763 Jacob Funk purchased a tract of 130 acres, located generally between what is now 19th and 24th Streets, H Street, and the Potomac River, where he laid out the town of Hamburg. Also known as Funkstown, the area was one of a series of port towns situated along the Potomac in the mid-eighteenth century, of which Georgetown and Alexandria were the most successful. Throughout the remainder of the century, little development occurred in Hamburg, and the area did not pose an obstacle to Pierre L'Enfant's street plan, which covered the Maryland side of the Potomac River as far north as Boundary Street (now Florida Avenue).

L'Enfant's plan set forth Washington Circle as the focus for growth in the Foggy Bottom area. The grid of numbered and lettered streets was cut through by radial avenues that tied the area to other focal points throughout the city. Market locations reinforced the growth plan, as did the residential and commercial development that clustered close to the president's house and along Pennsylvania Avenue.

In the nineteenth century, a thriving waterside settlement developed along the Potomac River and Rock Creek. On the high ground of Foggy Bottom, north of E Street and east of 23rd Street, substantial residences were built to house the fashionable scientific and military communities and the diplomatic corps. On the lower ground, west of 23rd Street, modest brick and wooden dwellings were built to accommodate workers who toiled in the nearby glassworks, breweries, cement company, and gas works. Foggy Bottom was home to predominately Irish and German immigrants who worked at the factories, and the area became predominantly African American in the early twentieth century. The badly built and much-polluted City Canal (along what is now Constitution Avenue) and the marshy lands merging into the Potomac underscored the undesirable nature of the lowlands. In fact, the combination of fog from the river bottom area and smoke from the industries is said to have given rise to Foggy Bottom's name.

After 1900, the departure of the affluent residents from east of 23rd Street to more fashionable neighborhoods elsewhere in the District, and a new appreciation of the proximity of the area to the White House and downtown, changed the residential character of Foggy Bottom. Apartment buildings were wedged between narrow brick townhouses. Remaining row houses were adapted to institutional use, as exemplified by the removal of George Washington University to Foggy Bottom in 1912.

By the 1950s, with the closure of the Washington Gas Works and removal of its huge tanks, the area was ripe for redevelopment. In the following decades, the area served as a battleground between proponents of high-density development and defenders of the surviving row houses, and between residents who prized Foggy Bottom's neighborly qualities and institutions that wished to expand their operations into office structures occupied only from nine to five. Foggy Bottom has also served as the stage for post–World War II urban renewal and highway plans, of which some were carried out and others were aborted. Notably plans for the northwest section of the "Inner Loop" highway were abandoned, but not before construction of the Potomac Freeway—an extension of I-66 from Roosevelt Bridge—was built in the mid-1960s. The highway construction displaced hundreds of residents, wiped out several blocks of historic Foggy Bottom, including renovated row houses, alleys, and the Briggs-Montgomery Elementary School. The area has been further transformed by luxury condominiums, cooperatives, and rental apartment buildings in the Watergate complex, including the extensive rehabilitation of the row houses throughout the neighborhood. The area now includes both the Foggy Bottom and the George Washington University/Old West End Historic Districts.

■ 1 Begin the tour at 17th and H Streets. The **Winder Building,** 600 17th Street, (1848, Richard A. Gilpin), was one of the first buildings built to be leased by the federal government and was the tallest and largest office building in DC at the time of its construction. Purchased by the federal government in 1854, it was used by the Navy, War, and Treasury Departments and now houses the US Trade Representative office.

Adjacent is **Liberty Plaza** (1977, Sasaki Associates), with a tree and stone tranquility garden. The area also contains sandstone medallions and other decorative elements from the historic Riggs Bank Building that stood on the site from 1923 to 1974. Across the plaza is the **Consumer Financial Protection Bureau,** 17th and G Streets NW (1977, Max Urbahn and Associates). An innovative and attractive design, the headquarters blends well with the renovated Winder Building, harmonizing new with old.

■ 2 At 18th and G Streets and 20th and G Streets are buildings occupied by the **World Bank** (International Bank for Reconstruction and Development) and the **International Monetary Fund**. The Mexican Embassy is located at 1911 Pennsylvania Avenue NW and retains the facade of two of the original Seven Buildings (1794), some of the earliest residences built in Washington. On the south side of the block, the most recent building stands on the site of the early nineteenth-century **Lenthall Houses,** which were moved by the George Washington University (GWU) to 21st Street, between F and G Streets, as part of a preservation compromise with the community. At the northeast corner of 20th and F Streets stands the official residence of the GWU president (formerly the F Street Club, 1849); it is one of the few remaining Greek revival–style houses in the city. On the same block, at the southeast corner of 20th and G Streets, stands the **United Church**, a combined United Church of Christ and United Methodist congregation. Originally built as the Concordia Lutheran Evangelical Church, it is a reminder of the former German settlement in Foggy Bottom. Services in German are still offered.

■ 3 The cross streets of 20th and G form one of the major entrances to **The George Washington University**. Founded in 1821, the university was first located on College Hill in the area now known as Columbia Heights. In the early 1880s, the university moved to 15th and H Streets and later spread into other locations throughout the downtown area. In 1912 it secured its first foothold in Foggy Bottom by purchasing the former Saint Rose's Industrial School at 2023 G Street NW. Over the following decades, the university increased its land holdings many times over, until it, along with the federal government, constituted the largest institutional presence in Foggy Bottom. In the early years of its growth and expansion in Foggy Bottom, GWU constructed a quadrangle of Georgian-style buildings on the block bounded by 20th, G, 21st, and H Streets. During the Great Depression, the university buildings followed modernist trends. In the post–World War II period, several limestone-faced buildings were constructed, including, most notably, the cube of Lisner Auditorium at 21st and H Streets. Designed by the GWU's unofficial architect, Waldron Faulkner, in a stripped classical style in 1940, it opened in 1946. The GWU Museum and Textile Museum at 701 21st Street NW contains the Albert H. Small Washingtoniana Collection. The collection comprises nearly two thousand maps, prints, newspapers, and artifacts that trace the history of Washington, DC, and a permanent display of the history of some buildings on the campus. For more information visit museum.gwu.edu/visit.

The university has constructed a variety of academic buildings; many appear to replicate the office structures found elsewhere along K Street. The university's growth and expansion have frequently brought it into conflict with the residents. The university has entered into a number of agreements with the District of Columbia and the community to limit the expansion of the campus into the residential areas of the Foggy Bottom/West End community. As part of its 2007 Campus Plan, the university created a historic district including some (but not all) historic buildings on campus. Buildings not protected continue to be demolished.

■ **4** Moving north along 20th Street, you can see the university's Law School complex—incorporating **Stockton Hall** (1924)—on the left and the **International Monetary Fund** on the right.

■ **5** After you turn left at 20th and I Streets, **Western Market** (1983, John Warnecke) comes into view. An early controversial preservation compromise struck between the university and the community, this assemblage attempts to preserve the front sections of a strip of nineteenth-century buildings referred to as the Red Lion Row, named after a popular eatery that formerly occupied one of the buildings. Behind the line of older buildings, a high-rise office structure looms. Critics have decried this preservation solution as only "facade deep" and one that does little to improve the quality of design of the larger office structure. The structure now houses the Western Market Foodhall (2021), which recalls the original Western Market (1803), one of three markets originally laid out for the city, which was in the grassy triangle across from the current buildings.

■ **6** Continuing along I Street, you will pass the side of the George Washington University Student Union. At the southeast corner of 22nd and I Streets, the **Academic Center** (Rome Hall, Phillips Hall, and Smith Hall of Art, 1982) represents a new architectural style for the university. Sheathed in glass, this building suggests a lighter touch to large buildings and, one might hope, a more creative era for the university's construction program. As of 2022, however, the buildings were slated for demolition to make way for denser development at the site.

■ **7** At 23rd and I Streets is another **entrance to the university**. The Foggy Bottom/GWU Metro stop is located here, at the conjunction of the new George Washington University Hospital (owned by Universal Health Services) and the university's School of Medicine and Health Services. The old hospital building (1948, Waldron Faulkner), to the west of the new hospital, was demolished in 2003. The closing of I Street between 23rd and 24th Streets provides for a pleasant plaza area at this juncture, which features a farmer's market on Wednesdays in the summer through the mid-fall.

During the first half of the twentieth century, the lowlands area was largely occupied by an African American population who inhabited modest row houses and interior alley dwellings. There were approximately ten predominantly African American churches, which anchored their Foggy Bottom community. Of these, the only church that remains is **Saint Mary's Episcopal Church** (1886), located at 728 23rd Street NW. It was designed by James Renwick in

Saint Mary's Episcopal Church

red brick Gothic style with tile and marble floors and Tiffany Studio glass windows. Renwick was also the architect of the Renwick Gallery at 17th Street and Pennsylvania Avenue and the original Smithsonian Castle building.

8 Crossing over New Hampshire Avenue/24th Street is the four-block **Foggy Bottom Historic District** (designated 1987). Here you can still see groups of modest townhouses that formerly housed workers associated with Foggy Bottom's industrial past, some of which were built by Irish American immigrants themselves. Many of these houses were destroyed by highway construction (south of 26th Street) and urban renewal (1960s apartment buildings). But the community fought to retain the historic buildings, forming a group that is now the Foggy Bottom Association, which has produced a detailed online walking tour, https://foggybottomassociation.org/walking-tour. These row houses have been fully rehabilitated and are in high demand, even at more than a million dollars each. The neighborhood is also home to several murals and sculptures by recognized artists and urban garden areas.

800 Block of New Hampshire Avenue NW

9 Washington Circle is one of the many circles and squares that formed important elements of the L'Enfant plan. The center of the circle contains an imposing bronze equestrian statue of Gen. George Washington. Created by Clark Mills (who produced the Andrew Jackson statue in Lafayette Park) and erected in 1860, it depicts Washington advancing against the British lines in the Battle of Princeton. The statue is oriented to the east, looking toward the White House and Capitol. Shortly after the statute was erected, the area south of Washington Circle became US Army Camp Fry, a hub for collecting and distributing supplies to Union soldiers in and near the capital during the Civil War. It was also home to disabled soldiers in the Veteran Reserve Corps, who fought bravely at Fort Stevens when the city was threatened.

■ **10 K Street between 24th and 25th Streets** represents the post–World War II planners' vision for Foggy Bottom: tall apartment buildings astride major thoroughfares. The construction of the K Street underpass was intended to facilitate commuter traffic to and from the Virginia suburbs. However, the traffic density and speed also effectively cut off the area south of K Street from its natural commercial strip along Pennsylvania Avenue. The high-rises along K Street represent an interesting mix of styles: art deco, modern, and postmodern.

On the south side of K Street is the northern border of the Historic District. You will pass the former Manila House row house (1874), a gathering place for Filipinos, which is recognized as a literary landmark honoring author Bienvenido N. Santos (1911–96), who wrote about the house in his award-winning collection of short stories, "Scent of Apples." Next door is **Saint Paul's Episcopal Parish** (1948). The church lost its original property on 23rd Street to eminent domain exercised on behalf of GWU when it built its old hospital (1944). The current church was designed in the Gothic style by Philip H. Frohman, who had been the architect of Washington National Cathedral since 1912.

■ **11** Turning south on **25th Street**, you pass through the center of the Foggy Bottom Historic District, with late nineteenth-century working-class row houses. Several houses also feature art pieces permanently installed after their showing in the biennial *Arts in Foggy Bottom* exhibition, which started in 2008. Halfway down the first block of residential rows are passageways—the one on the left leads to Snows Court, one of DC's first occupied alleys. It contains about twenty-five row houses, most built in the 1880–90s, as well as the three-story Nash's Stable (1914), one of the few commercial horse stables remaining in DC alleys. The passage on the right takes you to Hughes Mews, another alley community that retains a small group of original row houses.

■ **12** At Virginia Avenue, look southeast for a unique direct view of the Washington Monument. The **Watergate Complex** at 25th Street and Virginia Avenue (1962–1971) was developed by the Societa Generale Immobiliare of Rome and designed by Luigi Moretti in a modern curvilinear style. It is an example of "packaged living"—with residential units and offices, restaurants, a hotel with rooftop views, an art gallery, and shops. The Watergate remains one of Washington's premier addresses, and the 1972 Watergate scandal in no way diminished the complex's reputation. As you continue along New Hampshire Avenue toward the Kennedy Center, a major office section of the Watergate complex comes into view. Directly north is a condominium that replaced the Howard Johnson hotel that was associated with the Watergate scandal.

■ **13** The **John F. Kennedy Center for the Performing Arts** now comes into view. Completed in 1971 after the designs of Edward Durell Stone, it represents the culmination of nearly two decades of plans to locate a major auditorium in Washington. The center houses eight venues as well as two restaurants and sweeping terraces along the Potomac River side of the center. In 2019, the Kennedy Center opened the REACH—a new building complex featuring community arts spaces, rehearsal spaces, and an extensive garden with modern sculptures. The views of Rosslyn, Georgetown, and the Potomac River from the main-floor and rooftop terraces should not be missed.

■ **14** On the way back to Virginia Avenue, you will pass a structure that was built as a privately owned office building for the Peoples Life Insurance Company in the late 1950s. The building now houses the Saudi Arabian embassy. The building, together with **Potomac Plaza** across Virginia Avenue (completed in 1955 on the former site of the Washington Gas holding tank), was an early high-rise entrant into the lowlands of Foggy Bottom.

A statue of Mexican President Benito Pablo Juárez García (erected 1966) on Virginia Avenue at 25th Street was a gift from Mexico. It is one of a series of monuments honoring Latin American leaders donated to the United States from 1950 to 1976. Their presence lends the avenue the informal name of "Foggy Bottom's Avenue of the Americas." Additional statues along the avenue depict Bernardo Vicente de Gálvez y Madrid, first Viscount of Galveston (a Spanish general who fought against the British in the American Revolution), and liberators General José de San Martín (Argentina), General José Simón Bolivar (Venezuela, Colombia [then including Panama], Ecuador, Peru, and Bolivia) and Gervasio Artigas (Uruguay).

■ **15** **Columbia Plaza** (1968, Keyes, Lethbridge and Condon) comes next into view at 23rd Street and Virginia Avenue. Another packaged living complex of apartments, offices, and shops located in a large plaza area, Columbia Plaza represents the completed urban renewal project envisioned for Foggy Bottom in the post–World War II era. The development replaced nearly two hundred modest row houses with eight hundred upscale apartments. Across 23rd Street is the headquarters of the Pan American Health Organization (1965, Román Fresnedo Siri), one of Washington's outstanding examples of midcentury modern architecture.

■ **16** Continuing south along 23rd Street, you come upon the **Potomac Hill** on the right; it is now a secure **State Department** facility, but over the years it

Columbia Plaza

was the former home of the first US Naval Observatory (which discovered the moons of Mars, Phobos and Deimos, in 1886), the Naval Hospital, the Office of Strategic Services, and the Central Intelligence Agency. The State Department, on the left, was relocated to Foggy Bottom in the 1940s, first taking over the War Department Building and then growing into the largest office building in DC. The State Department's National Museum of American Diplomacy, diplomacy.state.gov/, located on 21st Street, opened in 2017. The area between E Street and Constitution Avenue and 23rd and 17th Streets is known as the Northwest Rectangle and contains several federal and institutional buildings, including buildings of international organizations.

■ **16a** At the **United States Institute of Peace**, 2301 Constitution Avenue NW (2011, Moshe Safdie Architects), the 150,000-square-foot glass-and-concrete building makes a striking symbolic statement of the nation's commitment to peace. It features a public education center, a conference center, and working space for nearly two hundred staff members. Atriums link the three components, which are covered by a series of steel frames with translucent glass and a billowing, winglike roof. More information can be found at www.usip.org /pages/visit-us or by calling 202-457-1700.

■ **17** At the crossroads of 23rd Street and Constitution Avenue, the **Lincoln Memorial** is in view (see Tour 4, The Mall—West, no. 10). The memorial (1922), with its sculpture of a seated Lincoln by Daniel Chester French overlooking the Reflecting Pool, was a favorite among the followers of the City Beautiful movement (around 1900). The **Arlington Memorial Bridge** to the west opened in May 1932 and carries traffic into Arlington Cemetery and points beyond.

■ **18** Turning east on **Constitution Avenue**, you now face the ceremonial street, with its views and monumental buildings that are seen on countless postcards. This area was carved out of the reclaimed lowlands and filled-in City Canal in the first half of the twentieth century. On the left, you will see a series of institutional and federal buildings designed by a host of nationally famous architects.

At the northeast corner of 23rd Street and Constitution Avenue is the **American Pharmaceutical Association Building** (1933, John Russell Pope). The next building is the **National Academy of Sciences** (1924, Bertram Grosvenor Goodhue). Don't miss the academy's oversize **sculpture of Albert Einstein** just to the left of its building. Dedicated in 1979 on the centennial of Einstein's birthday, this statue was based on a bust that Robert Berks sculpted from life in 1953. Einstein sat for Berks in his study, dressed in casual attire, in a pose that translated into this sculpture as the scientist gazing down into the stars, arrayed at his feet. As you continue east, the following buildings come into view: the **Federal Reserve Board** (1937, Paul Cret); the **Federal Reserve Board—East Building / Public Health Service** (1931, Jules Henri de Sibour); the **Organization of American States Annex** (1948, Harbeson, Hough, Livingston and Larson); and the **Organization of American States** (1910, Albert Kelsey and Paul Cret). On the right are the parklands of the Mall, including the site of the **Vietnam Veterans Memorial** and Constitution Gardens (including the Constitution Signers Memorial on the small island), and the recently restored stone Washington Canal Lockkeeper's House (1835) and a Visitor's Information Center).

■ **19** As you walk north along 18th Street, the large main **Department of the Interior Building** (1937, Waddy Butler Wood) comes into view on the left. The building includes New Deal murals and a museum. More information can be found at www.doi.gov/interiormuseum.

■ **20** To the north at E Street is **Rawlins Park**, a pocket of tranquility that reaches its zenith in the early spring, when its magnolia trees are in full bloom.

■ **21** At the northeast corner of 18th Street and New York Avenue is the **Octagon House** (1800, William Thornton). The Octagon, originally the home of Col. John Tayloe III, served as the temporary site of the president's house after the burning of the capital city by the British in 1814 and was the site of the signing of the Treaty of Ghent, which ended the War of 1812. The Octagon House is now operated by the American Institute of Architects and serves as a historic house museum and exhibition gallery. More information can be found at https://architectsfoundation.org/octagon-museum/.

Octagon House / AIA headquarters

■ **22** Behind the Octagon is the headquarters of the **American Institute of Architects**, completed in 1973 after the designs of the Architects Collaborative. Although criticized by some as a less-than-distinguished effort, the AIA building does not try to compete with its historic frontispiece. The lobby area contains an exhibition gallery, and its conference facilities are used by many design-related organizations in the city.

■ **23** The **General Services Administration Building** stands on the left, the symbolic, if not actual, center of the federal government's public building design operations. The GSA Building was built for the Department of the Interior in 1917 after designs produced by the Office of the Supervising Architect of the Treasury but was vacated by that department when its building to the south on C Street was completed in 1937.

■ **24** The crossroads of 18th and F Streets contains two architectural oddities. To the west is the DACOR Bacon House (1825), which houses the **Ringgold-Marshall Museum,** http://dacorbacon.org/ringgold_-_marshall _museum.php. The house is the headquarters of DACOR, the organization for Diplomatic and Consular Officers, Retired. The house and its garden are protected from development by a preservation easement held by the National Trust for Historic Preservation. To the east stand the remnants of **Michler Row,** cemented onto a modern office facade (1981, Skidimore, Owings & Merrill).

Michler Row had been constructed in the 1870s and named for Gen. Nathaniel Michler of the Department of Public Buildings and Grounds (1866–1971).

White House

(White House, Renwick Gallery, Lafayette Square, Corcoran Gallery)

John J. Protopappas, updated by Denise Vogt and Frank Leone

Distance: 1¾ miles
Time: 1½ hours
Bus: 32, 33, and 36
Metro: Farragut West (Blue, Orange, and Silver Lines)

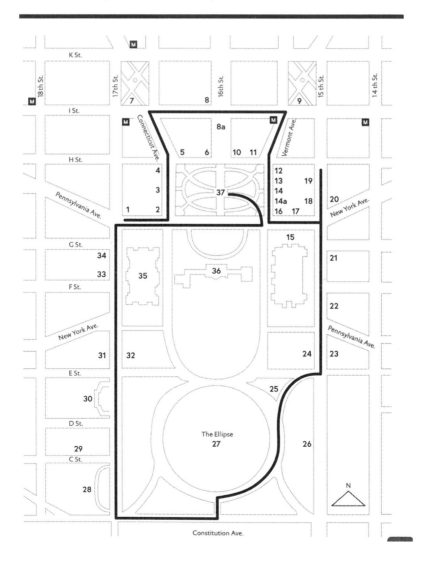

■ **1 Renwick Gallery of the Smithsonian American Art Museum** (Old Corcoran Gallery and US Court of Claims), 17th Street and Pennsylvania Avenue (1859, James Renwick; 1972 restoration, John Carl Warnecke and Hugh Newell Jacobsen) was designed as an art gallery for banker and art collector W. W. Corcoran. The Second Empire–style building housed the US Department of State during the Civil War, while Corcoran, a Southern sympathizer, was in London. When he regained occupation, Corcoran found that the building was too small for his collection, so he built a larger gallery at 17th Street and New York Avenue. The US Court of Claims took possession of the building in 1899 and used it for the next sixty-five years. The Smithsonian undertook the meticulous exterior and interior restoration beginning in 1965, and in 1972 the building was returned to its original function as an art gallery. The Renwick is dedicated to contemporary craft and decorative arts from the nineteenth to the twenty-first century created by American artists. The Renwick Gallery is open 10:00 a.m.–5:30 p.m. daily, except December 25. Admission is free. More information can be found at www.americanart.si.edu or by calling 202-633-7970

Renwick Gallery

■ **2 Blair-Lee Houses**, 1651 Pennsylvania Avenue NW (1824; 1931 restoration, Waldron Faulkner). This complex of four connected houses, one with a distinctive green awning, combined in 1943, constitute the president's guest house. When the White House underwent renovations from 1948 to 1952, President Harry S. Truman and his family resided at there, and White House police officers thwarted an assassination attempt on Truman in 1950 in front of the house.

■ **3 Lafayette Square Building Restoration**. Architect John Carl Warnecke was engaged by the Kennedy administration to study the of development for Lafayette Square. The result was the integration of new buildings with the restored and infilling row houses. The row houses are used as offices for the various commissions created during presidential terms of office. The two office buildings referred to as "bookends" flank the square on the west and east and contain secluded courtyards with fountains. They are the **New Executive Office Building** (west), at 17th and H Streets, and the **US Court of Claims** (east), at 717 Madison Place NW (both are closed to the public).

■ **4 Decatur House**, 748 Jackson Place NW (1818, Benjamin Latrobe). The house of Commodore Stephen Decatur, the suppressor of the Barbary pirates, was the first private house to be built on Lafayette Square. The Federal-style corner building, owned by the National Trust for Historic Preservation, displays historic furnishings and houses the National Center for White House History. The center supports research efforts and offers education programs related to the White House's history. The adjoining carriage house (1610 H Street) functions as the White House History Shop. More information can be found at https://www.whitehousehistory.org/.

■ **5 US Chamber of Commerce**, 1615 H Street NW (1925, Cass Gilbert). The Chamber of Commerce and the Freedman's Bank (Treasury Annex; see this tour, no. 14a) Buildings are the only completed portions of the McMillian Commission (1902–02) plan to unify the architecture of Lafayette Square in the neoclassical style of the older Treasury Building.

■ **6 Hay-Adams Hotel**, northwest corner of 16th and H Streets (1927, Mirham Mesrobian). This elegant hotel was built on the site of H. H. Richardson's houses for Henry Adams and John Hay. The hotel's roof bar, the *Top of the Hay*, offers amazing views of the White House and Lafayette Square.

■ **7** "Damn the torpedoes! Full speed ahead!" said Adm. David G. Farragut during a Civil War battle in 1864 in Mobile Bay. A statue to the naval hero, whose father was born in Spain and fought in the American Revolutionary War, is the centerpiece of lovely Farragut Square—and a roosting place for scores of pigeons. With good reason, **Farragut Square** is one of the most heavily used urban parks in Washington.

■ **8** The striking hexagonal **Third Church of Christ, Scientist** and the **Christian Science Monitor Building** (which stood at the northwest corner of 16th and I Streets) were designed by I. M. Pei & Associates in 1972. Although designated as a DC historic landmark, the brutalist building was demolished in 2014. The

Farragut Square

church, however, now meets in a portion of the building behind a dramatic mirrored glass entrance on 16th Street.

■ **8a Black Lives Matter Plaza** occupies 16th Street between K and H Streets. Originally a site of protests in the summer of 2020, DC officially renamed the area and commissioned a mural spelling out BLACK LIVES MATTER in thirty-five-foot high yellow letters on the street pavement. The street mural painted by city workers and volunteer artists honors the movement for freedom, equality, and justice as a permanent installation.

■ **9 McPherson Square**, the eastern counterpart to Farragut Square, is one of the many public spaces provided in the L'Enfant plan. A statue of Brig. Gen. James B. McPherson, who commanded the Army of the Tennessee in the Civil War, was erected in 1876.

■ **10 Saint John's Church**, 16th and H Streets (1816, Benjamin Latrobe; 1883, James Renwick). Saint John's is among the oldest Episcopal churches in the city. The Greek revival building is commonly referred to as the "Church of the Presidents" because a pew has been set aside for the president of the United States and the First Family. Since its first services in 1816, every president has visited the church.

■ **11 Saint John's Parish House** (Old British Embassy), 1525 H Street NW (1822–24, Matthew St. Clair Clarke). This house was designed by its owner, St. Clair Clarke, and in the 1840s served as the British prime minister's residence. Saint John's Church acquired the building in 1954 for use as a parish house. Visit www.stjohns-dc.org for information about history, services, tours, and concerts.

■ **12 Cutts Madison House** (Dolley Madison House), at the corner of H Street and Madison Place, was built in 1820 in the American colonial style. This yellow house was originally owned by James Madison, and upon his death his widow, Dolley, took up residence here from 1837 until her death in 1849. The house was restored as part of the Federal Judicial Center in 1968.

■ **13** The **Benjamin Ogle Tayloe House**, at 21 Madison Place NW, was built in 1828. This Federal-style house served as a prominent social center for high-ranking politicians for the next four decades and was later referred to by President McKinley as the "Little White House."

■ **14** **Howard T. Markey National Courts Building**, 717 Madison Place NW. An arcaded passageway leads pedestrians from H Street through a pleasant courtyard to Madison Place and Lafayette Square, but it is currently closed to the public.

■ **14a** The **Freedman's Bank Building**, Pennsylvania Avenue and Madison Place (1919, Cass Gilbert). Originally known as the Treasury Annex building, it was renamed in 2016 in recognition of the site of the principal office of the Freedman's Savings and Trust Co. The bank was founded in 1865 to receive deposits from formerly enslaved people but closed in 1874. The building was sold in 1882 and razed a few years later.

Treasury Building

■ **15** **Treasury Building**, 1500 Pennsylvania Avenue NW (1836–69, Robert Mills, Thomas U. Walter, Ammi B. Young, Isaiah Rogers, and Alfred B. Mullett). The Greek revival–style Treasury Building is the third oldest federal building in Washington. It features statues of Treasury secretaries Albert Gallatin on the north side and Alexander Hamilton on the south. The site, selected by Andrew Jackson, disrupts L'Enfant's grand concourse uniting the Capitol and the White House. Note the dramatic view down Pennsylvania Avenue as you walk past the Treasury. Free tours of the building's interior are available. For more information, see https://home.treasury.gov/services/tours-and-library /tours-of-the-historic- treasury-building.

The following five buildings (nos. 16–20) are included in the 15th Street Financial Historic District, clustering in front of the Treasury Building and along 15th Street. The buildings have elaborate architectural details including mosaics, medallions, and impressive iron grillwork on windows and entry doors.

■ **16 Treasury Annex**, Pennsylvania Avenue and Madison Place (1919, Cass Gilbert).

■ **17** The **Riggs National Bank**, 1503 Pennsylvania Avenue NW (1891, James G. Hill), and

■ **18 American Security and Trust Co. Building**, 1501 Pennsylvania Avenue (1899, York and Sawyer) contained two separate buildings that were merged in 2022. The new building will house the **Milken Center for Advancing the American Dream**, scheduled to open in 2023. The buildings occupied the prestigious location across from the Treasury Department. Next door (734 15th Street) is the Walker Building (1937, Porter & Lockie), a twelve-story office building with the smooth finish and stylized detail typical of 1930s buildings. It is notable for the colorful mosaics composed of exposed aggregate concrete above the three portals, produced by artisan John J. Earley. (Earley's office and studio, a DC Historic Landmark, is in Foggy Bottom at 2131 G Street.)

■ **19 Union Trust Co. Building**, southwest corner of 15th and H Streets (1906, Wood, Donnard and Deming), originally built as the Union Trust and Storage Co., housed the DC office of the American Bar Association until 2013 and now contains commercial office space. At the corner, cross over 15th Street and proceed south.

■ **19a** Financial brokerage buildings on this block include the narrow, Jacobean-style Securities/Walker Building, 729 15th Street (1929, Wardman), the Swartzell, Rheem & Hensey/Playhouse Theater Building, and 727 15th Street (1907, Bruce Price & de Sibour), with its arched glass entry flanked on each side by eagles with their wings outstretched.

■ **20 National Savings & Trust Co. Building**, northeast corner of 15th Street and New York Avenue (1880, James Windrim). This red brick, Victorian-style structure, with its copper-clad bay and prominent clock, provides a delightful relief from its more classical neighbors in the old financial district. Across New York Avenue is the stylized classical-revival Washington Building (1927, Coolidge, Shepley, Bullfinch & Abbott), originally the Washington Central Trust Building (renovated in 1986).

■ **21 Metropolitan Square** (1986, Vlastimil Koubek and Skidmore, Owings & Merrill), southeast corner of 15th and G Streets. Construction of this private office and retail complex involved the demolition of Rhodes Tavern (1801), but the facade of the Keith-Albee theater building (1911–12, Jules Henri de Sibour) was preserved. The building houses the Old Ebbitt Grill restaurant, "Washington's oldest saloon" (originally at another location) with the original restaurant's long wooden bar.

■ **22** The Hotel Washington, which occupies the corner of 15th and F Streets (1917–18, Carrère and Hastings), is Washington's oldest hotel in continuous use. The corner location of this fine hotel is one of the best in the city. The hotel's rooftop terrace is open for dining and offers wonderful views of the White House, the Mall, the Potomac River, and Virginia (see Tour 12, Downtown—West, no. 38).

The luxury Beaux-Arts **Willard InterContinental Hotel**, at 14th Street and Pennsylvania Avenue, opened in 1901 and was one of Washington's top hotels for many years. In an earlier Willard Hotel on this site, Julia Ward Howe composed "The Battle Hymn of the Republic." Over the decades, several US presidents have temporarily resided at the hotel. In 1963, Martin Luther King Jr. wrote his famous "I Have a Dream" speech in his hotel room. The hotel closed in 1968. Early plans for Pennsylvania Avenue called for tearing it down and building a huge national square at the west end of the avenue. The plans were changed in 1974, when the Pennsylvania Avenue plan was revised to place more emphasis on historic preservation. The restoration of the hotel and an office building addition were completed in 1986 (see Tour 12, Downtown—West, no. 37).

■ **23 Pershing Park/World War I Memorial**, between 15th and 14th Streets on Pennsylvania Avenue (1981, M. Paul Friedberg and Jerome Lindsey; 2021, Joe Weishaar and David Rubin). Originally a small park featuring a memorial to Gen. John J. Pershing, the tree-lined park has been converted to a National World War I Memorial. The statue of General Pershing remains, the pool that doubled as an ice rink has been replaced by educational elements, and Sabin Howard's fifty-eight-foot-long bronze frieze is scheduled for completion in 2024. For more information, see https://doughboy.org/education/apps/.

■ **24 Sherman Monument**, 15th Street and Hamilton Place. In addition to the statue of Gen. William T. Sherman, this monument includes the names of Sherman's battles and a chronology of his military assignments. The statues at the four corners represent branches of the army: infantry, artillery, cavalry, and engineers.

■ **25** The **National Park Service's Ellipse Visitor Pavilion** on the west corner of 15th and E Streets features tourist information and restrooms.

■ **26** In the areas surrounding the Ellipse are a number of notable monuments and points of interest. The **Boy Scout Memorial** and the **Original Patentees** of DC Memorial (the eighteen original owners who granted their property to form the City of Washington, DC) are located along 15th Street. Along Constitution Avenue stand the granite block **Haupt Fountains**, installed by Lady Bird Johnson in 1968 to "frame the White House in water," and the **Second Infantry Division Monument**—the eighteen-foot-tall, flaming golden sword symbolizes the division's defense of Paris during World War I and added wings honor service in World War II and the Korean War. Facing the White House across E Street are the **Butt-Miller Memorial Fountain** (1913, honoring two US officials who died in the sinking of the *Titanic*), the Zero Milestone Marker, and the National Christmas Tree.

■ **27** The **Ellipse**, officially known as President's Park South, is a fifty-two-acre park south of the White House fence. Like Lafayette Square, the Ellipse (bordered by 15th and 17th Streets and Constitution Avenue) was part of the presidential grounds included in L'Enfant's original plan for the city. Note the visual relationship between the White House and the Jefferson Memorial and the strong axial relationship along 16th Street, through the White House to the Jefferson Memorial, enhanced by the Haupt Fountains. L'Enfant intended the monument to George Washington to be located along this north-south axis, but soil conditions prevented its construction there.

As you progress north along 17th Street to Pennsylvania Avenue, note the imposing variety of architectural styles of the upcoming buildings.

■ **28** **Pan American Union** (Organization of American States), 17th Street and Constitution Avenue (1910, Albert Kelsey and Paul Cret). This building is the headquarters for the General Secretariat of the Organization of American States (thirty-five member states are represented). The architectural styles of North and South America are blended into the building. The interior court, filled with many tropical plants, creates a wonderful space. Behind the main building is the lovely "Aztec Garden," and the building is surrounded by sculptures honoring Latin American authors and leaders. The Museum of Modern Art of Latin America is open Tuesday through Saturday, 10:00 a.m.–5:00 p.m.; entrance on 18th Street NW. More information can be found at www.oas.org.

■ **29** **Daughters of the American Revolution**, 1778 D Street NW (about 1930, John Russell Pope). The DAR complex consists of Memorial Continental Hall, a library, a museum, archives, an administration building, and Constitution Hall, which hosts performances, concerts, and lectures. The Revolutionary period museum tour is given weekdays, 9:00 a.m.–4:00 p.m.; Sundays, 1:00–5:00 p.m. More information can be found at www.dar.org.

■ **30** **American Red Cross**, 17th, D, and E Streets (1917, Trowbridge and Livingston). The classical-revival style building is a monument to the women of the Civil War and serves as national headquarters for the American National

Corcoran Flagg Building

Red Cross. There are memorials, gardens, and a large lawn between the main building and more recent additions. Tours of Red Cross Square are available— see https://redcross.org/about-us/who-we-are/history.html.

■ **31 Corcoran Flagg Building**, 17th Street and New York Avenue (1897, Ernest Flagg). This was once one of Washington's finest art galleries, specializing in American art, fine art photography, modern art, and the education of artists. In 2014, the gallery closed and most of the original artwork was donated to the National Gallery of Art. The building was transferred to the nearby George Washington University and is occupied by its Corcoran School of Arts and Design. A fine example of Beaux-Arts style, the Corcoran has a magnificent atrium gallery. Information on exhibits and events can be found at corcoran .gwu.edu/exhibitions-performances-conversations.

■ **32** The **First Infantry Division Memorial** (1924, Cass Gilbert) is the US Army's testimonial to those of the First Infantry Division who died in the World Wars, with additions honoring veterans of World War I and II, Vietnam (1955–75), and Operation Desert Storm (1990–91). The symbol of the First Division is "the Big Red One," and a large bed of red flowers in the shape of the numeral 1 lies at the base in front of the memorial.

■ **33 Winder Building**, 604 17th Street NW (1847–48, Richard Gilpin). The Italianate-style building pioneered the use of central heating and cast-iron beams and was a veritable high-rise in its time. Its significance is more historical than architectural. It was the first, among many more to come, of the inexpensive, speculative office buildings designed for use by the federal government—its use today, housing the US Trade Representative's office.

■ 34 **Consumer Financial Protection Bureau**, 17th and G Streets, NW (1977, Max Urbahn and Associates). An innovative and attractive design, the headquarters blends well with the renovated Winder Building, harmonizing new with old. The courtyard between the buildings, Liberty Plaza (1977, Sasaki Associates) invites calm with a garden of bean pod–shaped stone chairs and geometrically placed trees. This Asian-style garden replaces the original ice-skating rink. The area also contains sandstone medallions displayed on the interior walls and other decorative elements from the historic Riggs Bank Building that stood on this site from 1923 to 1974.

■ 35 The **Eisenhower Executive Office Building** (Old State, War, and Navy Building), Pennsylvania Avenue and 17th Street, NW (1871–88, Alfred B. Mullett). Behind the nine hundred Doric columns was the world's largest office building at the time it was built. With its wealth of detail, it is probably the most eloquent government building in Washington. At times controversial, the Gilded Age building was preserved from demolition a number of times and is the most notable Second Empire–style building in DC. Today it houses various agencies composing the Executive Office of the President, including the vice presidential staff and the Office of Management and Budget. It is closed to the public.

■ 36 The **White House**, 1600 Pennsylvania Avenue NW (begun 1792, James Hoban, Benjamin Latrobe, and others). The simple, yet dignified, home of the US president contains six levels, including 132 rooms and thirty-five bathrooms in the residence. President John Adams and his family were the first presidential family to occupy the White House, and soon after, in 1814, the British burned it. Public tours of the White House are available, but requests must be

The White House

submitted through a member of Congress. More information can be found at https://www.whitehouse.gov/visit/.

■ **37 Lafayette Square**, during the 1700s, was at times a family graveyard, a racetrack, an apple orchard, and a slave market. The seven-acre-square public park was included in the President's Park in the L'Enfant plan of 1791. President Thomas Jefferson authorized its separation into a park for public use. In 1824 the park was named in honor of the Marquis de Lafayette, a French hero of the American Revolution, during his triumphal return visit to the United States. In 1851 landscape designer Andrew Jackson Downing developed the plan for the park and many other DC parks. Two years later the central statue of President Andrew Jackson, cast from the cannons captured by Jackson during the War of 1812, was installed. It was the first equestrian statue in Washington and the second in the United States. It was created by sculptor Clark Mills, who also created the statue of George Washington in Washington Circle near the historic district of Foggy Bottom (see Tour 7, no. 9). The four other statues are of other Revolutionary War heroes: General Lafayette (southeast corner, 1890); Comte Jean de Rochambeau (southwest corner, 1902); Gen. Thaddeus Kosciuszko (northeast corner, 1910); and Baron Friedrich Wilhelm von Steuben (northwest corner, 1910).

Federal Triangle

(World War I Memorial, government office buildings, Old Post Office with
National Park Service bell tower, Waldorf Astoria Hotel)

Christopher J. Alleva, updated by William J. Bonstra. WWI Memorial
description by Edwin Fountain

Distance: 1½ miles
Time: 1½ hours
Bus: 32, 33, and 36
Metro: Federal Triangle (Blue, Orange, and Silver Lines)

The Federal Triangle is formed by the intersection of Constitution Avenue with the diagonal Pennsylvania Avenue and is bounded on the west by 15th Street and on the east by 6th Street.

When Pierre L'Enfant created one of the most innovative land plans in the history of urban design, the Triangle was a swamp, subject to frequent flooding from the nearby Tiber Creek. L'Enfant transformed this barren wetland into the future sites of the buildings that now house much of the nation's federal government. Its exceptional location, south of Pennsylvania Avenue and north of the Mall between the White House and the Capitol, made it a natural place to locate the ministries and departments that run the day-to-day affairs of government.

After construction of the Tiber Canal in 1816 alleviated the flooding, the Triangle area developed rapidly, but as a commercial rather than a governmental center. The Center Market, between 7th and 9th Streets, lasted here from 1801 until 1870. Hotels, taverns, rooming houses, and printing and newspaper offices also filled the area. The Market Square development across the avenue from the National Archives Building recalls the historic markets in name only. It contains mostly offices with commercial space at the street.

The Triangle began to deteriorate after the Civil War. In 1899 the Old Post Office was erected at 12th Street and Pennsylvania Avenue, and it was hoped that this would be the beginning of a renaissance for the area. The McMillan Commission plan of 1902 pictured the Triangle as a park dotted with various municipal government buildings, and in 1908 the District Building was erected at 14th and E Streets, but no further action was taken. Conditions became increasingly scandalous: tattoo parlors, gas stations, and cheap hotels became prevalent, and Ohio Avenue (subsequently eliminated by Triangle construction) was lined with brothels. At the same time, the government's need for more office space was growing acute. The Public Buildings Bill, allocating $50 million for buildings in the District of Columbia, was finally passed by Congress and signed by President Calvin Coolidge on May 5, 1926. Two years later, Congress appropriated the money to buy the entire Triangle.

Secretary of the Treasury Andrew W. Mellon was responsible for the construction and design of the buildings, and in 1927 he appointed the Board of Architectural Consultants to draw up a plan for the entire Triangle area.

The architects and the members of the Commission of Fine Arts, who participated in formulating the plan, accepted the prevailing premise that the neoclassical style was the proper one for public buildings. They saw in the Triangle development a rare opportunity to plan a group of related monumental buildings designed to constitute a single great composition. Public enthusiasm was high for the project, and the capital was caught up in a quest for grandeur. Everyone looked forward to Washington becoming the "Paris of America" and talked of a capital "worthy of a great nation."

In 1929 a model of the composition designed by the Board of Architectural Consultants went on display. The Triangle had been given a treatment somewhat similar to that of the Louvre, with buildings reflecting a classical-revival style. A series of courtyards surrounded a central circular court. Vistas from this court extended into the other plazas, one of which—the Great Plaza—was to be as large as Lafayette Square. The main entrances of the buildings were planned to open onto these courts, so that a sense of quiet would pervade the scheme. The buildings had a uniform cornice line drawn from the Natural History Museum and following the diagonal of Pennsylvania Avenue. Pylons at the entrances and specially designed sidewalks served to unify the composition.

Unfortunately, the Triangle never achieved the perfection for which its designers strove. The Great Depression—and the automobile—would sadly alter the final composition. The Great Plaza became a parking lot. The sweeping drives turned into major traffic arteries, and the pylons that were to flank them were declared a traffic hazard and were never constructed. The circular court was never completed because the Old Post Office, anathema to the Triangle's designers, was never demolished. Depression economies put the future of the final structure, at the apex, in doubt. When the Federal Trade Commission Building was finally constructed in 1937, it was a simplified version of the original design. By that time the neoclassical style was out of favor, and there was little interest in the buildings or in completing the design. The Triangle's imperial facade was deemed inappropriate for a democratic country.

For over sixty years, the finished facade along Constitution Avenue has been somewhat forbidding, and the Pennsylvania Avenue street line, broken at 13th Street, exposed to view the huge, unfinished parking lot that was to have been the Great Plaza. In 1981 GSA commissioned Harry Weese and Associates to design a master plan for the Triangle, including the completion of this area. The intent was to create an urban design that would be more inviting to the public, exposing the historic courtyards and handsome architecture and providing new office, public use, and commercial space, thus creating a link between the Mall and downtown. This idea evolved into the International Trade Center and DC Visitors Center, now the Ronald Reagan Building. Start your walking tour at the Federal Triangle Metro Station on the 12th Street side, facing the Old Post Office Building (Waldorf Astoria Hotel). Walk north to Pennsylvania Avenue and then west along Pennsylvania Avenue to Freedom Plaza. Then cross 14th Street to the National World War I Memorial opposite the Willard Hotel.

■ 1 Across 14th Street from Freedom Plaza is Pershing Park, site of the **National World War I Memorial.** Pershing Park was designed in tandem with Freedom Plaza and opened in 1981. The park landscape was designed by M. Paul

Friedberg, while the Pershing Memorial in the southeast corner, constructed by the American Battle Monuments Commission, was designed by Wallace K. Harrison, with a sculpture of General Pershing by Robert White (grandson of American architect Stanford White).

In 2014, Congress authorized the World War I Centennial Commission to enhance and rededicate the site as the National World War I Memorial. (The Commemorative Works Act had declared the Mall a "substantially completed work of civic art," and prohibited new memorials on the Mall.) An international design competition was won by Joseph Weishaar, a twenty-five-year-old graduate of the University of Arkansas School of Architecture, and Sabin Howard, a leading American figurative sculptor. Weishaar and Howard teamed with GWWO Architects of Baltimore and the Philadelphia landscape architecture firm David Rubin Land Collective to preserve and modernize the existing park while adding significant new commemorative elements.

The central feature of the memorial is a fifty-eight-foot-long sculpture of thirty-eight figures that is the largest free-standing bronze sculpture in the Western Hemisphere. The figures include seven women and four African Americans, as well as a Native American, Latino, Asian American, and representatives of other ethnic groups that contributed to the American war effort. Titled *A Soldier's Journey* and patterned after the archetypal myth of the hero's journey, the sculpture depicts a recurring figure of an American doughboy as he takes his helmet from his daughter and leaves his family, joins the parade to war, endures the hell of combat, emerges in the aftermath a transformed man, and returns home to his daughter, who looks into his helmet and sees the future—World War II. On a second level, the sculpture also represents the wartime experience of America as a nation. While most figures in the work move left to right across the tableau, at one point the hero stops, turns, and looks toward the viewer, as if to ask, "What happened here? What was it for? What did it cost? Was it worth it?"

The memorial is unique in that it includes a message of peace. On the reverse of the sculpture wall is the Peace Fountain, which includes lines from Archibald MacLeish's poem "The Young Dead Soldiers Do Not Speak," a call to the reader to bring a peace that gives meaning to the sacrifice of those who fell in the war—including MacLeish's own brother, Kenneth. Water cascades from both sides of the wall, and the shallow scrim in the middle of the viewing platform, which serves as a reflecting pool, can be drained to permit concerts and other events. Other commemorative features include inscribed quotations from President Woodrow Wilson, Army nurse Alta May Andrews, and renowned American author Willa Cather. In the round belvedere, interpretive panels are complemented by a bronze medallion that depicts the victory medal awarded to American troops. Visitors who stand on the medallion and speak aloud will hear an amusing echoing effect.

■ **2** The **Department of Commerce Building** (14th Street between E Street and Constitution Avenue) was designed by Louis Ayres of the firm of York and Sawyer and housed all the bureaus of the department under one roof, except for the National Bureau of Standards. At the time of its construction in 1931, it was the largest government office building in the world—1,050 feet long, exceeding the Capitol by three hundred feet. Arched gateways two stories high give direct access through the building at what used to be C and D Streets. The central section of the 14th Street facade is patterned after the Perrault facade at the Louvre. The relief panels, designed by James Earle Fraser, represent the various agencies of the department. The building encloses six courtyards providing light and ventilation, a design that was necessary before air conditioning. Enter the lobby to view the coffered ceiling with gilded accents and richly colored marble floors and columns. Look out the windows into the landscaped courtyards, and you will begin to sense the feeling the planners and architects had in mind when the building was laid out.

■ **3** The **Oscar Straus Memorial Fountain** in front of the Ronald Reagan Building was designed by John Russell Pope, but a simplified version of his design was actually built. The figures were sculpted by Adolph A. Weinman.

■ **4** **Ronald Reagan Building and International Trade Center (ITC)** at 1300 14th Street NW. In 1987, the Federal Triangle Development Act authorized the construction of a federal building complex and International Cultural and Trade Center on the eleven-acre Federal Triangle property.

The complex was designed by Pei, Cobb, Freed & Partners of New York City, in association with Ellerbe Becket, Architects and Engineers, of Washington, DC. Lead architect James Ingo Freed and his design team had a truly unique challenge. They would define the last vacant piece of land on Pennsylvania Avenue between the Capitol and the White House. They would complete the great complex of buildings whose construction was halted by the Depression. And, almost at the dawn of the twenty-first century, they would leave a statement about the relationship between traditional and contemporary architecture for future generations.

The building was originally designed to house operations for the International Cultural and Trade Center (ICTC) and offices for the Department of Justice. Some of the ICTC program components included an international club and reception center, two performing arts theaters, an IMAX theater, exhibition space, and retail and food services. The building was originally designed to house operations for the ICTC and offices for the Department of Justice.

In 1992, the program for the project was revised to abandon the ICTC and retain approximately five hundred thousand square feet of space for the ITC. Plans included an auditorium and conference center, reception spaces, exhibit space, retail and food services, and office space for private-sector trade-related firms. Parking for approximately two thousand cars remained unchanged, as did the tunnels connecting the building to the Commerce Building, the Customs Building, and the Federal Triangle Metro station at the Ariel Rios Building. The ITC Building opened in 1999. More information can be found at www.rrbitc.com.

Walk south along 14th Street and turn left into the courtyard known as Woodrow Wilson Plaza. Continue around the back of the Ronald Reagan Building to visit the National Children's Museum.

■ 5 The **National Children's Museum** is located on the east side (rear) of the Ronald Reagan Building at 1300 Pennsylvania Avenue NW off Woodrow Wilson Plaza. This museum combines science center content with a children's museum experience, with hands-on spaces to ignite curiosity and inspire young children to explore science, technology, engineering, arts, and math (or STEAM) through whimsical exhibits and engaging programs. Advanced tickets are required for all visitors and all tickets are timed entry. See www.nationalchildrensmuseum.org/tickets to reserve your spot today.

■ 6 Arthur Brown Jr. of San Francisco, designer of the City Hall and War Memorial Opera House in that city, was the architect of the complex (between 12th and 14th Streets on Constitution Avenue) originally built for the Department of Labor, the **Andrew W. Mellon Auditorium**, and the Interstate Commerce Commission, and now occupied by the **Environmental Protection Agency**. Of particular interest is the second-story relief panel of the Departmental Auditorium, which diverges from the neoclassical allegorical sculpture typical of the building's exteriors. Designed by Edmond Romulus Amateis, it depicts Gen. George Washington with Maj. Gens. Nathanael Greene and John Sullivan. Greene's face is that of architect Brown, and Sullivan's is that of sculptor Edgar Walter.

Continue walking east along Constitution Avenue. As you cross 12th Street, note the glimpses of the Old Post Office Building to the north (opposite where you came out of the Metro station at the start of the tour).

■ 7 After crossing 12th Street, you will be looking across Constitution Avenue at the headquarters of the **US Department of the Treasury Building** and **Internal Revenue Service** at 1111 Constitution Avenue NW and the words of Oliver Wendell Holmes inscribed on it: "Taxes are what we pay for a civilized society." The building was designed by the Office of the Supervising Architect of the Treasury Department under the direction of Louis Simon. It was completed in 1930, the first of the group to be finished. It is constructed of Indiana limestone and granite with columns of Tennessee marble. The building has four handsomely landscaped inner courtyards, like the Commerce Department Building. The final wing, meant to form the eastern side of the circular court, was never completed.

8 When you have crossed 10th Street, you are opposite the **Robert F. Kennedy Department of Justice Building** at 950 Pennsylvania Avenue NW (entrance on the north side on Pennsylvania Avenue). It was designed by the Philadelphia firm of Zantzinger, Borie and Medary and completed in 1934. Its architecture is notably simplified, reflecting the influence of the art deco or modern styles of the period. This is reflected in the extensive use of aluminum in decorative lighting fixtures and monumental doors, as well as in the polychrome details at the cornice and the soffits at the entries.

Department of Justice Building

9 As you proceed across 9th Street, stop to admire John Russell Pope's **National Archives Building**. This was to be the most important and tallest building in the complex, designed as a shrine for the nation's most treasured documents. The structure is purely classical with completely plain walls, except for windows to accommodate the offices on the Pennsylvania Avenue side. It is adorned by seventy-two Corinthian pillars, fifty-two feet high, grouped in colonnades about the building. The great pediment on the Constitution Avenue facade displays a figure representing the Recorder of the Archives and two eagles standing guard at the sides. The sculptor was James Earle Fraser, who also designed the large, seated figures that flank the monumental steps leading into a public hall housing the **Declaration of Independence**, the **Constitution**, and the **Bill of Rights**. The National Archives is open 10:00 a.m.–5:30 p.m., with extended summer hours, except on Thanksgiving Day and December 25. Admission is free. Guided tours are offered at 10:00 a.m., Monday through Friday, and may be reserved online. More information is available at www.museum.archives.gov.

10 Proceed along Constitution Avenue to the last of the Triangle group, the **Federal Trade Commission Building**, with entry at 600 Pennsylvania Avenue NW. This building, designed by Bennett, Parsons and Frost, was considerably

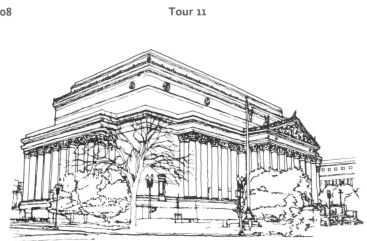

National Archives

altered from the original model to be acceptable to a nation in the throes of a depression. It is still a satisfying building, however. This rounded colonnade of Doric columns, reminiscent of a blunted ship's bow, makes an excellent terminus to the Triangle composition.

■ **11** The **Canadian Chancery**, designed by one of Canada's most decorated architects, Arthur Erickson, across Pennsylvania Avenue toward the Capitol, opened in 1989. It has long horizontals, wide open spaces, and water features—trying to evoke a sense of Canada. In the large, airy courtyard, you can see a sculpture by Bill Reid, *Spirit of Haida Gwaii*.

■ **12** The **H. Carl Moultrie I Court House of the District of Columbia** at 300 Indiana Avenue NW opened in 1977. It has one appellate and forty-four trial courtrooms, plus ancillary space.

■ **13** The **E. Barrett Prettyman US Court House** on the east side of John Marshall Park has been the scene of many famous trials, including those held in connection with the Watergate and Iran-Contra affairs, and the trial of former DC mayor Marion Barry.

■ **14 555 Pennsylvania Avenue NW** exists as a 420,000-square-foot academic building under Johns Hopkins University, standing as a complete renovation of the Newseum originally constructed in 2008. It includes 555 sports classrooms, offices, conferencing space, media suites, roof terraces, restaurants, and picturesque views along Pennsylvania Avenue and the Capitol Building. Several divisions of the university occupy the building, including the School of Advanced International Studies, the Carey Business School, and the Krieger School of Arts and Sciences. This conversion to academic pursuits bolsters the presence of the university in the nation's capital.

■ **15** The **Andrew W. Mellon Memorial Fountain**, across 6th Street from the Federal Trade Commission Building, is an exclamation point to the Triangle.

The fountain, completed in 1952, could not be in a more appropriate position, filling the last sliver of the great Triangle that Mellon's influence brought to fruition and situated directly across from the National Gallery of Art, which he gave to the nation. The fountain was designed by architect Otto R. Eggers in bronze and granite. The signs of the zodiac, visible under the sheet of water formed by the overflow from the basins, are the work of sculptor Sidney Waugh. There are also benches to rest on before beginning the walk back along Pennsylvania Avenue.

The Pennsylvania Avenue side of the Federal Triangle has been completely reconstructed. It is noticeable here that, in designing the National Archives Building, John Russell Pope did not follow the diagonal of the avenue as did the other architects. The resulting triangular slice of land is a small park, a memorial to Franklin Delano Roosevelt, located there according to his wishes. The flanking statues at the building's entrance are the work of Robert Aiken.

The Justice Department Building returns to the concept of filling the entire block. Walk to the vehicular entrance in the center of its 9th Street facade for a glimpse of the largest and most elaborate of the Triangle's interior courtyards. Note the polychrome decorations of the soffits above the driveways.

At 11th Street, the short, truncated facade of the Internal Revenue Service Building testifies that the design here was never completed, awaiting the planned demolition of the Old Post Office. It is here that some of the most dramatic proposals of GSA's master plan will be realized.

■ 16 The **Old Post Office** was designed by Willoughby Edbrooke in the Richardsonian Romanesque style popular at the time of its construction in 1899. It was considered an "object of permanent regret" by the neoclassicists, and the Triangle designers drew up a plan that demanded its demolition. Its bulk cuts across the space that would have been the pivotal circular court designed after the "gay fashion of Paris." It is worth walking down 12th Street to see the great eastern facade of the Old Post Office that was to form half of that court. A small segment of the opposite side of the circular court is visible on the Internal Revenue Service Building behind the Old Post Office.

When completed in 1899, it was thought that the Post Office Building would stimulate revitalization of one of the worst neighborhoods in Washington. But the hoped-for results were not forthcoming. The early years of the building's history were marked with controversy and disappointment. The Old Post Office Building was less than ten years old when cries were heard that it should be torn down. One local man, Nathan Rubinton, carved by hand a model of the building so that when it was torn down people would remember how it looked. In 1914, the District of Columbia Mail Depot was moved to a larger building constructed next to Union Station. Although only fifteen years old, the building at 12th Street and Pennsylvania Avenue was dubbed the "old" post office.

The postmaster general moved to a newly constructed office building directly across 12th Street in 1934. The only reason that the Old Post Office was not then razed was the lack of money caused by the Great Depression. For the next forty years the building served as overflow space for several government agencies. In the 1970s, when Congress finally appropriated the money to remove the Old Post Office, local citizens banded together for a desperate final struggle to save it. Nancy Hanks, the politically influential chairperson of the National Endowment for the Arts, joined the effort and prevailed in convincing Congress to reverse its decision. The Old Post Office was rescued.

The Old Post Office Building was lavishly renovated and home to the ill-fated Trump Hotel for several years during Donald Trump's presidency. It has been gloriously renovated to its historic grandeur and is now home to the Waldorf Astoria Hotel DC, complete with a new restaurant by famed chef and philanthropist José Andrés.

The National Park Service provides tours of the Old Post Office Tower (enter in the courtyard at the rear of the hotel), which affords one of the most spectacular views of Washington, DC, from a 270-foot-high observation deck. An exhibit depicts the struggle for survival of the Old Post Office. While touring the tower, visitors can also view the Congress Bells, one of the largest sets of change-ringing bells in North America and the official bells of the US Congress. For more information, please visit www.nps.gov/thingstodo/old-post-office-tower.htm.

Old Post Office Building

■ **17** The **John A. Wilson Building** (1908, Cope and Stewardson) is Washington's city hall, the site of the offices of the mayor and the Council of the District of Columbia and some other city offices. By the late 1980s the building was out-dated and had deteriorated, and the mayor and council temporarily moved out in the early 1990s. The Beaux-Arts building was renovated and enlarged by filling in a U-shaped space on the back frontage, creating a new atrium space. Shalom Baranes was the architect for the restoration and addition.

■ **18** In front of the Wilson Building is **Freedom Plaza**, designed by Venturi, Rauch and Scott Brown for the Pennsylvania Avenue Development Corporation. The design incorporates a partial plan of the city into the paving of its raised platform. A water feature was added to the plaza at the western portion in the mid-1990s. This plaza is the site of concerts, and a destination for skateboarders and roller bladers.

Downtown—West of 9th Street

(Central business district, Franklin Square, CityCenterDC, Ford's Theater,
FBI Building, Pennsylvania Avenue)

John Fondersmith, updated by William J. Bonstra

Distance: 2 ¾ miles

Time: 2½ hours

Bus: 32, 36, 70, 79, P6, and D6

Metro: Metro Center (Red, Blue, Orange, and Silver Lines); Gallery
Place/Chinatown (Red, Yellow, and Green Lines); McPherson
Square (Blue, Orange, and Silver Lines); Archives/Navy
Memorial (Yellow and Green Lines); Federal Triangle (Blue,
Orange, and Silver Lines)

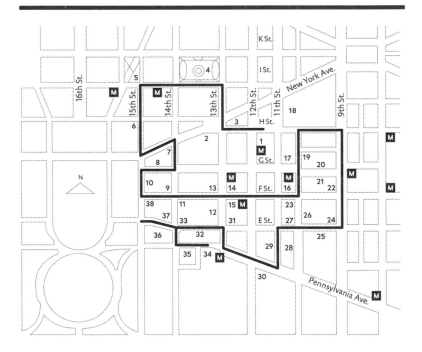

Beginning in the 1950s, Washington's original downtown area north of
Pennsylvania Avenue underwent the decline and change of functions that have
affected other large American cities. In the early 1980s, the reversal of this trend
began, stimulated by the still-expanding Metrorail system and a recognition
of the area's economic potential by developers, the District of Columbia government, business leaders, and citizens. With guidance from the downtown

element of the comprehensive plan, extensive rebuilding continues, with the aim of achieving a "living downtown." The work of the Pennsylvania Avenue Development Corporation (PADC), a federal development corporation, was important along Pennsylvania Avenue between 1972 and 1996, when the agency was closed. A Downtown Business Improvement District (BID) was formed and began work in 1997. The District government, through its Office of Planning and its development agencies, continues its work to transform downtown. Revitalization—new development and the reuse of older buildings—has largely been completed in the area of this tour, west of 9th Street.

1 Metro Center is at the core of the Metro system and has one of the most heavily used of the ninety-eight Metro stations that serve the completed 128-mile regional rapid rail system. A twenty-three-mile extension to and beyond Washington Dulles International Airport opened in 2022. Metrorail service on a limited 4.5-mile segment through downtown started in 1976.

In the early 1970s, the District government acquired four renewal sites along G Street adjacent to the Metro Center station. The **Macy's Department Store** on G Street between 12th and 13th Streets is the largest freestanding department store built in any American downtown since 1945. It has two direct connections to the Metro Center station. The original building was designed for additional development. **One Metro Center**, an additional six-story office building, was developed on top of the department store by Tishman Speyer Properties (completed in 2003). On the west side of 13th Street is **700 13th Street NW**. The building lobby relates to a garden space adjacent to the historic **Church of the Epiphany** (1844, with later additions) Between 11th and 12th Streets is another office building, **700 11th Street NW**. This complex also includes the 450-room Marriott Metro Center Hotel at 775 12th Street NW, opened in 1989 These three buildings were designed by Skidmore, Owings & Merrill and developed by the Oliver T. Carr Company and the Theodore Hagans interests.

2 The InterAmerican Development Bank Building at 1300 New York Avenue NW, designed by Skidmore, Owings & Merrill, is one of the largest buildings in downtown. It has a spectacular atrium space, which, unfortunately, is difficult for visitors to see because of security restrictions.

3 The National Museum of Women in the Arts (NMWA) is housed in the landmark Masonic Building; Keyes Condon Florance (now SmithGroup) were the architects of the renovation. The museum, which opened in 1987, is the only one in the United States exclusively devoted to art by women. The NMWA is undergoing a complete interior renovation and will reopen in later 2023. Sandra Vicchio & Associates designed the project. More information can be found at www.nmwa.org/renovation

Franklin Square

■ **4 Franklin Square** is both a park, bounded by K, I, 13th, and 14th Streets, and the name of a larger section that has developed as a prestigious office area since 1980. **Franklin Park** is the second-largest space owned by the National Park Service in downtown Washington, DC, and was created in the 1800s to protect the primary water source serving the White House. The revitalization of historic Franklin Park is the first-ever joint venture between the Park Service, the DowntownDC Business Improvement District (BID), and the Department of General Services (DGS). As part of the agreement, the DowntownDC BID will operate, manage, and program events in the park. In collaboration, STUDIOS Architecture and David Rubin Land Collective are revivifying the open spaces and adding a café within the 4.79-acre park. The reimagined historic, urban square is designed for inclusion, to provide improved environmental function, and to introduce new, programmable spaces and areas for play, while celebrating the history of water on the site.

The park is surrounded by striking new buildings. On the southeast corner of the square, **1300 I Street NW** was developed by Gerald D. Hines Interests and designed by John Burgee Architects with Philip Johnson. On the east side of the square, the exterior of the landmark **Franklin School** (1869) was restored in the early 1990s as one of the amenities of the **Franklin Plaza** office project to the east. Planet Word Museum's home is in the Franklin School, the fifty-thousand-square-foot, five-story building originally opened in 1869 and completely rehabilitated between 2018 and 2020. Renowned architect Adolf Cluss designed the Franklin School as the flagship of eight modern urban public school buildings in DC. The building served as a model for the modern public school system and offered free education to as many as nine hundred white boys and girls per year (DC schools were segregated at this time).

Planet Word opened in 2020 as a new kind of interactive and self-guided museum. Using the museum's state-of-the-art technology, visitors determine their experience through their own words and choices. Planet Word is a bold and imaginative response to the life-long importance of literacy and to the challenge of growing a love of language. General admission is free, but visit planetwordmuseum.org/plan-your-visit/ for museum hours and ticket reservations.

The large **One Franklin Square Building**, designed by Hartman-Cox Architects, now frames the north side of the square. The two large towers add a new design feature. Use of towers on commercial buildings in Washington was popular in the 1980s as a way to give buildings a special design character even though the main building height is limited (generally to 130 feet in the central area of the city). Several other new and renovated buildings are located around the square. The office building at the southwest corner, designed by Arthur Cotton Moore, incorporates the western entrance to the McPherson Square Metro station (Orange and Blue Lines). The square was improved in the early 1990s (plantings, new sidewalks, lighting, new fountain) through a cooperative effort of the District government, the National Park Service, and the Franklin Square Association.

■ **5 McPherson Square** is one of two squares centered on avenues radiating north from the White House (the other is Farragut Square, two blocks west). A mix of old and new buildings borders the square. At the southwest corner of the square is the former University Club (1911), later the headquarters of the United Mine Workers. The building, now known as the **Summit Grand Parc**, was renovated with a new building added to the west in 2002 for housing (105 units) by Martinez Johnson Architects. The lower level is home to the **Victims of Communism Museum** at 900 15th Street NW. It is open Monday through Friday, between the hours of 9:00 a.m. and 3:00 p.m.

■ **6 15th Street** between New York Avenue and K Street was once known as "Washington's Wall Street" because of the concentration of financial institutions. The area is now incorporated into the 15th Street Financial Historic District. The Bowen Building at the southwest corner of 15th and I Streets NW began construction in 2003 (a major facadomy project) and was completed in 2005 (see no. 7 for discussion of "facadomies"). The Shoreham Building (formerly offices) on the northwest corner of 15th and H Streets NW was converted to a 225-room Sofitel Hotel (opened 2002). Buildings of special interest are the **Southern Building** (1912) at 15th and H Streets, restored with two stories added on top, and the **National Savings and Trust Building** (1888), now a part of SunTrust Bank, also restored with a skillful addition. The **Wells Fargo Bank** and **PNC Bank** buildings, both with impressive banking halls and neoclassical facades, face the **Treasury Building** at the corner of 15th Street and Pennsylvania Avenue.

■ **7 New York Avenue** extends northeast from the White House to Mount Vernon Square. Along the **south side of the 1400 block of New York Avenue**, notice the **Washington Building**, renovated in 1989 with two floors added on top, and the new section of the **National Commercial Bank** project (1420 New York Avenue NW). The **Bond Building**, designed by Shalom Baranes Associates at the southwest corner of New York Avenue and 14th Street, is a facadomy—a project retaining the historic exterior facade of the building while a new building is built behind, below, and with the addition rising taller from within.

Commercial National Bank Building

■ **8** The landmark **Commercial National Bank Building** was renovated by the Oliver T. Carr Company in 1989 and joined to new construction to the west, which extends through to New York Avenue. Removal of an interim dropped ceiling revealed the full height of the impressive two-story banking hall, which now serves as the building's lobby off 14th Street. The **Colorado Building** (1921) across 14th Street was also renovated in 1989, by Greycoat Real Estate Corporation, and two stories were added on top. The renovation of these and other landmark buildings in the western portion of downtown provides a link to an earlier era.

■ **9 Hamilton Square** (600 14th Street) at the northwest corner of 14th and F Streets is an office / retail building (renovation completed in 1998). The building formerly housed Garfinckel's, long downtown's most fashionable department store; Garfinckel's closed in 1990.

It may be a good time to pull up a stool at the Hamilton, a popular dining and concert venue by the Clyde's Restaurant Group.

■ **10** The **Metropolitan Square** complex (office/retail), developed by the Oliver T. Carr Company and designed by Skidmore, Owings & Merrill, was built in two stages between 1980 and 1986 and marked the movement of new development east of 15th Street. The landmark facades of the Keith-Albee and Metropolitan Bank Buildings along 15th Street facing the Treasury Building were retained as part of the project. The project occupies about three-quarters of Square 224. (City blocks in Washington are called squares no matter what their shape and are identified by numbers that date from 1792 in the original city.) The complex has a large central atrium that includes the Old Ebbitt Grill, now in its third location. Some original furnishings were incorporated into the new space. The second phase of the project involved the controversial demolition of Rhodes Tavern.

■ **11** The **National Press Club Building**, at 14th and F Streets, has housed a concentration of media offices since it opened in 1924. The top floor is often the scene of talks by national and foreign leaders. The building underwent renovation in 1984, including a new facade, a central atrium, and a two-level shopping mall, which connects it to the adjacent National Place complex.

■ **12** **National Place** is a retail/office/hotel project extending from F Street to E Street, developed by the Quadrangle Development Corporation, the Marriott Corporation, and the Rouse Company in the early 1980s. The Shops, a two-level mall, connects with the retail mall space in the National Press Building. The Shops offers stores, restaurants, and a food court.

■ **13** The **north side of the 1300 block of F Street** has a mix of old and new buildings. The new Westory at 14th and F Streets, designed by Shalom Baranes Associates and developed by the Steven A. Goldberg Company, incorporates the earlier Westory Building. The entrance canopy and lobby are noteworthy. The Romanesque nineteenth-century **Sun Building** at 1315–17 F Street NW, designed by Alfred B. Mullet in 1887, was Washington's first "skyscraper." Fahrney's Pens, in the Sun Building, is one of Washington's distinctive older businesses.

■ **14** The **Homer Building** was built in the 1920s as a four-story structure with provision for additional stories. In view of that history, the District's Historic Preservation Review Board approved a design by Shalom Baranes Associates that retained the landmark facade and incorporated it into a large new building (developed by the John Akridge Company and completed in 1990). The structure has a dramatic atrium and an entrance to the Metro Center Metro station in an arcade in the corner at 13th and G Streets. Despite its success, this building illustrates some of the conflicts between the design goals of office-building developers and the city's interest in obtaining more retail space.

■ **15 Columbia Square** was the first new building along F Street, designed by I. M. Pei & Associates and built by Gerald D. Hines Interests. It is another successful office complex with a spectacular atrium but limited retail space. An entrance to the Metro Center Metro station is in an arcade at the corner of 12th and F Streets.

■ **16** The **Woodward and Lothrop department store**, known to Washingtonians as "Woodies," was once the area's leading department store. It was the first retail establishment to move to F Street from Pennsylvania Avenue after the Civil War, beginning the present retail core. Its two buildings were built from 1901 to 1926, when they were joined to form one building. Woodward and Lothrop closed in 1995. The Douglas Development Corporation, with Shalom Baranes Associates as architect, renovated the Woodies Building for office use with retail space on three levels. H&M Clothiers opened in the Woodies Building in August 2003. The Woodies Building remains an anchor in the retail area of the neighborhood.

■ **17 Washington Center** fills the entire block (Square 345) to the north. Designed by RTKL and developed by Quadrangle Development Corporation, it includes the 989-room Grand Hyatt Hotel on the north (built facing the old Convention Center), with a grand atrium and an office building with a second atrium. The complex skillfully incorporates the landmark McLachlen Bank Building at the corner of 10th and G Streets. There is a direct link to the Metro Center station.

■ **18** The **Washington Convention Center** was begun in 1998, and the new facility (see Tour 13, Downtown—East, no. 22), which opened nearby, north of Mount Vernon Square, was dedicated in March 2003. The old convention center closed at that time and was demolished. The almost ten-acre site, after remaining a parking lot for many years, has been transformed into **CityCenterDC** by Foster+Partners, along with Shalom Baranes Associates, a 2.5-million-square-foot housing, ultra-luxury retail, and Class A office development. The $850 million project was built in three phases and completed in 2015. The **Conrad Hotel**, by Swiss architects Herzog & de Meuron, also provides luxury retail environments. At **1100 New York Avenue NW**, an office building west of the old convention center site was designed by Keyes Condon Florance (now SmithGroup) and developed by Manufacturers Realty, a Canadian firm active in Washington development in the 1980s. The complex is notable for retaining much of the 1930s art deco Greyhound Bus Terminal on New York Avenue. The old bus terminal lobby has been reconstructed as a focal point in the new building.

■ **19** The **First Congregational United Church of Christ (FCUCC)** has been located at the corner of 10th and G Streets since the Civil War. This building is their third church. With the goal of rebuilding their congregation, funding their social service programs, and remaining at this site in a new sanctuary, FCUCC partnered with a local developer to create a project to maximize the site's development potential and ensure the economic survival of the church.

Acknowledging the color palette of the adjacent Martin Luther King Jr. Memorial Library, the masonry base anchors the building at the corner of 10th and G Streets. Glowing glass boxes adorn the base, providing natural light to the sanctuary and chapel. A glass canopy on the west side marks the office entrance. The simply detailed, shimmering glass geode floats above the masonry base, cantilevering at the corner to mark the church entry. The sculpted glass tower tapers to maintain long views to the MLK Jr. library and surrounding buildings while reflecting the adjacent architecture. This mixed-use project (completed in 2011) includes Class A office space, ground floor retail, and church worship space for three hundred congregants and associated programs.

■ **20** The **Martin Luther King Jr. Memorial Library**, at 9th and G Streets, is the city's central library and the only work of the architect Mies van der Rohe in Washington. A mural in the library depicts the life of Dr. King. The Washington DC Public Library (DCPL) embarked on an ambitious initiative to renovate and imbue its aging infrastructures with a renewed sense of purpose in the digital information age. Chief amidst this program is the reimagining of the MLK Jr. Memorial Library. In partnership with Dutch architecture firm Mecanoo Architecten, OTJ Architects led this internationally significant test case on the sensitive transformation of a 1970s cultural complex into a socially sustainable engine for the exchange of knowledge. The renovated library now functions as an agile vehicle for the many platforms through which end-users access information. Four existing lower floors are connected to a fifth-floor addition and a rooftop garden via bold, sculptural staircases and intuitive way-finding devices, forming a more legible route through the building.

■ **21** Across the street are the Mather Studio Lofts by Cunningham and Quill Architects. The **Mather Building** was built in 1917 as RKO Studios in Washington, DC, at 7th and G Streets NW. The adaptive reuse and renovation completed in 2004 ended ten years of abandonment and neglect for the building, which later was the home of the University of the District of Columbia Visual Arts program. After extensive historic research and documentation, and a collaborative effort with community groups, the project gained unanimous approval from municipal authorities. The project team restored the building's existing structure and terra-cotta facade using original photographs and survey drawings. Two floors of affordable live/work artist lofts and seven floors of condominiums occupy the upper levels, while a new rooftop penthouse and private terraces offer spectacular views of the National Mall. The street-level public arts space is a community arts venue for education, theater, and an exhibition that engages residents and neighbors alike.

■ **22** The **900 block of F Street** is interesting because of the eclectic mix of old buildings, because it is a transition area between the retail core and Gallery Place, and because it is the last block in downtown west of 9th Street to undergo transformation. Two important landmark buildings anchor the eastern corners of the block. The **Courtyard Washington Convention Center Hotel** occupies the Richardsonian granite building at the southwest corner of 9th and F Streets (originally designed by James G. Hill for the Washington Loan and Trust Company in 1891 and for many years a branch of Riggs National Bank). Renovation was completed in 2000. The Gordon Biersch Brewery and Restaurant occupies the old banking hall on the first floor. On the northwest corner, the old Masonic Temple (1870) was renovated with a modern addition to house the Gallup Organization with McCormick & Schmick's Seafood Restaurant on the ground floor. These two buildings are part of a cluster of landmarks surrounding Gallery Place

■ **23** At **1000 F Street NW** is an eleven-story office and retail building located near Metro Center. Working on a challenging narrow site, new construction is surgically inserted adjacent to a two-story designated historic structure whose facades and renovated interiors are integrated into the development. A higher and lower volume frame the historic building, with extensive outdoor terrace spaces at roof levels and setbacks. The LEED-Gold development includes ten levels of office space above ground floor retail with two levels of below-grade parking.

■ **24** The **E Street Theater Row** is a key element of the Downtown Arts District. It has retail, restaurants, and entertainment along E Street, linking the National, Warner, Ford's, and Shakespeare theaters as well as the **E Street Cinema** complex in Lincoln Square and the Woolly Mammoth Theatre at 7th and E Streets.

■ **25** The huge **J. Edgar Hoover FBI Building** (between 9th and 10th Streets and Pennsylvania Avenue and E Street), completed in 1972, provides space for more than eight thousand employees. Its brutalist architectural style reflects design ideas of the 1960s, and recent security restrictions have made its frontages even more unfriendly.

■ **26 Ford's Theatre**, where Abraham Lincoln was assassinated, was restored by the National Park Service and reopened as a museum and a theater in 1965. Across 10th Street, the **Petersen House** has also been restored to its appearance on April 14, 1865, when the dying president was carried there for treatment. The brick-paved portion of 10th Street between E and F Streets is known as "Lincoln Place." Just south of Ford's Theatre is another cultural monument: Washington's **Hard Rock Cafe**, in the renovated 999 E Street building.

■ **27** Two recent buildings to the west provide more office space for Washington law firms and add activity on E Street. **Lincoln Square** (555 11th Street), designed by Hartman-Cox and developed by the Lawrence Ruben Company, combines office, retail, and cinema space. It integrates portions of older building elements with the new building and relates well to 1001 Pennsylvania Avenue across E Street, also designed by Hartman-Cox. **E Street Cinema**, an eight-screen art cinema complex operated by Landmark Theatres, has an E Street lobby in Lincoln Square. The **Thurman Arnold Building** (555 12th Street) occupies the entire block to the west and is home to Arnold and Porter, one of the city's largest law firms.

■ **28 1001 Pennsylvania Avenue**, designed by Hartman-Cox Architects, is considered one of the most successful of the newer buildings along Pennsylvania Avenue. Completed in 1985, it has a strong but subdued Pennsylvania Avenue facade. Facades of several older buildings on 10th and 11th Streets were retained and skillfully integrated into the overall design. Intersecting interior arcades meet in the center of the building in an impressive domed space.

■ **29** The old **Evening Star Building** (1898, Marsh and Peter), on Pennsylvania Avenue at 11th Street, has a beautiful neoclassical facade. The facade along 11th Street is especially prominent because of the setback of the FBI Building. The Jonathan Woodner Company, with Skidmore, Owings & Merrill as architects, completed renovation of the building in 1989. The project included the skillful integration of a slim new building element on Pennsylvania between the original building and a larger addition on 11th Street.

■ **30** The **Old Post Office** (see Federal Triangle, Tour 11, no. 14).

■ **31** The **Warner Theatre**, at 13th and E Streets, has a long history as an entertainment center in downtown Washington. The theater was renovated as part of the Warner, an office/retail/theater complex at 1299 Pennsylvania Avenue. Shalom Baranes Associates was the restoration architect of the Warner Building and theater renovation, which includes improvements to the "back of the house" theater facilities. Pei Cobb Freed & Partners were the architects for the related new office/retail building, with an interesting atrium, extending east along E Street to 12th Street. More information can be found at www.warnertheatre.com.

■ **32 Freedom Plaza**, designed by Venturi, Rauch and Scott Brown under the original Pennsylvania Avenue Development Corporation (PADC) guidelines, is an important open space used by skateboarders and bicyclists, concerts, and frequent national and local political rallies also organized along Pennsylvania

Avenue to the east. It occupies a key site between the retail core and the monumental Federal Triangle complex to the south. The central part of the L'Enfant plan is outlined in stone and grass in the center of the plaza, and there are interesting inscriptions about Washington, DC. The overall design of the plaza is not fully satisfactory (hot in summer, not user friendly, and too hard edged), but attempts to humanize the space are being made.

■ **33** The Pennsylvania Avenue frontage of the **National Place** complex (a joint design venture of Mitchell / Giurgola and Frank Schlesinger Associates) includes offices, the 774-room **J. W. Marriott Hotel**, and the entrance to the retail mall. As part of the project, the adjacent **National Theatre** was renovated in 1983.

■ **34** The **Ronald Reagan Building and International Trade Center** (see Tour 11, Federal Triangle, no. 4).

■ **35** The **John A. Wilson Building** (see Tour 11, Federal Triangle, no. 17).

■ **36 Pershing Park and the World War I Memorial** (see Tour 11, Federal Triangle, no. 1).

■ **37** The landmark **Willard InterContinental Hotel**, at 14th Street and Pennsylvania Avenue, opened in 1901 and was one of Washington's top hotels for many years. In an earlier Willard Hotel on this site, Julia Ward Howe composed "The Battle Hymn of the Republic." The hotel building closed in 1968.

Willard InterContinental Hotel

Early plans for Pennsylvania Avenue called for tearing it down and building a huge national square at the west end of the avenue. The plans were changed in 1974, when the Pennsylvania Avenue plan was revised to emphasize historic preservation. Restoration of the hotel and an office building addition were completed in 1986. Hardy Holzman Pfeiffer was the original renovation. Walk into the Pennsylvania Avenue entrance to see the restored lobby and then proceed along "Peacock Alley," the grand hallway extending north to F Street.

38 The **Hotel Washington** anchors the west end of Pennsylvania Avenue. Notice the sgraffito (etching in the stucco) frieze around the top of the hotel, restored in 1989 with assistance from PADC. Inside are a restored lobby and the J&G Steakhouse. If you take this tour in late spring or summer, you would do well to end your walk with a visit to the P.O.V. lounge's rooftop terrace overlooking 15th Street. This offers a splendid view over the White House grounds and other parts of monumental Washington. Information and reservations are available at www.thehotelwashington.com.

Downtown—East

(Penn Quarter, Navy Memorial, Gallery Place, Smithsonian Donald W. Reynolds Center for American Art and Portraiture, Verizon Center, Chinatown, Mount Vernon Square, City Museum, Washington Convention Center, Judiciary Square, National Building Museum, National Law Enforcement Officers Memorial, National Postal Museum, Union Station, Canadian Embassy, Newseum)

John Fondersmith, updated by William J. Bonstra

Distance:	3 miles
Time:	4 hours
Bus:	70, 96, D5, P6, and X8
Metro:	Archives/Navy Memorial (Yellow and Green Lines), Gallery Place/Chinatown (Red, Yellow, and Green Lines)

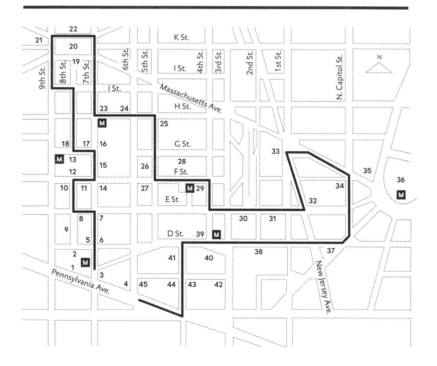

Seventh Street between Pennsylvania Avenue and Mount Vernon Square was once a primary retail street. Now it has emerged as an office/retail/residential/arts corridor, with a mix of old and new buildings. There are many restaurants of various cuisines in and near this corridor. This tour provides a view of the development that has been completed and is underway along 7th and

9th Streets between Pennsylvania Avenue and Mount Vernon Square. The
tour extends east through Chinatown, Judiciary Square, and downtown to
North Capitol Street, providing an opportunity to visit Union Station before
returning to the Municipal Center area and ending at the Canadian Embassy
and 555 Pennsylvania Avenue NW on Pennsylvania Avenue.

Between 1972 and 1996, the Pennsylvania Avenue Department Corporation
(PADC) took the lead in the development of the southern portion of this area
(Penn Quarter). Thereafter, the District government has worked to encour-
age development in the Gallery Place area and to preserve and enhance
Chinatown. Attention is being focused on the Mount Vernon Square area and
Shaw to the north.

The Downtown Business Improvement District (BID) has been important
in providing security and maintenance services. Capital One Arena (built in
1997 and designed by SmithGroup) and the new Convention Center (2003)
have spurred revitalization. Most encouraging is the amount of new residential
development downtown and in adjacent areas along New York Avenue and
Massachusetts Avenue east of 7th Street.

1 The **US Navy Memorial** at 8th Streets and Pennsylvania Avenue NW is a circular plaza flanked by fountains, highlighting the oceans of the world in stone.
The sculpture of the "lone sailor" by Stanley Bleifeld symbolically represents
all Americans who have served in the US Navy since the American Revolution.
Bas-reliefs surround the base of the fountains, illustrating the various branches
of the Navy. A theater and information center in the adjacent Market Square
East Building provides orientation and sources for ex-Navy personnel seeking
information about their ships and former crewmates. The memorial, designed
by Conklin and Rossant, provides space for concerts. The Navy Memorial is
part of Market Square Park, one of five open spaces along Pennsylvania Avenue developed by the PADC.

Market Square on Pennsylvania Avenue

■ **2 Market Square** is a mixed-use complex (retail and office space and 210 apartments) developed by the Trammell Crow Company. Hartman-Cox Architects designed the monumental complex. The two buildings frame the important **8th Street vista** extending north from the National Archives Building to the Smithsonian's Donald W. Reynolds Center for American Art and Portraiture at Gallery Place. There are several good places to eat before beginning the tour.

The area around Pennsylvania Avenue and 7th Street was Washington's first commercial center. A market was established in 1801 on the site where the National Archives Building now stands south of Pennsylvania Avenue. The new residential/commercial/arts area adjacent to Pennsylvania Avenue (approximately 1,500 residential units) is now called **Penn Quarter**.

■ **3 Indiana Plaza** is another open space created by closing several streets and combining small park spaces into one plaza. Notice the **Temperance Monument** and the **Grand Army of the Republic** memorial. On the edge of the plaza is the Richardsonian **Argentine Naval Attaché Building** (1886). To the south on Pennsylvania Avenue is the renovated former Apex Building, which was joined to several historic buildings in a complex designed by Hartman-Cox Architects. This is now the **Dorothy I. Height Building**, the headquarters of the National Council of Negro Women.

■ **4 Pennsylvania Plaza** is an office/residential/retail complex facing Indiana Avenue (technically it is joined to 601 Pennsylvania Avenue NW and thus has a Pennsylvania Avenue address). Notice the attractive entrances and the corner campanile structure at the corner of 6th Street and Indiana Avenue. The complex (completed 1990) was developed by the Sigal/Zuckerman Company and designed by Hartman-Cox Architects.

■ **5 Liberty Place** is an office building at 7th and D Streets, completed in 1990 by the Oliver T. Carr Company. The architect was Keyes Condon Florance. The project included the restoration of the Fireman's Insurance Company Building at 7th Street and Pennsylvania Avenue. As part of the restoration, the former gold dome on the building was replaced. The three smaller buildings to the east on Indiana Avenue, housing the Artifactory, the Penn Quarter Sports Tavern, and Potbelly Sandwich Works, are some of the oldest commercial buildings in Washington, dating from the 1820s. The **Litwin Building** (637 Indiana Avenue) had one of the earliest elevators in the country.

■ **6 Gallery Row** at 7th and D Streets was developed under the auspices of the PADC. The landmark facades were placed back onto a modern building, designed by Hartman-Cox Architects.

■ **7 The Jefferson at Penn Quarter** (completed 2003) includes 428 residential units, retail space, and the Woolly Mammoth Theatre (265-seat, courtyard-style theater, opened fall 2004). One building, which included a post–Civil War office of Clara Barton, has been retained and the space may be restored as a museum. This complex is being developed by JPI with Esocoff & Associates as architects. It is one of three major complexes completed along 7th Street in 2003–4, essentially completing major development along 7th Street (see this tour, nos. 14 and 16).

■ **8** The **Lansburgh** is one of the most interesting building complexes along 7th Street. Developed under the auspices of the PADC, the complex was designed by Graham Gund Architects and developed by the Gunwyn Company. The project includes 385 apartments, the Shakespeare Theatre's five-hundred-seat Lansburgh Theatre, and retail space. The design includes retention of a portion of the former Lansburgh's department store on 8th Street and two landmark facades, with a bold, colorful building along 7th Street.

■ **9** Eighth Street from Pennsylvania Avenue to F Street is part of an important axis derived from the L'Enfant plan. In this section, the National Archives Building is to the south and the portico of the National Portrait Gallery is to the north. **Market Square North**, an office/residential/retail complex, occupies most of the remainder of Square 407. Market Square North includes a major office building (401 9th Street NW) extending along the entire 9th Street frontage, developed by Gould Properties/Boston Properties, and two apartment buildings on 8th Street, the **Lexington** (eighty-six units) at D Street and the **Lexington North** (forty-nine units) at E Street. Guy Martin at Studios Architecture was the architect for these three buildings. The Lexington houses Teaism, an unusual teashop and café.

■ **10** A renovated row of landmark buildings lines the south side of the **800 block of F Street**, including the **LeDroit Building**, joined to new construction to the south. The LeDroit Building was an early Victorian office building (1875). The entire complex, which includes office space and twelve residential units, was designed by Shalom Baranes Associates.

■ **11** The **Hotel Monaco** now occupies the landmark Greek-revival former **US General Post Office Building**, also known as the **Tariff Commission Building** (1829–69, Robert Mills) at 700 F Street NW. This building first housed the Post Office Department and the city's post office and has provided space for other government agencies over the years, including the Tariff Commission. However, the building had deteriorated and was not suited for modern office use. In the late 1990s the General Services Administration decided to lease this historic building for private development. The resulting Hotel Monaco, developed by Kimpton Boutique Hotels, is one of the most interesting hotels in Washington. The renovation has made good use of the classical rooms and hallways. Turn through the archway from 8th Street into the courtyard to reach Poste Moderne Brasserie, the hotel's restaurant, in the former mail handling room. An attached contemporary glass pavilion houses the bar.

■ **12** The **Donald W. Reynolds Center for American Art and Portraiture**, which includes the National Portrait Gallery and Smithsonian American Art Museum, is located between F, G, 7th, and 9th Streets. It was formerly the US Patent Office, a repository for the Declaration of Independence, and a Civil War hospital, among other uses, before its initial renovation and reuse by the Smithsonian Institution in 1968 for these two important art museums. The building, erected in stages from 1836 to 1857 on a site that the L'Enfant plan indicated for a national nondenominational church and pantheon, is an excellent example of Greek-revival architecture. Architects included Robert Mills and Thomas U. Walter. Of particular note is the Robert and Arlene Kogod Courtyard, designed by Foster + Partners in London. The glass-covered courtyard, which opened in 2007, includes live plants and provides a large area for relaxation while still receiving plenty of natural light. Visitors can also enjoy food and beverages from the Courtyard Café, attached to the space. The Donald W. Reynolds Center for American Art and Portraiture is open daily, 11:30 a.m.–7:00 p.m., except December 25. Admission is free.

■ **13** The wide expanse of F Street between 7th and 9th Streets, created by the slightly offset alignment of F Street for those two blocks, forms a space framed by surrounding buildings. This space, known as **Gallery Place**, has the largest grouping of landmark buildings downtown and will become even more interesting as nearby buildings are completed. In the 1970s this portion of F Street and the related section of 8th Street from E to F Streets were closed to traffic and converted to pedestrian areas as part of a "Streets for People" program. Over time, that program did not work. In 1997 the pedestrian areas were rebuilt to conventional street design and reopened to traffic.

■ **14 Terrell Place** is a mixed-use complex (completed 2003) focused at 7th and F Streets that occupies much of Square 456. The Macy's department store at 7th and F Streets (formerly Hecht's) was a cornerstone of 7th Street retail activity, and the store eventually grew to encompass almost the entire block. In 1985 Hecht's moved to a new store at Metro Center. The old Hecht Company main building at 7th and F streets (1924) and older buildings that had been joined together were closed. The new complex includes reuse of the completely renovated old Hecht Company building, a new building to the east on F Street, and new construction behind retained facades further south on 7th Street for office and related retail use. The building at 7th and E Streets has been increased in height (facade retained) for residential use (twenty-nine units). CarrAmerica was the developer. Terrell Place is named for Mary Church Terrell, a civil rights leader who led the fight in 1951 to integrate Hecht's lunch counter.

The **Harman Center for the Arts** is composed of the Lansburgh Theatre at 450 7th Street NW and Sidney Harman Hall at 6th and F Streets. Both theaters are home to the Shakespeare Theatre Company. The Harman Center has greatly increased Washington's role as a destination for classical theater in the United States. Its construction completes the first phase of rebuilding this square that began in the 1980s with the Oliver T. Carr Company's dramatic neoclassical building at 6th and E Streets, the headquarters of the **American Association of Retired Persons**. The building was designed by Kohn Pedersen Fox Associates. Schedule and ticket information for the Harman Center can be found at www.shakespearetheatre.org.

15 Capital One Arena was developed by Washington businessman and team owner Abe Pollin, who decided in the early 1990s that the time was right to build a modern arena downtown to replace a 1970s arena located near the suburban Beltway. Capital One Arena was built on a site that included a previously cleared but undeveloped urban renewal site, the closing of the 600 block of G Street, and additional land to the north. The complex includes a sporting goods store, sports exhibit space, a steakhouse, and other eateries. A large arcade entrance to the Gallery Place/Chinatown Metro station is built into the 7th and F Streets corner of the building, providing excellent Metrorail access from all parts of the Washington region. Capital One Arena opened in December 1997 and has been a major catalyst for development in adjacent areas of downtown, especially Penn Quarter, Gallery Place, and Chinatown.

16 Gallery Place is a new, mixed-use complex on 7th Street at H Street, in the center of Chinatown (opened 2004). It includes 250,000 square feet of retail space (including a fourteen-screen United Artists Cinema, dining, and other retailers), a new office building, 192 residential condominiums, and space for Chinatown community functions. A lively pedestrian walk, G Street Alley, provides a connection between 7th and 6th Streets along the north side of the Capital One Arena. The Chinatown entrance to the Gallery Place/Chinatown Metro station is built in an arcade in the north end of Gallery Place at 7th and H Streets, adjacent to the Chinatown Archway. Gallery Place is a joint venture of Akridge and Western Development, designed by Arquitectonica and HKS Architects.

17 The **buildings along the west side of the 700 block of 7th Street**, between G and H Streets, are the best remaining row of late nineteenth and early twentieth century commercial buildings downtown. The Douglas Development Corporation has undertaken the historic restoration of these buildings, with ground-floor retail (mostly restaurants and food stores) and office space above. GTM Architects have provided design services. This row of buildings adds a special character to this section of 7th Street.

■ **18 Eighth Street** extends north from G Street to Mount Vernon Square, a continuation of the strong north–south axis derived from the L'Enfant plan. Major development has taken place in this corridor. At 8th and G Streets, the Trammel Crow Company has constructed the **Portrait Building** (office with ground floor retail) with Leo A. Daly as architect. The project was undertaken in association with **Calvary Baptist Church**. The program included the development of a new building behind the retained Greene Building facade for church use and restoration of significant historic elements on the church sanctuary, including reconstruction of the church's long-lost, 150-foot-tall corner tower at 8th and H Streets. On the west side of 8th Street at G Street is the headquarters of the **Family Research Council** and, at 9th and G Streets, the new and striking **Edison Place** building, designed by Devrouax and Purnell. The building is headquarters for PEPCO, the local electric utility. The dramatic Zaytinya restaurant is a popular gathering place, one of several restaurants encircling the Donald W. Reynolds Center for American Art and Portraiture. Among the other new buildings between 8th and 9th Streets, notice the **Greater New Hope Baptist Church** north of H Street (originally built in 1897 as the Washington Hebrew Congregation).

■ **19** The **two city blocks bordering the south side of Mount Vernon Square** between 7th and 9th Streets, with 8th Street converted to a pedestrian plaza, constitute an interesting complex of four buildings, each with its own core and all built atop a common parking facility. The 8th Street pedestrian area passes below the four-story glass-faced bridge connecting two of the four buildings of the complex, creating a frame for the view between the north facade of the Donald W. Reynolds Center for American Art and Portraiture to the south and the DC History Center and new Convention Center to the north. The complex has meeting and exhibit area space underground. There are also two Chinese gardens.

■ **20** In an open green space in Mount Vernon Square stands the historic **Carnegie Library**, which was constructed in 1902 to serve as the city's central library until 1972, when it moved to the nearby Martin Luther King Jr. Memorial Library. The Beaux-Arts gem was recently restored by Foster+Partners with Beyer Blinder Belle, and now houses the DC History Center, as well as an Apple store. Founded in 1894, the DC History Center uplifts the District's diverse communities and their stories, through its library and collections, exhibits, and adult and youth programming. Admission is free. Check www. dchistory.org for hours.

■ **21 Mount Vernon Square** is also the name of a larger area extending from 12th Street on the west to New Jersey Avenue on the east and generally for several blocks to the north and south, overlapping part of Chinatown to the south. Mount Vernon Square has become a prominent urban neighborhood with an eclectic mix of housing, retail, commercial office, and parks centered on the DC History Center and Apple Store. East of 9th Street the pattern will be mainly commercial with some residential. Just southwest of the square a new office building, **901 New York Avenue NW**, was completed in 2004. A major **Marriott convention headquarters hotel** is under construction at 9th Street and Massachusetts Avenue, just west of the convention center. The Mount Vernon Triangle east of 7th Street is proposed for residential development, approximately five thousand units, with initial projects under construction along the south side of Massachusetts Avenue.

■ 22 The **Walter E. Washington Convention Center** welcomes visitors from around the world and is located at Mount Vernon Square to serve the conference and exhibition needs of the city. With over 2.3 million square feet of space on almost six city blocks, it is the largest building in Washington. It has 725,000 square feet of column-free exhibit space, seventy meeting rooms, restaurant space, and a fifty-two-thousand-square-foot ballroom. It also has a grand lobby facing Mount Vernon Square with magnificent stairways and views over the city from the upper ballroom floor. Although the building is huge, its size is less apparent because the building is broken into separate components and burrows into the slope of the land toward the north. The Mount Vernon Square/7th Street/Convention Center Metro station on 7th Street (Green Line) provides convenient Metro access. The Washington Convention and Sports Authority operates the convention center. A team of Thompson, Ventulett, Stainback & Associates; Mariani Architects and Engineers; and Devrouax and Purnell designed this large and innovative complex. The convention center has been important in promoting activity and spurring economic growth and new development. Most important, however, it attracts thousands of additional visitors to explore and appreciate Washington, DC.

■ 23 The **Chinatown Archway** at 7th and H Streets marks the heart of Chinatown. With its seven colorful pagoda roofs, the archway is said to be the largest of its kind outside China. Erected in 1986, it was a joint project of the District of Columbia government and the Municipality of Beijing (Washington, DC, and Beijing are sister cities.) Alfred Liu was the architect for the District.

■ 24 The **600 block of H Street** forms the center of Washington's Chinatown, with many Chinese restaurants. It is an ideal place to stop for lunch or a snack. The **Wah Luck House**, at the northwest corner of 6th and H Streets, provides 153 apartments, a Chinatown community room, and a Chinese meditation garden. This modern building incorporates Chinese design features. The Office of Planning works with the Chinatown Steering Community to obtain Chinese design features and calligraphy on new and renovated buildings as part of the city's program to preserve and enhance Chinatown.

Chinatown Archway

■ **25 Saint Mary's Catholic Church**, at 5th and H Streets, was established in the mid-nineteenth century to serve German Catholic immigrants. The design of the present church building (1891) was influenced by German Gothic architecture. The large but not very inspiring **General Accounting Office** wraps around the Saint Mary's Church complex on two sides.

■ **26** The **Jackson Graham Building**, designed by Keyes, Lethbridge and Condon, is the headquarters of the Washington Metropolitan Area Transit Authority, operators of Metrorail and Metrobus. It will soon be vacated to a development group that will remake the forty-six-year-old building into a modern commercial office space that could house more than 1,500 employees and bring new life to solemn Judiciary Square.

■ **27** The **Keck Center of the National Academies** (Science, Engineering, and Medicine) at 500 5th Street NW is a striking modern building, which also retains elements of previous historic buildings (designed by the SmithGroup). The lobby has interesting and stimulating murals by Larry Kirkland. There is also a bookstore for scientific publications and the Marian E. Koshland Science Museum (entrance at 6th and E Streets).

■ **28** The **National Building Museum** is housed in the **Pension Building** (1882), 5th and G Streets, a Category I landmark in **Judiciary Square**. Montgomery C. Meigs, engineer of the Capitol dome and the Cabin John Bridge, designed the building. Its huge central hall, an innovation in lighting and ventilation at the

Pension Building / National Building Museum

time, continues to be used for presidential inaugural balls and many special events today. The National Building Museum is a center for study and display of American building arts, including architecture, city planning, landscape architecture, and construction. The exhibit *Washington: Symbol and City* provides an overview of the planning and development of the city. The museum offers many programs and has an especially interesting gift shop. The National Building Museum is open 10:00 a.m.–5:00 p.m., Monday through Saturday, and 11:00 a.m.–5:00 p.m. on Sunday, except Thanksgiving and December 25. More information can be found at www.nbm.org.

■ **29** The **National Law Enforcement Officers Memorial**, designed by Davis Buckley, provides a landscaped setting in the center of Judiciary Square, just south of the National Building Museum. Names of law enforcement officers who have been killed in the line of duty are carved on two elliptical walls flanking the landscaped space. The northern entrance to the Judiciary Square Metro station is incorporated into the edge of the memorial. Dedicated in 1990, its meaning has increased with time. It was one of the first major national memorials to be built outside the monumental core.

■ **30** The **US Tax Court**, east of 3rd Street between D and E Streets, designed by Victor Lundy, uses innovative structural concepts of post-tensioning to support a cantilevered courthouse on six columns. A landscaped pedestrian plaza spans the adjacent Center Leg Freeway (I-395). Because the dramatic front of this building faces the freeway, most visitors do not see it. The original **Adas Israel Synagogue** is now located two blocks north of E Street at 701 3rd Street NW, on land next to the freeway. Dedicated a few blocks away in 1876, this was the first building constructed as a synagogue in the District of Columbia.

It was moved to its present site in 1969, and restoration was completed in 1974. It now serves as the Lillian and Albert Small Jewish Museum.

■ **31** The **Community for Creative Non-Violence Shelter** occupies the previous temporary federal office building on the east side of 2nd Street between D and E Streets. The shelter provides accommodations and facilities for homeless men and women.

■ **32** **New Jersey Avenue** is the eastern spine of downtown. The **Capitol Place** complex, at New Jersey Avenue and F Street, includes the 265-room Washington Court Hotel and office space. The national headquarters of the **National Association of Realtors** was constructed on a challenging triangular site at New Jersey Avenue and E Street. This was the first new "green" office building in Washington.

■ **33** The **Georgetown University Law Center** now includes four buildings: the original semiclassical building (McDonough Hall, 1971) facing New Jersey Avenue at F Street, designed by Edward D. Stone; the neoclassical Edward Bennett Williams Law Library (1990) at the intersection of New Jersey and Massachusetts Avenues, designed by Hartman-Cox Architects; the Bernard S. and Sarah M. Gewirz Student Center; and the Eric Hotung International Law Center and Georgetown Sports and Fitness Center (completed 2004), designed by Shepley, Bullfinch, Richardson and Abbott. To create a campus environment, F and G Streets between 1st and 2nd Streets have been closed to traffic.

■ **34** **North Capitol Street** is the eastern edge of downtown and the dividing line between the Northwest and Northeast quadrants of the city. Beyond North Capitol Street are the grounds of the Capitol complex. A cluster of hotels once extended along the west side of North Capitol Street, providing accommodations to rail travelers passing through nearby Union Station. Office buildings have replaced most of these hotels. The **Phoenix Park Hotel** at North Capitol and F Streets is the result of the renovation and expansion of an earlier hotel. The **Dubliner** is a popular Irish pub on the ground floor.

■ **35** **Postal Square** is a strong classical building originally constructed (1915, expanded 1935) as Washington's main post office. It was designed to relate to Union Station just to the east and to help form the northern edge of the Capitol grounds. The building was extensively restored and restructured in the early 1990s (completed 1993) by the Hines Interests (Shalom Baranes, architect) working under the direction of the Office of the Architect of the Capitol. The classical facades were retained, as was the impressive former Post Office lobby that extends the length of the building along Massachusetts Avenue. The building is now used primarily for federal office space (the US Bureau of Labor Statistics), and there is a small post office accessible from North Capitol Street.

Visitors will be most interested in the **National Postal Museum,** part of the Smithsonian Institution, which tells the story of the postal system in its intriguing exhibits. More information can be found at www.postalmuseum.si.edu.

■ **36 Union Station** was designed by Daniel H. Burnham (1908) to provide a monumental entrance into Washington during the heyday of rail travel. The agreement to build this station and to remove railroad tracks from the future National Mall was a key element of the McMillan Commission plan of 1902. By the 1970s, rail travel had declined. A program to use the station as a visitors center for the 1976 Bicentennial was not successful, and deterioration of the main part of the building led to its closing in the late 1970s and early 1980s. A joint effort by federal, District, and private entities, under the direction of the Union Station Redevelopment Corporation, rescued the building. The renovated Union Station reopened in 1988 with a two-hundred-thousand-square-foot retail mall, nine movie theaters (now closed), an improved Amtrak station, a huge parking garage, and office space. The former main waiting room is now the focal point of the complex. There are many specialized shops, a large food court, and four major restaurants. The Union Station Metro station provides direct access to the Red Line. The **Columbus Monument** with fountain is located in front of the station.

Development continues around Union Station. East of the station is the **Thurgood Marshall Federal Judiciary Building** (1992, designed by Edward Larrabee Barnes Associates), a striking modern building with an interesting atrium.

■ **37** The **Japanese American Memorial to Patriotism during World War II** is on Louisiana Avenue at the edge of the Capitol Grounds. Designed by Davis Buckley, it is a reminder of the time during World War II when Japanese Americans were moved to detention camps. It also commemorates other Japanese Americans who served in the military during the war.

■ **38** The **Department of Labor Building,** between 2nd and 3rd Streets south of D Street, accommodates approximately four thousand employees. Below this large federal building is the Center Leg Freeway, which tunnels under the Mall. The Department of Labor Building incorporates ventilation shafts for the freeway tunnel.

■ **39** The **Old City Hall** (1820–81, George Hadfield) is a fine Greek-revival building in Judiciary Square. The first public building constructed to house the District of Columbia government, it is now occupied by the Superior Court of the District of Columbia.

■ **40** The **District of Columbia Municipal Center (Henry J. Daly Building)** houses the headquarters of the Metropolitan Police Department and other District government agencies.

■ **41** The H. Carl Moultrie I Courthouse of the **District of Columbia Court-house** at 300 Indiana Avenue NW opened in 1977. It has one appellate and forty-four trial courtrooms, plus ancillary space.

■ **42** The **E. Barrett Prettyman US Courthouse** on the east side of John Marshall Park has been the scene of many famous trials, including those held in connection with the Watergate and Iran-Contra affairs and the trial of former mayor Marion Barry. A bold new courthouse addition on the Constitution Avenue frontage at 3rd Street, designed by Michael Graves, opened in 2004.

■ **43** **John Marshall Park**, created by closing John Marshall Place, is the fifth of five open spaces along Pennsylvania Avenue created by the PADC. Designed by Carol R. Johnson Associates, the park offers a quiet oasis for visitors and employees from the nearby court buildings.

■ **44** The striking **Canadian Embassy**, designed by Arthur Erickson and opened in 1989, frames John Marshall Place on the west and relates to the East Wing of the National Gallery of Art diagonally across Pennsylvania Avenue. The courtyard has a rotunda of twelve columns, representing Canada's ten provinces and two territories, and an interesting sculpture, *The Spirit of Haida Gwaii*, by Bill Reid. The embassy includes a theater and an art gallery.

■ **45** **555 Pennsylvania Avenue NW** exists as a 420,000-square-foot academic building under Johns Hopkins University, standing as a complete renovation of the Newseum originally constructed in 2008. It contains 555 sports classrooms, offices, conferencing space, media suites, roof terraces, restaurants, and picturesque views along Pennsylvania Avenue and the Capitol Building. Several divisions of the university occupy the building, including the School of Advanced International Studies, the Carey Business School, and the Krieger School of Arts and Sciences. This conversion to academic pursuits bolsters the presence of the university in the nation's capital.

From this point, you can proceed west or east along Pennsylvania Avenue, south to the Mall, or back north into downtown.

16th Street and Meridian Hill

(Elegant mansions, established churches, new and restored residential areas)

Ryan Harris, updated by John DeFerrari and Peter Sefton

Distance: 1½ miles
Time: 2 hours
Bus: 42, 43, 90, 96, D6, and G2
Metro: Farragut North or Dupont Circle (Red Line)

Sixteenth Street, the most prominent of the numbered streets of Washington, is laid out along the north–south center line of the White House, just slightly east of the central meridian of the District of Columbia. Beyond the original border of the City of Washington at "Boundary Street" (today's Florida Avenue), the impressive boulevard mounts a series of gentle terraces shaped in the glacial period. One of the highest terraces, stretching across Meridian Hill and Mount Pleasant at an average elevation of about two hundred feet, is bisected by 16th Street's modern-day route from Lafayette Square to Silver Spring, Maryland.

The lower 16th Street corridor and the Meridian Hill district occupy land that at the time of the establishment of Washington was part of large estates stemming from seventeenth-century patents. When L'Enfant submitted his plan for the City of Washington in July 1791, development in this section of the Territory of Columbia was typical of the tidewater region of the time. County estates, most of which were worked by enslaved African Americans, and smaller farms occupied Meridian Hill and its environs. Before the Civil War, some widely scattered clusters of shacklike frame houses, brick kilns, and small slaughterhouses grew up south of Boundary Street, a marshy district surrounding a stream known as "Slash Run" for the best method of traversing the dense underbrush on its banks. Sixteenth Street north of M Street and the future site of Scott Circle remained largely vacant throughout the first three-quarters of the nineteenth century.

The territorial government Congress imposed upon the District of Columbia in 1871 and the ambitious public works programs initiated by Gov. Alexander Robey Shepherd laid the foundations for the development of 16th Street as a modern thoroughfare. Shepherd's ambitious program of municipal improvements saw the encasing of Slash Run in a sewer, the draining of the marshes, and the paving of 16th Street with wooden blocks. During the last quarter of the nineteenth century, the blocks of 16th Street north of the newly established Scott Circle gradually developed as a mix of middle-class housing and grand mansions.

■ **1 Scott Circle** (Massachusetts Avenue, Rhode Island Avenue, and 16th Street) is one of the original federal reservations planned by L'Enfant. In the mid-1870s the original rectangular reservation and its dusty crossroads were landscaped as a park and transformed into a circle as the setting for an equestrian statue of Gen. Winfield Scott. The statue, which was sculpted by Henry Kirke Brown, was cast from cannon captured in the Mexican War and erected in 1874. (See Tour 8, White House, for more information on the area south of the circle).

By the early twentieth century, the circle was ringed with mansions, upper-middle-class homes, and monuments. Although 16th Street was classified as residential, with embassies and hotels permitted by the original District of Columbia zoning act of 1920, the blocks south of Scott Circle were rezoned to also allow limited commercial use in 1947. Today the grand houses to the circle's south have been replaced by apartment buildings, embassies, and commercial structures. North of the circle, 16th Street's residential character remains intact, with the incorporation of numerous apartment houses.

The automobile underpass along 16th Street was completed in 1942.

■ **2 Doctor Samuel Hahnemann Memorial.** In the small triangular park just to the circle's east is a statue commemorating Christian Friedrich Samuel Hahnemann (1775–1843), founder of the homeopathic school of medicine. The memorial was designed by Charles Henry Niehaus and erected in 1900 by the American Institute of Homeopathy.

■ **3 Daniel Webster Statue.** In the corresponding small triangular park just to the west of 16th Street is Gaetano Trentanove's statue of Daniel Webster. Scott Circle resident Stilson Hutchins, founder of the *Washington Post*, presented the statue to the nation in 1900.

■ **4 1500 Massachusetts Avenue NW apartment house.** This was the original site of the Louise Home, erected in 1871 by William Wilson Corcoran, Washington banker, art patron, and philanthropist. The Louise Home, named for both Corcoran's wife and daughter, was founded as a refuge for "Protestant women of refinement and culture who have become reduced in circumstances in their old age." The ornate Victorian building was replaced by the current apartment house in the early 1950s after the home moved to Kalorama (see Tour 15, Kalorama, no. 10).

■ **5 Embassy of Hungary,** 1500 Rhode Island Avenue NW. The present exterior of this building is John Russell Pope's 1912 classical entombment for most of architect John Fraser's 1879 house for John T. Brodhead, a wealthy Marine Corps officer from Detroit. In 1882 Brodhead sold the house to Gardiner Greene Hubbard, founder of the National Geographic Society, as a home for his daughter and son-in-law, inventor Alexander Graham Bell. In 1889 the Bells sold their mansion to Levi P. Morton, newly elected vice president, who later commissioned Pope's transformation of the house. After eighty years as the headquarters of a trade association, the house was purchased by the government of Hungary and converted to its embassy in 2016.

For an example of architect Fraser's great domestic commissions in Washington, you may view the James G. Blaine mansion (1881) at 2000 Massachusetts Avenue NW, a building very similar to the original Brodhead mansion (see Tour 13, Dupont Circle, no. 8).

■ **6 Embassy of Australia Chancery**, 1601 Massachusetts Avenue NW. The construction of a new Australian Embassy, which began in 2020, reflects 16th Street's continuing importance as a boulevard of diplomatic missions. The new embassy, designed by Australian architects Bates, Small, features an expansive glass atrium and is meant to "pay tribute to the unique Australian landscape and spirit of Australia" including "its distinctive geography, with bright and clear natural light and open skies, warm materiality, and vast scale." It replaces a 1965 building designed by the same firm.

■ **7** The **Johns Hopkins University School of Advanced International Studies**, 1619 Massachusetts Avenue NW. Commissioned by a trade association and originally known as the Forest Industries Building, this notable modernist building was designed by the local firm of Keyes, Lethbridge and Condon and erected in 1961. Its order and polish, the dignified restraint in the use of materials, and the proportioning of the main blocks and elements of the facade have pleased both critics and laypeople.

■ **8** The **Embassy of the Philippines** is located on the west side of Scott Circle, between Massachusetts Avenue and N Street, 17th Street, and Bataan Place. Erected between 1991 and 1993, it is a recent addition to the list of embassies and other diplomatic missions with addresses on 16th Street. Those in the immediate environs of Scott Circle include the reconstructed Australian Embassy on the circle's north side, the Russian ambassador's residence and previous embassy in the former George Pullman mansion at 1125 16th Street, as well as the embassies of Hungary and Kazakhstan.

■ **9 First Baptist Church**, southwest corner of 16th and O Streets NW. This church was designed in a neo-Gothic style in 1955 by Philadelphia architect Harold Wagoner. Wagoner designed hundreds of Protestant churches nationwide, and his notable Washington commissions include the National Presbyterian Church on Nebraska Avenue NW. However, a church of a different style once occupied the site. In 1890 architect W. Bruce Gray designed a red brick and sandstone church that combined Romanesque and Italian Renaissance styles. An impressive campanile, flanking the main church on the north, reached a height of 140 feet and became a landmark in the city skyline.

The 1890 First Baptist Church was built during the period when many downtown congregations sought new sites in the developing 16th Street and Dupont Circle areas. It was an important addition to a block that had been filling with the elegant homes of political, social, and business leaders throughout the 1880s.

■ **10 Embassy of the Republic of Kazakhstan** (former Susan Shields House), 1401 16th Street NW. H. H. Richardson, the most prominent American architect of the late nineteenth century, cast a long shadow on 16th Street. Richardson designed four magnificent houses on or near 16th Street. Richardson's continuing influence after his death at age forty-seven in 1886 is reflected in the numerous Richardsonian Romanesque houses erected in Washington's most fashionable neighborhoods in the late 1880s and 1890s. This house, one of many grand 16th Street houses commissioned by women, was built in 1888 for Susan Shields, the widow of a lawyer and newspaper publisher. Its builders, brothers Samuel and Charles Edmonston, had constructed two Washington houses designed by Richardson, and its design by one of the brothers heavily reflects Richardson's style. In the 1920s and 1930s, 16th Street addresses fell out of fashion, and, like many of its grand neighbors, the Shields House was repurposed as a rooming house. It was renovated during the 1980s as office space and became an embassy in 1992.

■ **11 Former Carnegie Institution for Science**, southeast corner of 16th and P Streets. The Carnegie Institution is an internationally respected sponsor of research in natural science. Its Beaux-Arts former headquarters was built of Indiana limestone in 1908 to the design of the New York architectural firm of Carrere and Hastings. It features an impressive rotunda and portico with a massive Ionic colonnade and magnificent urns. Its construction reflected the spread of important institutional edifices to 16th Street and the growth of the scientific community in Washington. In 2021, the Carnegie Institution sold the building to the government of Qatar

■ **12 Foundry United Methodist Church**, northwest corner of 16th and P Streets. Foundry Methodist was constructed in the period when 16th Street earned its nickname as "the Avenue of Churches." Founded by Georgetowner Henry Foxall (1758–1823), who operated the Foxall-Columbia Foundry on the Potomac, Foundry Methodist moved from downtown to its new church in 1904. The church was designed by prolific and versatile architect Appleton P. Clark Jr., whom the *Washington Post* called "the dean of Washington architects" at his death in 1955 after sixty years of practice.

Foundry United Methodist has always been a socially active congregation and has developed many programs in collaboration with the surrounding neighborhood.

■ **13 Jewish Community Center**, southeast corner of 16th and Q Streets. Designed by prolific architect B. Stanley Simmons, this limestone and granite structure's classical-revival style was perhaps inspired by the Carnegie Institution building, which stands one block to its south. For nearly fifty years the center was home to recreational and cultural activities, including one of the city's earliest concerts with a racially integrated audience and performers in 1942.

In 1968, after the center had followed most of its membership to the suburbs, the building was occupied by Federal City College, a precursor of the University of the District of Columbia. The building had been vacant for six years when it was purchased in 1990 by another group, which renovated it as a new Jewish Community Center. It now offers a theater, meeting rooms, a health club, and other cultural and recreational facilities to Jewish and non-Jewish members.

C. C. Huntley House

■ **14 C. C. Huntley House**, 1601 16th Street NW. This ornate Italianate house with bracketed cornices, arched window hoods, and a stable with finial was among the first upper-middle-class houses built on 16th Street north of Scott Circle. It was constructed in 1878 by Capt. Charles C. Huntley, a Civil War veteran who became wealthy by operating stagecoach lines and mail delivery routes on the western frontier. Although he died at an early age, Huntley also constructed the three houses to the north as speculative ventures.

■ **15** The **Cairo**, 1615 Q Street NW. This pioneering apartment building was designed and built in 1894 by Thomas Franklin Schneider, who eventually built more than two thousand structures in Washington, most in a very idiosyncratic interpretation of the Richardsonian Romanesque. Schneider here combines neo-Moorish and art nouveau elements in the facade of what is still the city's tallest commercial building. Note especially its wonderful carved elephants.

The Cairo

The Cairo's 165-foot height so shocked turn-of-the-century, row house Washington that Congress imposed severe height restrictions in 1899 that in large part continue to shape the skyline of city. The Cairo was opened as a first-class residential hotel but fell on hard times in the mid-twentieth century, before being restored as rental apartments in 1976. The sponsor of the restoration was the Georgetown Inland Corporation, and the architect was Arthur Cotton Moore. Although the partial federal funding of the rehabilitation required a percentage of low- to moderate-income tenants, ultimately only high-rent apartments were offered in the remodeled Cairo. The structure was converted to residential condominiums in 1979.

■ **16** The **Church of the Holy City**, southeast corner of 16th and Corcoran Streets. Built as the "national church" for the Swedenborgian faith, this architectural landmark was dedicated on May 3, 1896. It is constructed of Bedford limestone and designed on the English perpendicular order, with a good deal of French Gothic influence. Its bestiary of ornament includes jaguars, lions, and griffins, as well as snarling canine gargoyles. The church is also noted for the beauty and vividness of its stained glass.

The architect of this fine church was H. Langford Warren, head of the Department of Architecture at Harvard University, and Paul Pelz of Washington was construction overseer.

■ **17** The **1500 block of Corcoran Street**. This "minor" street, originally laid out as an alley, today presents a largely intact block of 1880s row houses in a composite of late nineteenth-century domestic architectural styles. Many houses were restored following the establishment of adjoining historic districts in the 1970s. The Sixteenth Street Historic District, created in 1978, now protects buildings between Lafayette Square and Florida Avenue constructed through 1959. The 1500 block of Corcoran Street is within the Fourteenth Street Historic District, whose period of significance ends in 1940. The establishment of these districts was marked by both enthusiasm and controversy over inclusivity, community control, and potential contributions to gentrification.

■ 18 The **Denman House**, 1623 16th Street NW. Like the Shields House (8), the Denman House is a fine example of the Richardsonian Romanesque style. It was built in 1886 for H. P. Denman, a lawyer and former mayor of Kansas City. The architects were Fuller and Wheeler of Albany, New York.

■ 19 The **Mulligan House**, 1601 R Street NW. The house was built in 1910 for Navy officer Richard T. Mulligan to the design of Jules Henri de Sibour, a gifted Beaux-Arts architect who designed numerous notable buildings on 16th Street and elsewhere. The Mulligan House reflects the importance of the Georgian revival in the large-scale domestic architecture of early twentieth-century Washington. It has served as a private club and currently houses the National Association of Colored Women's Clubs.

■ 20 **Chastleton Apartments**, 1781 16th Street NW. The elegant English Gothic revival-style Chastleton opened as a rental building in 1919. For a time in the 1920s it was part of legendary real estate developer Harry Wardman's empire. Although Wardman converted approximately a quarter of its more than three hundred apartments to hotel space, the building reverted to rental apartments after he surrendered his interest at the start of the Great Depression. In 2008, the Chastleton was converted from rental to a co-op.

■ 21 **Scottish Rite Temple**, 1733 16th Street NW. This is the headquarters of the Supreme Council of the Southern Jurisdiction of the Thirty-Third Degree of the Ancient and Accepted Scottish Rite of Freemasonry. The Scottish Rite Temple is one of the most architecturally significant buildings on lower 16th Street. John Russell Pope's design borrows from the famed Mausoleum of Halicarnassus. The cornerstone was laid in 1911, and the temple was dedicated in 1915. Two sphinxes by Adolph A. Weinman flank the main entrance to the building and represent Divine Wisdom and Power. The main space is beneath the ziggurat surmounting the Greek-temple base. The symbolism of the Masonic order is displayed in many facets of the design. For example, the Ionic columns of the colonnade are thirty-three feet high, representing the thirty-third degree of Masonry.

■ 22 **Justice Brown House**, 1720 16th Street NW. The 1880s German Renaissance–style mansion of Supreme Court Justice Henry B. Brown is a rare design in Washington. The wings and carriage house along adjoining Riggs Place are superb. The house is currently the embassy of the Republic of Congo.

23 Riggs Place NW, one of Washington's more charming side streets, is largely a product of the speculative building activities of the 1890s. The stained glass and copper work of these modest row houses are worth noting.

24 Proceed north on 16th Street through an area that is a mixture of **late nineteenth-century row houses** and small **early twentieth-century apartment buildings**. Some of the properties had deteriorated in this vicinity in the mid-twentieth century, but considerable restoration has taken place since that time. As 16th Street crosses U Street, it enters the **Meridian Hill district**. The major east–west artery connects the neighborhoods of Adams-Morgan and Shaw-Cardozo and in the early twentieth century was the heart of Black Washington. Entertainers such as Duke Ellington, Cab Alloway, Sarah Vaughn, and Billie Holiday played in the U Street theaters and nightclubs to the east, earning it the nickname "Black Broadway." With much revitalization following the 1991 opening of a Metro station on U Street at 13th and 10th Streets, U Street is now as highly gentrified as it is historic.

25/26 2001 16th Street NW (the Brittany) and 2101 16th Street (the Roosevelt). These two apartment buildings are emblematic of the rapid development of such structures to meet a housing crunch at the time of World War I and afterward. Developer Harry L. Wardman built the Brittany in 1916 on a triangular plot of land that some neighbors had hoped would remain open space. The mammoth Roosevelt, built by a New York development company in 1919, was originally an apartment hotel for the well-to-do called the Hadleigh. Expensive to maintain, it eventually went into decline but was revived as the Roosevelt Hotel for Senior Citizens from the early 1960s to the early 1990s. In 2001 the Roosevelt was renovated by a private development firm and converted back into high priced rental apartments.

27 Florida Avenue NW (the original city limit of Boundary Street) marks the location of the fall line, which divides the older and harder Piedmont plateau from the softer deposits of the coastal plain. Merchant and mayor of Georgetown Robert Peter had assembled by 1760 some parts of a patent for land in this vicinity to form Mount Pleasant. His country farmhouse stood in the square bounded by 13th, 14th, and W Streets and Florida Avenue until the 1890s. Meridian Hill was originally referred to as Peter's Hill. In 1821 Columbian College (which grew into the George Washington University) built its first building on Meridian Hill, where it remained until moving to the downtown financial district in the 1870s. Another educational institution on Meridian Hill was the Wayland Seminary for the training of Black Baptist preachers, which was built in the northeast corner of the present Meridian Hill Park in 1873.

The Meridian Hill area remained a combination of small-scale farms and country estates until after the Civil War. In 1867 developers Richard M. Hall and John R. Elvans subdivided Meridian Hill into building lots selling at ten cents per square foot. Dozens of modest frame buildings were constructed, and most were either sold or leased to working-class African Americans, who established a thriving community on the northeast portion of what is now Meridian Hill Park. Real estate values in this section of Washington peaked (in relation to the rest of the city) in the mid-twentieth century. In 1925, for example, so prestigious had the area become that the large houses on 16th Street sold for $250,000 and more. It was the extension of 16th Street north of Columbia Road along the true north–south line, and the bridging of Piney Branch Valley at the turn of the century, that prompted intensive development.

■ **28 Henderson Castle Tract**, northwest corner of 16th Street and Florida Avenue NW. It was Mary Foote Henderson, wife of John B. Henderson (the senator from Missouri who authored the Emancipation Amendment and cast the deciding vote that saved Andrew Johnson from conviction in his impeachment trial), who did the most to try to turn 16th Street into the premier residential and embassy boulevard of Washington from the late 1880s until her death in 1931. The Hendersons bought the tract in 1887 for about $31,000, the first purchase in what would be the eventual assembly by Mrs. Henderson of a real-estate holding of some three hundred city lots in the Meridian Hill area. The wall is all that remains of the turreted, crenelated, red Seneca sandstone house built in 1888 and popularly known as Henderson Castle. E. C. Gardner was the architect and J. H. Lane the builder. From her Meridian Hill tower Mary Henderson directed her preferred architect, George Oakley Totten Jr., in the improvement of 16th Street. She fought buses on the Avenue of the Presidents (she succeeded in having her street's name changed for one year) and the large apartment houses that obstructed her view of the White House and degraded the capital city of villas. She also preached the evils of alcohol and advocated for the construction of the great Meridian Hill Park opposite her home.

Henderson Castle was torn down in 1949. After many other plans and false starts, including proposals for a colony of homes for the elderly, the Henderson Castle tract was developed into a suburban-styled, gated "colonial" townhouse development during the 1980s.

■ **29 Meridian Hill Park** (Malcolm X Park), east side of 16th Street between Florida Avenue and Euclid Street NW. At the turn of the twentieth century, when the White House was in a bad state of repair, it was Meridian Hill that was seriously considered for a new presidential residence. Mrs. Henderson was the most vocal supporter of the movement. When it became clear that the presidential mansion would not be moved to Meridian Hill, Mrs. Henderson pressured Congress to buy the site for a public park. The purchase of the twelve acres that became Meridian Hill Park was authorized in 1910. Henderson's aim, in part, was to get rid of the modest frame houses (which she called shanties) that were home to African Americans and that did not fit in her grand vision for the neighborhood. After the government purchased the land, these residents were all forced to move and their homes were leveled.

Nevertheless, the beautiful park that was built on the site is one of the most important examples of formal garden design in the United States. Actual construction did not begin until 1917, and the lower part of the park was not opened until 1936. George Burnap was the original landscape architect, and Horace W. Peaslee was responsible for the final plan and architectural design. The magnificent concrete work was created using a technique in which aggregates were selected for varying sizes and colors, and the concrete was quickly washed with muriatic acid after it began to set to expose the aggregates. Pioneering architectural sculptor John Joseph Earley perfected this technique. The use of massive retaining walls heightens the drama of the natural topography. The upper two-thirds of the park are designed in the formal French manner, with a large *tapis vert* bordered by promenades. The lower part of the park is inspired by the great Italian formal gardens of the eighteenth century. An artificial cascade of thirteen waterfalls of graduated size, representing the location of the park on the fall line, is the principal feature of this section. In the late 1960s, many civil rights rallies and marches were held here, and the park became known as Malcolm X Park, in honor of the slain civil rights activist. While drugs and crime plagued the park in the 1970s and 1980s, an organized neighborhood coalition was successful in restoring a sense of safety, and the park is often busy with strollers, impromptu games of soccer, and a popular drum circle on Sunday afternoons.

30 Envoy Towers Apartments, 2400 16th Street NW. The Envoy Towers opened in the early 20th century as Meridian Mansions, a fashionable apartment hotel, and later acquired the name Hotel 2400. The enormous structure—some of the apartments have dining rooms that seat twenty-four people—changed hands repeatedly in the early 1960s. After the 1968 riots, the District of Columbia leased space in the building to house displaced victims of the 14th Street civil disturbances. The handsome structure's use as this kind of housing angered many of the nearby residents. It has since been totally renovated and turned into condominiums and rental units.

31 Crescent Place—White and Laughlin Houses. On the high ridge between Belmont and Crescent Places, opposite Meridian Hill Park, stand two of John Russell Pope's loveliest domestic commissions. Both represent departures from the usual ascetic classicism of Pope's work. The house at 1624 Crescent Place NW, in something of a Georgian-revival mode, was built about 1912 for Henry White, ambassador to France, and was long the residence of Eugene Meyer, publisher of the *Washington Post*. The building, which takes such command of a fine site, has been listed on the National Register of Historic Places

Meridian House (Laughlin House)

and restored to its former glory by the Meridian International Center, which purchased it in 1987.

■ **32 Meridian House (Laughlin House)**, 1630 Crescent Place NW, Pope's other Meridian Hill commission, is a richly decorated limestone house in the manner of an eighteenth-century French pavilion. It was built for Irwin Laughlin, ambassador to Spain, in 1915. The manicured garden, with its beautiful canopy of pollarded trees, is a rare example of landscaping art. The house is now the Meridian International Center.

■ **33 Council for Early Childhood Recognition**, 2460 16th Street NW. This chancery was built through the joint efforts of Mrs. Henderson and her architect, George Oakley Totten Jr. Between 1897 and 1925, it housed the French Embassy. It was the first of thirteen mansions erected speculatively to attract embassies to Meridian Hill. Totten, adept at Beaux-Arts architectural styles, here displays a particularly exuberant Beaux-Arts style fitting for its French tenants.

■ **34 Inter-American Defense Board ("The Pink Palace")**, 2600 16th Street NW. This fanciful Venetian palace, built by the Henderson-Totten team in 1906, was first occupied by Oscar Straus, Theodore Roosevelt's secretary of commerce and labor. Mrs. Marshall Field was another prominent occupant. The Inter-American Defense Board has been headquartered here since 1949.

35 Warder-Totten House, 2633 16th Street NW. Originally constructed in the 1500 block of K Street for a prominent real estate developer, Benjamin Warder, the sandstone house is a product of H. H. Richardson's office. George Oakley Totten bought the shell of the house from the wrecker in 1902 and stored the parts of the building until he was able to reconstruct it as his own residence. The mansion makes a far better detached villa than part of the original row house block. The building has been converted to apartments with a nine-story building on the back of the lot facing 15th Street.

36 Former **Embassy of Italy**, 2700 16th Street NW. Designed by the architects of Grand Central Station, Warren and Wetmore of New York, this house is an especially fine adaptation of the Italian Renaissance palazzo. The interiors originally were rich in works of medieval Italian art. In 2019, the renovated building opened as an apartment house with a new, nine-story building added at the rear.

37 Former **Embassy of Spain**, 2801 16th Street NW. The former Spanish Embassy at 2801 16th Street was built for Mrs. Henderson and designed by George Oakley Totten in 1921. In 1923, Mrs. Henderson offered the mansion to the federal government as the official residence of the vice president, but her offer was declined. The Spanish government purchased it for their embassy in 1927; it now serves as their cultural institute.

38 The **Mexican Cultural Institute**, 2829 16th Street, was built in 1911 for Franklin MacVeagh, Taft's secretary of the treasury, by his wife as a Christmas present. The architect was Washington designer Nathan Wyeth. The Italianate house is one of the most elaborate in Washington and has perhaps the largest private dining room in the city; it seats 250. The music room has an exact copy of the pipe organ at Fontainebleau. Beginning in 1934, Roberto Cueva del Río began his great series of murals for the new owner, the Mexican government.

39 **Rabaut Park**, at the intersection of 16th Street, Columbia Road, and Harvard Street. This intersection was originally planned as a circle in honor of Civil War hero Gen. George Meade. The pleasantly landscaped park just west of 16th Street is named for Louis C. Rabaut, a Michigan congressman who chaired the House Subcommittee on the District of Columbia in the 1950s, but most locals just call it "Pigeon Park." Around the busy intersection are three important church buildings, erected during the years when the neighborhood was one of Washington's best residential neighborhoods. Columbia Road was here long before any other construction; it was a trail used by Native Americans and later a post road to Georgetown from Baltimore. From this intersection, you can venture via Columbia Road to Adams Morgan, east on Columbia Road to Columbia Heights, and northwest on Mount Pleasant Street to Mount Pleasant.

■ **40 All Souls Unitarian Church**, southeast corner of 16th and Harvard Streets. The architects of this skillful copy of James Gibbs's Saint Martin-in-the-Fields, in London, were Coolidge and Shattuck of Boston. The church was constructed in 1924 at a cost of almost a million dollars.

Before the completion of the 16th Street church, the congregation was located downtown at 14th and L Streets. Welcoming its first African American members in 1950, the church became a pivotal force for civil rights and social justice, working with other area congregations to find housing and other assistance for those displaced by the 1968 civil disturbances on nearby 14th Street. The church's Pierce Hall Auditorium was where jazz musicians Charlie Byrd and Stan Getz recorded their landmark bossa nova album, *Jazz Samba*.

■ **41** Former **Washington Chapel of the Church of Jesus Christ of Latter-Day Saints**, southwest corner of 16th Street and Columbia Road. This is an interesting architectural period piece designed by Ramm Hansen and Joseph Don Carlos Young of Salt Lake City, completed in 1933. Young was a grandson of Brigham Young. Until September 1975, Washington Mormons used the elegant Utah-marble edifice for worship. A gleaming, goldleaf-covered statue of the Angel Moroni, which rested atop the lovely spire until the Mormons vacated the building, was a landmark seen from all parts of Washington. The building is now a branch of the Unification Church.

Dupont Circle

(Mixed uses and historic preservation; an area with diverse lifestyles and urban delights)

Sherry Mauch and Sharon Augustyn, updated by William J. Bonstra

Distance: 2 miles
Time: 2 hours
Bus: 42, 43, G2, L2, N2, and N4
Metro: Dupont Circle (Red Line)

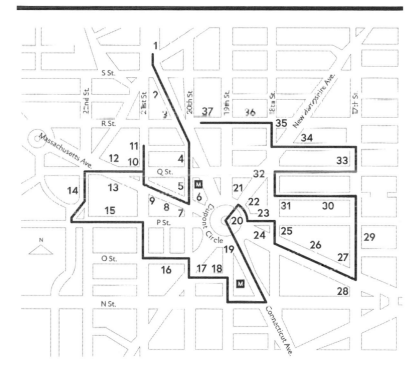

Dupont Circle is a fascinating area offering many points of interest. It was the prestige neighborhood in Washington at the beginning of the twentieth century. The large mansions built by the newly wealthy from across the country reflected Washington's increasing importance on the national and world scene. The mansions also reflect the Beaux-Arts influence of the period and help give the neighborhood a distinguished character. In addition to these great houses are smaller townhouses and row houses along many streets, creating an intimate scale.

With the stock market crash of 1929, Dupont Circle's fortunes began to decline, and by World War II the elegance and prestige that had been slowly

diminishing virtually disappeared as the mansions were converted into board-
ing houses for government workers. When the war was over, society had
changed: commercial interests were expanding, and families were moving to
the suburbs. This too was reflected in the Dupont Circle area, as many proud
old structures were razed to make way for modern office and apartment buildings. Other large townhouses were put to use as rental apartments.

Today Dupont Circle is an area of large row houses and apartment buildings that have been renovated and converted into single-family homes or
condominiums by people moving back into the city. It has an established
commercial office and retail component along with the many embassy and
nonprofit headquarters offices that support the demographic and economic
balance of the community. It is truly a "Live Work Plan" neighborhood.
The challenge facing Dupont Circle, as in any city, is to retain its historical
quality, scale, vitality, and mix of residential and commercial activities while
accommodating pressures for more intensive land uses and escalating housing costs.

■ 1 The tour begins at Connecticut and Florida Avenues NW. (Until 1902
Florida Avenue was known as Boundary Street, because it formed the original
northern boundary of the city.) **Connecticut Avenue** between Florida Avenue
and Dupont Circle (as well as the block south of the circle) has a bustling, cosmopolitan ambience; its array of bookstores, restaurants, cafés, antique stores,
and other shops makes this one of the liveliest mixed-use neighborhoods in the
city. Many of the newer buildings along this stretch of Connecticut Avenue
date from the late nineteenth or early twentieth century, and although many
times larger than their historic neighbors, they coexist and strengthen their
historic context.

■ 2 The building at **1718 Connecticut Avenue NW**, designed by David M.
Schwarz, was one of the first postmodernist buildings to go up in Washington.
The facade features several interesting elements: the clock tower, gabled mansard roof, contrasting brick and limestone surfaces, and arched windows, all of
which combine to create a modern structure that fits gracefully into its context
without too much literal mimicry of earlier historic styles.

■ 3 The block between Connecticut Avenue and Florida in the 2000 block of
R Street NW is lined with many small **art galleries** in renovated row houses.
More continue to open and expand, along with restaurants and neighborhood
professional offices.

Take time for a stroll down Hillyer Place, a short, quiet block lined with
lovely trees and row houses. This street was the original driveway for the
Townsend Mansion, now the Cosmos Club, when Massachusetts Avenue was
still unpaved. The 1987 movie, *Broadcast News*, was filmed there as the residence of the character played by William Hurt.

1719 Connecticut Avenue NW

◾ **4** The **row of buildings** on 20th Street between Q Street and Hillyer Place represents a successful effort at preservation of old structures. These turn-of-the-century townhouses, many by acclaimed architect/developer T. F. Schneider, are now occupied by offices, restaurants, and shops and are an attractive feature of this part of the neighborhood.

◾ **5** On the southwest corner of 20th and Q Streets, at 1520 20th Street NW, is the **Embassy of Colombia**. It was designed in 1920 by architect Jules Henri de Sibour, whose structures dot the Washington landscape. Built originally as a private residence, it was sold to the Colombian government in 1944. The house is designed in the style of a sixteenth- or seventeenth century French country château. Its striking mixture of brick and limestone blocks on the facade and its wrought iron and glass marquee above the entryway are among the features that make it an interesting contrast to the historic buildings around it.

◾ **6** Across from the embassy on Q Street is the northern entrance to the **Dupont Circle Metro station.** The precipitous descent on one of the longest escalators in the city through the circular entry into the station makes this a dramatic highlight of Washington's Metro system for tourists and commuters alike. This station is among the deepest in the system, as the Red line in this area featured a tunnel drilled in a rock deep enough to go below Rock Creek Park to the north. The steel and glass canopy was added to help protect travelers and the escalator mechanisms. This and other canopies across the system were designed by architect Jon Laurie, along with engineers ARUP, through a design competition.

■ **7** At 2000 Massachusetts Avenue NW stands the former **Blaine Mansion**, one of the oldest great houses to grace Dupont Circle. It was built in 1881 at a cost of $85,000 for James G. Blaine, a three-time presidential candidate. The dark-brick structure is an interesting combination of Victorian, Gothic, Romanesque, and Renaissance elements, with towers, seven chimneys, four skylights, and an elaborate covered carriage porch on Massachusetts Avenue. A 2010 aluminum-clad multiunit residential addition, designed by a notable local architect, was added within the original rear yard of the site and serves as a modern contrast to the original historic architecture.

Blaine Mansion

■ **8** Next to the Blaine Mansion at 2010 Massachusetts Avenue NW is the **Beale House**, a Renaissance-revival house constructed in 1898. The modern headquarters of **Optica**, it replaced a similar building to the east.

If you visit the area on a Sunday from 10 a.m. to 1:00 p.m., take time to view the produce available at the **Dupont Circle Farmers' Market**, in the 1500 block of 20th Street, a well-established public amenity and lively neighborhood market and gathering place of the neighborhood.

■ **9** The **Indonesian Embassy**, the former **Walsh-McLean House** at 2020 Massachusetts Avenue NW, is one of Washington's truly great residences. It was designed in 1903 by architect Henry Anderson for Thomas F. Walsh, whose wealth came from his discovery and development of one of the world's richest gold mines; it is rumored that a piece of gold from this mine is built into the foundation of the house. This ornate art nouveau mansion contains sixty rooms, some of which are among the largest and most elaborate in Washington. Throughout its history, the house has been the scene of many lavish parties, attended by such notables as Alice Roosevelt Longworth and Adm. George Dewey, among many others. Thomas Walsh's daughter, Evalyn Walsh McLean, who lived in the house until 1916, was the last private owner of the Hope Diamond. In 1951 the Indonesian government bought the mansion for $355,000 for use as its embassy. A modern addition to the old building was built so that offices could be moved out of the mansion itself. Set back from Massachusetts Avenue, the curving facade of the addition was designed to respect the undulating art nouveau exterior of the original structure. The back of the new portion, situated on P Street at the rear, presents complementary modern glass and brick.

■ **10** The **Statue of Mohandas K. (Mahatma) Gandhi** (1869–1948) was dedicated in June 2000 in the triangular park at Massachusetts Avenue, 21st Street, and Q Street. The Indian American community and the Indian government created the park and statue in this small park across from the Indian embassy. Gandhi began a political movement aimed at creating an India free of British rule, with the keynote of his political program centered on "nonviolent civil disobedience."

■ **11** At 1600–12 21st Street NW is the **Phillips Collection Gallery**, one of the nation's outstanding private art collections. The original brownstone structure, built in 1897, was the home of Duncan Phillips, the grandson of James Laughlin and an avid collector of the contemporary art that now fills the rooms. The collection was opened to the public in 1921. An initial extension, added in 1960, was renovated and reconceived in 1989 to better complement the warmth and scale of the old section. A more ambitious expansion, the Sant Building, was undertaken in 2006 with Arthur Cotton Moore / Associates by incorporating an adjacent former apartment building. Another renovation / addition was designed by award-winning architects Cox, Graae + Spack in 2002–4. The new spaces include expanded galleries, a 180-seat auditorium, an outdoor courtyard, and a café and shop. Two noteworthy features of the building are a winding, three-floor interior staircase and an external stone relief of a bird, echoing Georges Braque's painting *Bird*. The Phillips Collection is open 11:00 a.m.–6:00 p.m., Tuesday through Sunday, except New Year's Day, Independence Day, Thanksgiving, and December 24 and 25. More information can be found at phillipscollection.org.

■ **12** To the west, at 2121 Massachusetts Avenue NW, is the **Cosmos Club**, one of five surviving exceptionally grand residences built within two blocks of Dupont Circle, designed in the Beaux-Arts style. The structure was built in 1901 for railway magnate Richard M. Townsend and his wife, Mathilda, who superstitiously insisted that it be constructed around the shell of the home that formerly occupied this site. New York architects Carrère and Hastings designed and completely rebuilt the original Hillyer townhouse. The Townsend ballroom is a must-see example of Parisian interior design firm Jules Allard & Sons. The elegant building is individually listed in the National Register of Historic Places and is designated a DC Historic Landmark. The Cosmos Club, founded in 1878, is one of the most prestigious private social clubs in Washington. Its members include three presidents, two vice presidents, fourteen Supreme Court justices, thirty-six Nobel Prize winners, and sixty-one Pulitzer Prize winners.

■ **13** Across the street, at 2118 Massachusetts Avenue NW, is the **Larz Anderson House**, now the national headquarters of the **American Revolution Institute of the Society of the Cincinnati**, an organization of descendants of officers in the American Revolutionary Army, founded in 1783. Constructed in 1900, the beautiful Beaux-Arts residence was one of the largest and costliest in the city and is distinguished by its early eighteenth-century English-style walled entrance court. The society's museum is open to the public Tuesday through Saturday, 10 a.m. to 4 p.m., and Sunday 12 p.m. to 4 p.m., except Thanksgiving, Christmas, and New Year's Day. The research library is open Monday through Friday by appointment. More information can be found at www.societyofthecincinnati.org.

■ **14** The **Church of the Pilgrims**, at 2201 P Street NW just south of Massachusetts Avenue, is a landmark on the western edge of the neighborhood. Across from the church in a triangular park is a memorial to nineteenth-century Ukrainian national poet Taras Shevchenko. It consists of a modernistic frieze next to a traditional statue of Shevchenko, the Bard of Ukraine (1814–61). The monument was erected in 1964 amid controversy as to the suitability of a statue memorializing a "Soviet" national hero, but its defenders see it as a tribute to oppressed people everywhere.

■ **15** P Street west of Dupont Circle, in the 2000 and 2001 block of P Street, is a busy commercial strip, with many restaurants, stores, art galleries, and other establishments. Many of the older buildings have given way to modern high-rise apartments and hotels in which the lower floors include commercial and amenity spaces.

■ **16** **South of P Street**, between 22nd Street and New Hampshire Avenue, are several quiet, tree-lined blocks of older houses in varying stages of restoration and renovation. The residential character of this part of the neighborhood is a welcome respite from the high-rises and commercial activity of P Street and the large avenues crossing Dupont Circle.

■ **17** The **Christian Heurich Mansion**, at 1307 New Hampshire Avenue, commonly known as the Brewmaster's Castle, was built in 1894 for German immi-

Christian Heurich Mansion

grant and brewing magnate Christian Heurich. It is a splendid example of the Victorian architecture for which Washington is known. It is the most intact late Victorian home in the country, because only one family lived in the house and many of the original furnishings remain. The family foundation reopened the house in July 2003 as a historic house museum. The mansion's properties include the park and small carriage house along Sunderland Place. There is garden access Monday through Thursday, and the house is open for beer garden pickup and public tours on Thursday, Friday, and Saturday. More information can be found at www.heurichhouse.org. An earlier home designed by Christian Heurich in 1887 is located diagonally across the street in a building now occupied by the cultural and educational bureau of the **Embassy of the Arab Republic of Egypt**.

■ **18** The **Sunderland Building** (1969, Keyes, Lethbridge and Condon) at 1320 19th Street NW is a classically modern design based on the Casa del Popolo (formerly Casa del Fascio) by the Italian modernist architect Giuseppe Terragni.

■ **19** Walk northeast on New Hampshire Avenue to the **Euram Building**, 21 Dupont Circle NW. It is an exemplary office building designed by Hartman-Cox Architects and completed in 1970 (and one of the editors' favorite classic modern buildings in Washington, DC). Along with its commanding view of the historic circle to the north and streets on both sides, its "voluptuous" inner courtyard is an exemplary space offering a quite retreat from the urban conditions of the surrounding Dupont Circle neighborhood.

■ **20 Dupont Circle**. In 1882 an act of Congress changed the circle's name from Pacific Circle (so-called because it formed the western edge of the city) to Dupont Circle, in honor of Civil War hero RDML Samuel Francis Du Pont.

Euram Building

In 1884 a statue depicting Du Pont riding a horse was erected here. Public dissatisfaction with this memorial, combined with the erosion of its base, led to another congressional act in 1916 authorizing its removal and the installation of a marble memorial fountain in its place. Designed by Daniel Chester French (who also designed the statue of Lincoln in the Lincoln Memorial), the fountain consists of three figures representing sea, stars, and wind, traditional guardians of ships.

Over the years Dupont Circle has borne silent witness to the social and political changes taking place around it. It has been the starting point for political demonstrations and marches, and on warm days it is filled with people splashing in the fountain or relaxing on the benches around it. Permanent chess tables are located in the western part of the circle, and even on cold winter nights people congregate for spirited games.

Around the outside of the circle are entrances, now closed and filled with debris, to tunnels once used by trolleys. The two tunnels, built in 1949 to relieve congestion on the busy streetcar line, have been closed since 1962, when the streetcars stopped operating. For a time, they were used as fallout shelters. The tunnels are as wide as twenty-six feet in some sections, with fourteen-foot ceilings. The remnants of Dupont Down Under, an unsuccessful attempt to create an underground shopping venue in the tunnels, can be seen on either side of Massachusetts Avenue. Other cultural and art initiatives have been suggested and pursued by many preservation groups, but none have had the funding to catalyze long-term human experiences.

The windows of the twenty-four-hour CVS Pharmacy are many times decorated with interesting aerial photos and historical views of the streetcars in Dupont Circle.

■ **21** The **Dupont Circle Hotel** is typical of a type of design, especially for apartments, that was popular after World War II. The hotel replaced the famous Leiter Mansion, one of the most fabulous houses of the time, and was considered a notable example of modern architecture when it was built in 1949. It was fully renovated in 2018 by the Irish owners. A café was added in the 1990s. See www.boylecollection.com.

■ **22** The former **Patterson House** at 15 Dupont Circle NW, designed in 1903 by noted architect Stanford White of McKim, Mead, and White, has been converted and expanded with a modern addition designed by Hartman Cox Architects and rebranded as Oakwood Suites. It has suites and studios totaling ninety residences. The original owner, Eleanor "Cissy" Patterson, daughter of *Chicago Tribune* editor Robert Wilson Patterson and his wife Eleanor, used the house mostly for entertaining, usually in the form of gala dinner parties. In 1927 Mrs. Patterson lent the house to President and Mrs. Coolidge while the White House was being refurbished, and they entertained returning aviation hero Charles Lindbergh there. This building is an ornate example of neo classical Italianate architecture. The face, of marble and glazed terra-cotta, is replete with winged figures, fruit clusters, and other elaborate ornamentation. This structure gives us clues of what Dupont Circle must have been like in its heyday.

■ **23** The **Embassy of the Republic of Iraq**, formerly the **Boardman House**, at 1801 P Street NW, is considered one of the finest remaining Romanesque-revival houses in the city. Hornblower and Marshall designed and built it in 1893.

■ **24** The **Sulgrave Club**, at 1801 Massachusetts Avenue NW, occupies an entire block. One corner of the triangular building points to Dupont Circle, the back is on P Street, and the front is on Massachusetts Avenue; the building's unusual site was clearly an important factor in its design. It was built about 1900 as the residence of Herbert Wadsworth and has been the home of the Sulgrave Club, a private women's club, since 1933. This is one of the earliest Beaux-Arts mansions in the area and features interesting terra-cotta and cut-stone trim.

■ **25** The **National Trust for Historic Preservation** formally occupied the original **McCormick Apartments** at 1785 Massachusetts Avenue NW. Constructed in 1917, this monumental Beaux-Arts luxury apartment building originally contained six apartments, one on each floor, along with living space for forty servants. Considered the finest apartment building in the city, it was inhabited by such well-known personalities as Secretary of the Treasury Andrew W.

Mellon, who lived there while planning the National Gallery of Art. The building was designated a National Historic Landmark in 1977 when the Brookings Institution sold it to the Trust. The building was completely renovated in 2017 by the **American Enterprise Institute**.

■ **26** The **Brookings Institution**, at 1775 Massachusetts Avenue NW, is a noted national research center. The original building has been expanded with additional space and uses. Across the street from Brookings is the Peter G. Peterson Institute for International Economics. This glass-and-stainless-steel "insertion" was designed by Kohn Peterson Fox (KPF).

■ **27** The former **Moore Residence**, at 1746 Massachusetts Avenue, is occupied by the **Embassy of Uzbekistan**. Constructed in 1906–9 under commission from Clarence Moore (an investor who would later go down with the *Titanic*), this residence is considered by many to be one of the finest examples of Louis XV architecture in the city. Its granite and brick exterior, wrought-iron bar grilles, and casement windows present an orderly and symmetrical appearance.

■ **28** The section of **Massachusetts Avenue between 17th and 18th Streets** is part of the Dupont Circle Historic District. The buildings between the Embassy of Uzbekistan and the corner of 17th Street and Massachusetts Avenue exhibit diverse architectural styles in a variety of periods fitting together harmoniously.

 The southwest corner of 17th Street and Massachusetts Avenue, at 1700 Massachusetts Avenue, is occupied by the **Chancery of Peru,** a classical Italian structure whose entrance faces the intersection.

■ **29** **Seventeenth Street** between Massachusetts Avenue and S Street is a lively retail and restaurant district in the District of Columbia. Almost every block contains retail shops, restaurants and bars, and service establishments on the first and second floors for an often LGTBQ clientele. The annual "High Heel Race" there at Halloween showcases the unique athletic skills of the neighborhood's diverse occupants of this dynamic community.

■ **30** **Church Street** is another attractive block of townhouses. At 1742 Church Street NW is the **Keegan Theatre**, founded in 1996, which presents consistently fine productions of the works of young dramatists. Several of the houses on the west end of the block are used by small businesses and nonprofit organizations, while the street retains its residential quality.

■ **31** Several decades after an arson fire destroyed the original Saint Thomas Parish, the sixty-six-square-foot renovation reinvigorates the congregation's presence with a new eighteen-thousand-square-foot church while transforming the surviving parish hall and English Gothic church ruins into a fifty-one-unit multifamily residence on Church Street. Facing 18th Street, the new

Saint Thomas Parish (Episcopal) is inspired by the concept of ascension—or rising from the ashes—with a modern design to reflect its progressive values. Reaching sixty-five feet, the four-story church features an ascension stair, visible from the exterior, and a contemporary terra-cotta module facade. Above the entrance, a terra-cotta- and curtainwall-clad light tower, reminiscent of an Italian campanile, floods sunlight into the interior double-height sanctuary during morning services, while an embedded grand metal cross announces Saint Thomas Parish's triumphant return and serves as a beacon within the neighborhood.

■ **32** The **Whittemore House**, at 1526 New Hampshire Avenue NW, is now the home of the **Woman's National Democratic Club**. Constructed in 1892, this turreted Roman brick house has a modern wing added to the west on the Q Street side. Tours are available Tuesdays through Thursdays at 10 a.m. to 4 p.m. More information can be found at www.democraticwoman.org.

■ **33** The **row houses** on the 1700 block of Q Street provide an indication of popular residential architecture of the late nineteenth century. Designed by Thomas Franklin Schneider and built in 1889–92, these stone houses are a lively mixture of Victorian architectural features, such as Richardsonian Romanesque arches, full turrets, and projecting bays. Each is different, yet taken together they form a coherent and unified whole.

Southwest corner of 17th and Q Streets

■ **34** The buildings on **Corcoran Street** were among the first in the neighborhood to be rehabilitated. Notice the care and attention to detail reflected in the style and positioning of sculptures and reliefs in the houses on the south side of the street.

■ **35** Occupying a triangular site at the intersection of 18th Street and New Hampshire Avenue is the mammoth **Belmont House**, one of the largest on this tour. It was built in 1909 from the design of Ernest Sanson and Horace Trumbauer (the designer of the Philadelphia Art Museum) by Perry Belmont, who was a US congressman and minister to Spain at the time of the house's construction. Built in the Louis XVI style, it is massive and heavily ornamented, from the urns atop the eaves and the intricate wrought-iron balconies to the glass entrance doors. The Belmonts often held lavish parties in the exquisitely decorated rooms of this house.

■ **36** From the corner of New Hampshire Avenue and R Street, walk past the **Thomas Nelson Page House** at 1759 R Street NW. Built in 1897, it was designed in the Federal-revival style by architect Stanford White. Farther west, between 18th and 19th Streets, are the headquarters of the **American Institute for Cancer Research** and the **World Cancer Research Fund**. The **National Museum of American Jewish Military History** is located at 1811 R Street NW. More information can be found at www.nmajmh.org

■ **37** The final stop on the tour is at the northeast corner of 20th and R Streets. The **Fraser Mansion** is a registered historic landmark that has housed a string of restaurants and clubs since the 1930s. It is sometimes referred to as the Scott-Thropp House because it was incorrectly thought to have been built by Thomas A. Scott, assistant secretary of war under Abraham Lincoln. The Italian Renaissance mansion was actually built in 1890 by Hornblower and Marshall for New York merchant George S. Fraser. In 1901 Fraser's widow sold it to Scott's daughter, Miriam Thropp—hence the misnomer. Marshall was probably the designer of the spectacularly ornate interior, which has been restored to its original grandeur, complete with beautiful carved-wood paneling in many of the rooms. The building was restored by and was the home to the Founding Church of Scientology of Washington, DC, which has since relocated. The Fraser Mansion is undergoing additional restoration.

Logan Circle and 14th Street

(Historic residential neighborhood, converted automotive era showrooms, lively retail, and restaurants)

William J. Bonstra and Judith A. Meany

Distance: 1½ miles
Time: 1 hour
Bus: 52, 54, and G2
Metro: McPherson Square (Blue, Orange, and Silver Lines) and
U Street/African American Civil War Memorial/Cardozo
(Green Line)

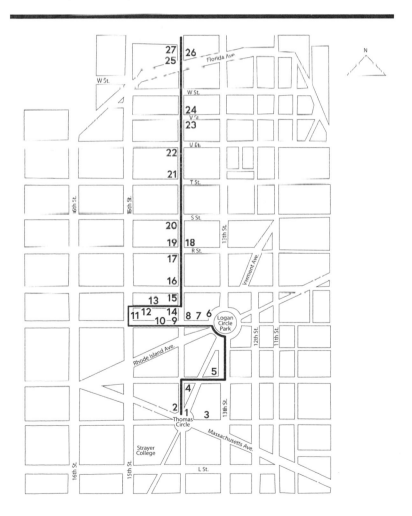

As the nation's capital, Washington is most often introduced to visitors as the monumental city. However, Washington is also a modern city with lively neighborhoods surrounding its commercial and monumental core. This tour showcases some of the emerging twenty-first-century architecture of Washington's historic residential neighborhoods.

The tour starts at Thomas Circle NW (located at the confluence of three major streets: Vermont Avenue, 14th Street, and Massachusetts Avenue), originally shown in the L'Enfant plan. Always an important route from the north into the Federal City, 14th Street finally experienced urbanization following the Civil War. Beginning in the 1870s, it became a thriving commercial corridor serving the surrounding residential neighborhoods. Thomas Circle was the southern axis from which the social and physical life of the city's residents expanded outward. The neighborhoods soon exhibited High Victorian urban dwellings and prosperous neighborhood retailers. By the 1930s, the 14th Street corridor was a major commercial area, focused primarily on automobile dealerships and supporting services. This remained a thriving commercial and residential area until violence erupted following the assassination of Martin Luther King Jr. in April 1968. Subsequently, the neighborhood experienced a decline of both population and commercial activity; many residents moved to the suburbs, and businesses closed for lack of patrons. It took a generation before business started to return to the 14th Street neighborhoods in the late 1990s. The next two decades have been an era of rebirth and renewal, bringing economic redevelopment and increased prosperity.

The *Washington Business Journal* recently commented on this neighborhood's rebirth, noting that, in addition to being one of the hottest restaurant destinations, the area increasingly supports a diversified retail development.

Visitors should start the tour standing in the center of Thomas Circle, in order to fully appreciate the view of the first three buildings.

■ **1 Thomas Circle**. The recently renovated circle honors Gen. George Henry Thomas, a Civil War hero known as the "Rock of Chickamauga." The circle's bronze statue of Thomas, by John Quincy Adams Ward, was erected in 1879, just as the surrounding neighborhood was beginning to push northward (thanks partly to the modern water and sewer lines being brought to this area of the city by Alexander "Boss" Shepherd).

The three important buildings that line the northern semicircle represent three important periods when significant numbers of new residents came to the area: the 1870s, the 1930s, and the 1960s.

■ **2 National City Christian Church**, 5 Thomas Circle NW. From the circle, stand facing north and look to your left. Designed by John Russell Pope in 1930, the imposing neoclassical church frames the entire circle, announcing both a significance of purpose and the streetscape beyond. Historians point to the fact that the architect took his inspiration from London's early eighteenth-century

Church of Saint Martin-in-the-Fields. However, Pope chose to enhance the architectural strength of the building with a portico entrance atop an architectural mound and terminated the tower with a small but delightful dome. The later wings of the church by Chatelain Architects, designed in the style of the Pope Church, are being renovated and converted to professional offices by a local developer.

■ **3 Washington Plaza Hotel** (formerly the International Inn), 10 Thomas Circle NW. Now turn your gaze across 14th Street and Vermont Avenue. Here the circle is wrapped by a modern, curvilinear building designed by architect Morris Lapidus in 1962. Lapidus was a somewhat controversial American architect whose motto was "Too much is never enough." He is known primarily as the designer of curvy, flamboyant neo-Baroque Miami Beach hotels.

■ **4 Luther Place Memorial Church**, 1226 Vermont Avenue NW. Set back from the circle, this church is the oldest structure on the circle. It was designed in 1873 by John C. Harkness and Henry S. Davis, based on an original design by Judson York. The acute space between Vermont Avenue and 14th Street significantly influenced the red sandstone, neo-Gothic design. The church has experienced numerous renovations and additions to support its mission to the homeless and low-income families in the community. Leaving the circle, proceed north on Vermont Avenue and then turn right on N Street.

■ **5 SoLo Piazza**, corner of N and 13th Streets, was one of the first residential projects to herald the return of the adjacent 14th Street commercial corridor. The building, designed by Bonstra | Haresign Architects in 2002, anchors the corner with a strong, modern design statement of form, materials, and space, emphasizing light as well as energy efficiency. The overall form of the building orients three soaring glass bay windows with balconies on each street facade; a corner tower with butt-glazed windows maximizes views to the south. In tribute to its historic neighbors to the north, a glass ribbon of windows cuts through the building, splitting it horizontally at the fifth floor. As wonderful as the front facade is for passersby to view, the seemingly rectangular building conceals an unusual cylindrical courtyard that affords residents both a green oasis and views to the distant Washington National Cathedral. The entrance to the courtyard is through a back alley on N Street in midblock. Leaving SoLo Piazza, walk along 13th Street north to Logan Circle, which offers more outstanding examples of Victorian architecture from the 1870s. Walk along the southwestern side of the circle, turning left at P Street NW.

■ **6** Row houses located at **4–7 Logan Circle NW** are contributing properties to the Logan Circle Historic District and the Greater Fourteenth Street Historic District. Originally known as Iowa Circle, the park was renamed by Congress in 1930 in honor of John A. Logan, commander of the Army of the Tennessee during the Civil War, commander of the Grand Army of the Republic, and US representative and senator for the state of Illinois, who lived at 4 Logan Circle NW. At the center of the circle is an equestrian statue of Maj. Gen. John A. Logan.

5 **Logan Circle NW** was built in 1883 for patent attorney, diplomat, and violin collector Dwight J. Partello and designed by notable architect Emil S. Friedrich, who worked for Robert Mills and the architect of the Capitol. While no name is listed for the builder, it is likely that Partello's brother, William Z. Partello, a carpenter, was involved in the property's erection. A unique floor plan with octagonal rooms and an internal skylit atrium bringing light into the center of the house showcases the residence's original preserved cherry millwork and three-story hand-carved cherry stair.

Dwight J. Partello died on August 13, 1920, after falling ill at the home of a friend, at which time newspapers listed his residence as 5 Iowa Circle. The property remained under the trust of Partello's estate for seven years until it was deeded to Partello's granddaughter, Florence Shipley Partello. Florence Partello retained the property for only four months before deeding it to James W. Good, who served as a member of the US House of Representatives from 1909 to 1921. In March 1929 Good was appointed secretary of war by President Hoover and deeded 5 Logan Circle NW the following month. This historic mansion has recently been restored by Bonstra | Haresign Architects, with AllenBuilt Construction for its current owners.

◼ 7 The **Lofts at Logan Circle**, 1309 P Street NW. Working in 1990 at an early stage in the area's revitalization, A+B+S Architects Group chose to marry the residential strength of Logan Circle to the east with the highly commercial development along 14th Street. Lacking older industrial buildings for adaptive use that have created loft oppor-tunities in other urban neighbor-hoods, the architects designed a new building to recreate the spatial advantages of lofts. The hierarchi-cal facade and reddish brick mate-rials appeal to the neighborhood's urbanites.

◼ 8 **Studio Theatre**, corner of 14th and P Streets. At this strategic corner in the Greater 14th Street Historic District, Bonstra | Haresign Architects were tasked in 2002 with designing a catalytic project to anchor the revitalizing neigh-borhood. The existing building's 1930s-era automotive showrooms provided an architectural backdrop

Studio Theatre

for two new two-hundred-seat theaters, a new entrance lobby with box office, and multiple classroom spaces. An added two-story glass atrium provides a common gathering area and nucleus for the facility. The vertical glass structure and composite fins reinforce the existing facade rhythms and firmly establish the adapted building's place in its historic context. At the sidewalk level, the theater's current productions are prominently and colorfully displayed. These backlit colored glass panels, along with zigzag strands of neon, form lively interplays of color and light that activate the street and add whimsy to the historic district. The theater has embarked upon a recent renovation and rebranding campaign that has added a few exterior features, such as a large, backlit STUDIO sign above the 14th Street entry, and painting and signage upgrades.

■ **9 Cooper Lewis Condos**, corner of 14th and P Streets. The original 1897 building was designed by architect Paul J. Pelz, renowned as the architect of the Library of Congress's original Thomas Jefferson Building. From 1925 to 1975, the building was centrally located in the bustling 14th Street commercial corridor, operating as the Cooper Hardware Store. RTKL undertook its creative preservation in 2006. The facade and main spaces at the front were restored inside and out, and spacious apartments with private terraces and balconies were formed within the historic design.

■ **10** The **Hudson**, 1425 P Street NW. One of several sophisticated mixed-use projects designed by Eric Colbert & Associates for PN Hoffman and SJG Properties, these apartments have contributed to the regeneration of the surrounding neighborhood since 2003. The first floor is dedicated to retail uses and the lobby. The design elements take cues from the former car showrooms and auto body shops in the area, combining an industrial-age vocabulary with contemporary materials. The facade includes horizontal cast-stone bands, each defining a two-story base and a one-story top. Gentle arches help define the upper stories. Changes in brick color establish the ends of the building and add definition to the center. The grid of the windows is a unifying element that helps give the facade a human scale. Instead of masonry, horizontal bands of metal panels cover the edges of the fourth and sixth floors, creating further visual hierarchy.

■ **11 Metropole**, 1515 15th Street NW. The 2009 RTKL-designed Metropole is located on the nexus of three architecturally distinct streets: P Street, 15th Street, and Church Street. The seven-story, ninety-eight-unit building celebrates this diversity with a design that responds to the eclectic character of each street. The building's south facade faces P Street, a busy thoroughfare with a strong urban edge and vibrant retail activity, while the building's west side fronts 15th Street, which is lined with elegant and stately brownstones. These historic buildings display highly sculpted massing and a diverse composition of architectural elements. In response, Metropole's west face is designed with masonry detailing, metal and glass bay windows, balconies, and a variety of fenestration patterns that complement the adjacent brownstones. Metropole's north side faces Church Street with trellises and other details to echo the more subdued character of Church Street. Recessed horizontal brick courses create a consistent architectural thread between this building and others on Church Street.

■ **12 CITTA 50**, 1450 Church Street NW. Designed by Bonstra | Haresign Architects in 2009, this adaptive use incorporates a historic coal distribution facility designed over a hundred years ago by Washington's first registered African American architect, John A. Lankford. The historic Lankford building was retained in its entirety to anchor the twenty-seven-unit loft-style residential building. Articulated as a lively composition of multicolored, textured brick planes, the new facades relate effectively to the historic industrial context, appearing to have been built over time. Respecting its varied streetscapes, the building allows for maximum views and open spaces on three faces.

■ **13 Rainbow Lofts**, 1445 Church Street NW. The winner of an American Institute of Architects Award for Excellence for Eric Colbert & Associates in

1450 Church Street NW

2006, Rainbow Lofts is a twenty-one-unit condominium featuring the adaptive use of a 1929 auto body shop with a new addition adjacent to and on top of the existing building. The project was subject to Historic Preservation Review Board approval. The original building is well proportioned, with a facade of dark, rough-faced brick, industrial steel windows, and poured-in-place concrete sills. The addition aims for a similar utilitarian elegance, expressed in a contrasting vocabulary of sleek aluminum panels, glass guardrails, and white painted aluminum sunshades. The old steel industrial sash windows were duplicated with the flanges reset into the concrete sills, matching the original detailing. Glass roof-deck guardrails were used so that the proportions of the front facade and its subtle cornice line would not be visually altered.

■ **14 Lofts 14**, 1400 Church Street NW. This sensitive historic restoration by RTKL was completed in 2006. The project site initially consisted of three 1920s era brick- and limestone-faced buildings next to the Pelz structure (see this tour, no. 10). To maintain as much of the structures as possible, the buildings were temporarily shored up and suspended while parking was excavated and built below. The design incorporated original structural elements such as beams, ribbed slabs, and exterior masonry walls, many with the remnants of earlier uses such as lifting hooks and electrical insets. The missing storefronts and damaged windows were replaced with modern versions, keeping the sight lines consistent with those of the original buildings. The design and detailing for the window bays were guided by previous construction drawings obtained from the Library of Congress. The profiles of the glazing system were researched from the archives of the original window manufacturer, and a custom extrusion was made to match what was used in the buildings' initial construction.

■ **15 Gallery plan b**, 1530 14th Street NW, offers an excellent example of architectural intervention to achieve the dual goals of historic preservation and economic viability. In 1986 architect Darrel Rippeteau purchased what he has described as a "crummy little" one-story warehouse, previously used to store street vendors' carts at night. By 2002, Rippeteau Architects' vision of a truly mixed-use building emerged with street-level retail, a second floor for architectural offices, and two residential units on the third floor. The power of functional design is on exhibit with this building.

■ **16 Q14 Condominium**, corner of 14th and Q Streets NW. Designed by Bonstra | Haresign Architects and completed in 2007, the building exhibits a fresh, contemporary street presence, fitting comfortably within its varied historic context. The building's playful geometric massing and rhythms and carefully composed facades, detailed with modest materials, embody the architecture of the modern era and reflect its occupants' urban lifestyles.

■ **17** The **Aston**, corner of 14th and R Streets NW. Continuing the redevelopment of the 14th Street Corridor from a commercial to mixed-use neighborhood,

Corner of 14th and Q Streets

Bonstra | Haresign Architects has designed this new seven-story residential con-
dominium building at the key corner of 14th and R Streets. Patterned after the
many showrooms of the area's former "automobile row," the 14th Street facade
has two projecting bays of metal and glass stitched together with a lattice of ornamental metals bands. More closely matching the height of the adjacent historical
Harry Wardman–built apartments, a five-story facade extends along R Street.

■ **18 Liz**, at 1357 R Street NW, includes two historic facades, the former
Elizabeth Taylor Medical Center building and the Belmont Garage, here
retained within this seven-story residential and office building. Included within
that preservation, the Whitman-Walker Cultural Center will utilize the former
front door of the clinic. This door—once used for LGBTQ community members who needed a space to receive stigma-free care and treatment—will now
be used to celebrate life and the resilience of the LGBTQ community.

The most distinctive transformative gesture of Liz is its striking architecture, designed to integrate history, community, and purpose. Liz was designed
by Selldorf Architects. The beautifully crafted building with colored terra-cotta
panels reflects both warm integrity and high design and includes seventy-eight
apartment residences across four floors, sixty thousand square feet of office
space across two floors, and twenty thousand square feet of ground-floor retail
and cultural spaces.

Liz honors the care to the community that Whitman-Walker provided at
the Elizabeth Taylor Medical Center, whose original dedication twenty-five

years ago was made through the generosity of actress and HIV/AIDS activist Elizabeth Taylor.

■ **19 1728 14th Street NW** is a contemporary mixed-use commercial building fitting comfortably into a varied historic context rich in architectural styles and changing land-use patterns. An infill building on a fast-redeveloping commercial street within the Greater Fourteenth Street Historic District, the project integrates two levels of commercial office above two integrated levels of street-front retail in a design that pays homage to the area's rich commercial past. The project design is formally composed around a central three-story display window. Humane, craft-derived masonry detailing in rich colors and textures organizes the building facade. Vertical steel columns mark the site's three former structures and support the horizontal louvers and a glazed retail canopy.

■ **20 District Condos**, corner of 14th and S Streets NW. The architects of Shalom Baranes Associates have designed a sleek and sophisticated new tower to complement and contrast modernity with the restored Whitman-Walker historic landmark that will be incorporated. The strong retail-focused street presence will be carried through the upper residential floors to emphasize the building's mixed-use character. The new building will read independently from the historic building yet is scaled to respect its character while reinforcing the pedestrian experience at ground level.

■ **21** The **Louis** at 1920 14th Street NW occupies a prominent site at the corner of two major commercial corridors: 14th Street and U Street NW. The building is a mix of old and new as it steps down from north to south, mirroring the shift from dense development along U Street to row houses along T Street. Varied brick colors and window profiles break down the apparent mass of the building, while still creating a coherent composition. The project includes the renovation of a row of commercial buildings and the addition of a service corridor and loading dock for the existing restaurants there.

■ **22 14th and U Streets**. On the evening of April 4, 1968, following the assassination of Martin Luther King Jr., civil rights leader Stokely Carmichael and demonstrators assembled at this historic corner to lead protesters to local businesses, requesting that they close in respect for Dr. King. Violence ensued over the next four days, resulting in the destruction of over 1,200 buildings in the neighborhood and the utter devastation of Washington's inner-city economy. The opening of the U Street/African American Civil War Memorial/Cardozo and Columbia Heights Metro stations in the 1990s finally sparked the beginning of reinvestment and renewal.

■ **23 Langston Lofts**, corner of 14th and V Streets. A strong twenty-first-century architectural style situated at this corner marks the entry into Washington's historic center of the city's lively jazz and art scene. Designed in 2005 by

Shalom Baranes Associates, the project takes cues from both the commercial storefront facades and the residential bay protrusions seen throughout the neighborhood. Simple massing and careful detailing, along with an expanse of glass, especially at the building's corners, provide a refreshingly urban vibe, as well as panoramic views of the Washington Monument and the Capitol dome.

■ **24** The **Flats at Union Row**, 2125 14th Street NW. The SK&I Architectural Design Group is responsible for joining two projects in one, blending historic warehouses with new construction. The contemporary condominium tower, completed in 2007, is divided into three distinct facades to moderate the block-long scale of the building. The two warehouses are preserved within the block's interior, renovated into fifty-nine loft-style units fronting on a landscaped gallery. The gallery acts as a pedestrian walkway between the residential units and the retail edge of 14th Street.

■ **25** The **Solea**, corner of 14th and Belmont Streets. Completed in 2009 and built on a challenging sloped site, this project features live-work units interspersed among ground-floor retail and upper-floor residential. Over 20 percent of the units are designed as live-work units with a mission to incubate and preserve local microenterprises and neighborhood start-ups. The project was undertaken on District-owned land in partnership with the city's Office of the Deputy Mayor for Planning and Economic Development. The design, by Sorg Architects, was carefully sculpted to harness sustainable aspects of light and volume with affordable materiality such as corrugated metal panels, while respecting Washington's traditional residential rhythms with projected bays interpreted in a modern vocabulary. As a LEED for Neighborhood Development pilot project, emphasis was placed on recycled materials, water-saving fixtures, low-emissivity windows, and reflective roofing materials.

■ **26** **View 14**, 2303 14th Street NW. Designed by SK&I Architectural Design Group, this 2009 apartment building, set on a hillside, clearly announces its contemporary identity. The design connects strongly with the view of the city below, while the building's industrial base is reminiscent of the twentieth-century automobile showrooms that preceded it.

■ **27** **Capitol View on 14th**, 2420 14th Street NW, is a ten-story mixed-use residential planned unit development in the burgeoning neighborhood between U Street and Columbia Heights. Designed by Shalom Baranes Associates, the project is situated on a sloping grade, the LEED-Platinum 260,000-square-foot building includes 255 rental apartments, sixteen-thousand square feet of retail space, and two levels of below-grade parking. Luxury amenities include a rooftop pool with year-round fireplace, open-air kitchen, and zen water garden. Floor-to-ceiling glazing maximizes daylight and affords sweeping views from within the open, clean-lined units.

Kalorama

Composed of two historic districts: Kalorama Triangle east of Connecticut Avenue and Sheridan-Kalorama west of it. The larger, grander houses, many of which have been converted to embassies, are in the western section. (Zoning allows embassies, which are the ambassadors' residences, but not chanceries, which are the offices of the foreign countries, in Sheridan-Kalorama.)

John J. Protopappas

Distance: 1½ miles

Time: 2 hours

Bus: 42, 43, L2, N2, N4, and N6

Metro: Dupont Circle (Red Line); transfer to bus routes, above, or walk to Sheridan Circle

Kalorama to the west of Connecticut Avenue is the center of the foreign diplomatic community and has been home to six presidents: Franklin Delano
Roosevelt, Warren G. Harding, Herbert Hoover, Woodrow Wilson, William
Howard Taft, and Barack Obama. It contains one of the finest collections of
revival architecture mansions in the United States. Richly treed and topograph-
ically varied, Kalorama is an enclave of quiet urbanity.

For almost a century after the founding of Washington, DC, much of the
district was part of a large estate of great natural beauty. Superbly sited, the
Kalorama estate looked out over the Potomac, Northern Virginia, and the infant
capital city. The estate bore the same name as the modern neighborhood and
was noted for its fine manor house, which stood until 1888. Kalorama was
carved out of the Widow's Mite, a colonial patent of approximately 660 acres
granted in 1664 to John Langworth by Lord Baltimore. Kalorama, well known
for the concentration of embassies and chanceries in its large mansions, is a
phenomenon of the early twentieth-century expansion of Washington. Its evolution into a beautiful and sophisticated neighborhood was closely related to
several important developments: the termination in 1890 of the distinction
between the City of Washington and the County of Washington (that is, the
area of the District of Columbia outside Florida Avenue); the extension of Massachusetts Avenue beyond Florida Avenue in the same period; the new bridges
across Rock Creek; the commitment made in 1890 to preserve the Rock Creek
Valley as a scenic and recreational resource; the proximity of Kalorama to
established wealthy neighborhoods like Dupont Circle; and the filling up of
older portions of the city in the dynamic post–Civil War years.

From the outset, Kalorama was intended to become a prime residential
area. Intelligent and aggressive real estate promotion, attractive building sites,
and the astounding growth of the colony of wealthy people in Washington
who wanted the most fashionable town residences made Kalorama desirable.
These developments provided an opportunity for architects working in the
Beaux-Arts-influenced styles of the general classical-revival period following
the Chicago World's Columbian Exposition of 1893.

■ **1 Sheridan Circle** (Massachusetts Avenue at 23rd Street). In November 1886
the commissioners of the District of Columbia held public hearings to discuss
plans for the extension of Massachusetts Avenue and a traffic circle in honor of
Stephen Decatur. The widow of George Lovett, the last private owner of the
Kalorama estate, protested the proposed improvements affecting her property.
However, a New York real estate firm paid the Lovett heirs $354,000 for the
remaining sixty acres of the estate. At an astonishing $5,900 an acre (in 1887),
subsequent development by owners of the planned Kalorama Heights subdivision had to be either for a very wealthy population or for a very high-density
population. It is clear to anyone standing in Sheridan Circle today that the new
owners decided on the former type of development.

Decatur Circle became Sheridan Circle in 1890, when the officers of the Army of the Cumberland received authorization to commission a statue of Gen. Philip H. Sheridan, a Civil War hero who had died in 1888. Gutzon Borglum (sculptor of Mount Rushmore) was commissioned, and the model of his equestrian statue of Sheridan was accepted in January 1908. The statue was erected the following year. In the past, the statue has been compared to a traffic cop stuck in mud, but the harshness of critical opinion of the work has lessened over time. To be close to it, Mrs. Sheridan commissioned the house at 2211 Massachusetts Avenue NW, designed by the firm of Wood, Donn, and Demin, 1903.

Sheridan Circle was the earliest part of the Kalorama neighborhood to develop. It is enclosed by a group of early twentieth-century mansions whose mass, detailing, and styles are reflective of the wide, baroque boulevards of L'Enfant's original plan for the capital city. Embassies are now located in these buildings. Around the circle you can see the embassies of Greece (227 Massachusetts Avenue), Romania (1607 23rd Street), Egypt, and Kenya (2249 R Street).

■ **2** The **Alice Pike Barney Studio House**, 2306 Massachusetts Avenue (1903, Waddy B. Wood, architect), is now the **Latvian Embassy**. Barney, a wealthy playwright and painter, commissioned the house for her many artistic pursuits and informal entertainments. Influenced by the Mission style, the house includes a studio, stage facilities, and an interesting collection of seventeenth-century Spanish furniture. The Barrymores, Enrico Caruso, and James Whistler were among those Alice Barney entertained here.

■ **3** The **Edward H. Everett House**, 1606 23rd Street, is now the **Embassy of the Republic of Turkey**. It was commissioned by Everett, a multimillionaire capitalist-industrialist. Much of his fortune was the result of his patent on the modern fluted bottlecap. The architect was George Oakley Totten Jr. Begun in 1910, the house was not completed until 1915. As in so many of Totten's buildings, classical details are combined in a personal and idiosyncratic manner. Totten was too aware of architectural developments in America to remain uninfluenced by the pioneering work of Midwestern and California architects that was contemporary with the full-blown Beaux-Arts. This native influence shows in features like the trellised roof garden on the Q Street side of the house. Similarly, the impact of Totten's time in Turkey shows in such features as the elaborate interior carving. It is hardly surprising that the Turkish government admired this house and has occupied it since late 1932.

■ **4** The **Egyptian Embassy**, 2301 Massachusetts Avenue, was commissioned by **Joseph Beale** in 1907. The gently curved facade of this magnificent eighteenth-century Italian–inspired palazzo creates a transition from R Street to Massachusetts Avenue. The architect was Glenn Brown, who from 1899 to 1913 was secretary of the American Institute of Architects. Brown is perhaps best known as the architect of the Dumbarton Bridge (1915, also known as the Q Street Bridge

Embassy of the Republic of Turkey

and the Buffalo Bridge), connecting Sheridan-Kalorama with Georgetown. The austerity of the exterior of the limestone and stucco mansion is not matched within. In 1928 Egypt acquired the Beale House for its ambassadorial residence.

■ **5** The **Philippine ambassador's official residence**, 2253 R Street NW, was originally the **Gen. Charles and Emma Fitzhugh Residence** (1904, Waddy B. Wood, architect). The scale of the building is somewhat smaller than that of most of the houses around Sheridan Circle, but the building holds its own important position by clarity of form, plain surfaces, clearly articulated openings, and basic horizontality. During the early period of his career, Wood was inclined toward Mediterranean design. The use of segmentally arched windows under the eaves is a typical Wood curiosity.

■ **6** Of the **three houses** at 2225, 2223, and 2221 R Street (George Oakley Totten Jr., architect), the central one was constructed first. It was built in 1904 for Alice Pike Barney, who just a year earlier had opened her studio house on Sheridan Circle. The other two houses were built in 1908 and 1909. They harmonize well with the earlier Fitzhugh residence. In 1931 Charles Evans Hughes, chief justice of the United States, purchased the house and lived there until his death in 1948. As the result of his residency, it was later designated a National Historic Landmark. The government of Burma has been the owner since Hughes's death.

■ **7** The **Gardner Frederick Williams House**, 2201 R Street (1906–7, George Oakley Totten Jr., architect). This imposing, straightforward, clean-lined house was built for Gardner Frederick Williams, a mining engineer who had been associated with Cecil Rhodes in Africa.

■ **8** The **A. Mitchell Palmer House**, 2132 R Street (1915, Clarke Waggaman, architect), a Georgian row house, was home to Palmer while he served as Woodrow Wilson's attorney general. Palmer was one of the chief figures in the

"Red Scare" paranoia that swept the country after World War I; he saw communists everywhere. On June 2, 1919, an unidentified terrorist tossed a bomb into the Palmer home and in the process destroyed himself. Palmer was in the house at the time but was uninjured.

■ **9** The **Franklin D. Roosevelt Residence**, now the **Embassy of Mali**, 2130 R Street (1921, Frederick H. Brooke, architect), is where Franklin Roosevelt lived from 1917 to 1920, while serving as assistant secretary of the navy. The house has seventeen rooms and six and a half baths and was well suited to the needs of the growing Roosevelt family. (Brooke worked with Sir Edwin Lutyens, architect, on the design of the British embassy in the late 1920s.)

■ **10** The **Codman-Davis House**, 2145 Decatur Place (1906, Ogden Codman, architect) was commissioned by wealthy Boston resident Martha Codman to serve as her Washington home. Her cousin, Ogden Codman, was well known as a New York society architect. The house is notable for its dark red brick, dressed stone, grand vehicular courtyard entry—recalling a Parisian hotel—and because its garden terrace serves as a retaining wall for the adjacent Decatur Terrace. The Codman Davis House became the Louise Home in the early 1950s, when the original Louise Home for poor but genteel Southern Protestant ladies was demolished to make way for the apartment building at 1500 Massachusetts Avenue NW.

■ **11** **Decatur Terrace and Fountain**, 22nd Street between Decatur Place and S Street (1911–12, Robert E. Cook, architect), is a project of the Office of Public Buildings and Grounds. Known affectionately as the Spanish Steps, it solved the problem of connecting Decatur Place with the much higher S Street, in favor of the pedestrian. It is a rare occurrence in an American city of a street becoming a staircase and is little known to most Washingtonians.

■ **12** The **Charles D. Walcott House**, 1743 22nd Street (1904–5, George Oakley Totten Jr., architect), was commissioned by the secretary of the Smithsonian Institution, who was also a real estate promoter in northwest Washington. The house has been enlarged and modified in design but was originally an Italianate Mission–style house. It still commands a fine site at the top of Decatur Terrace.

■ **13** Closer to Connecticut Avenue, the character of Kalorama changes. As early as 1873, streetcars ran along Connecticut Avenue from 17th Street to Florida Avenue. In the blocks of Kalorama adjacent to this major diagonal avenue of L'Enfant's plan is the speculative row-house development typical of a streetcar suburb; **1801–9 Phelps Place** (Joseph O. Johnson, architect) is a good example of the pattern. The row was built in 1896 by William Alexander Kimmel, a speculator and building contractor responsible for seventeen Washington churches in addition to countless houses. Most of the Phelps Place buildings now serve as foundations or educational sites. The row houses of the nearby blocks of S Street near Connecticut Avenue, as well as Bancroft and Leroy Places, have long been popular with government officials. An especially heavy concentration of prominent New Deal person-alities lived in this section of Kalorama. Most of the pleasant row houses in this favored district were built between 1900 and 1915.

■ **14** The **Conrad Miller Residence**, 1825 Phelps Place NW (1896–97, Thomas F. Schneider, architect), is one of the earliest houses in Sheridan-Kalorama. Commissioned by Miller, a celebrated lecturer and publisher, and his wife, Anna Jenness Miller, it displays the full-blown mannerisms of Schneider's early career.

■ **15** At the southwest corner of Phelps Place and California Street NW is **Saint Rose's Industrial School**. Organized in 1872 and originally downtown, the school for the training of orphan girls in home economics and "feminine" manual arts was built in its current location in 1908 (Francis E. Toomey, architect). An almost identical building is on North Charles Street in Baltimore. When Saint Rose's Industrial School was built, Washington was part of the archdiocese of Baltimore. Later, the building became the Saint Ann's Infant Asylum. In the 1960s it was the Cathedral Latin School and the Mackin Catholic High School. Today, it is home to the archbishop of Washington. The massive Roman brick and brownstone structure is one of the few buildings in Kalorama not intended as a residence.

■ **16** The **2100 and 2200 blocks of California Street**, Connecticut Avenue in this location, and Columbia Road constitute the only concentration of large apartment buildings in Kalorama. At the turn of the century, the heights above Florida Avenue attracted massive apartment development, which aroused the ire of many residents who felt that such structures were alien to the char-acter of the neighborhood.

■ **17** Typical of the grander apartment buildings is **California House** (originally Florence Court), 2205 California Street (1905, Thomas F. Schneider, architect), which has large, handsomely appointed apartments, some with views of the Washington Monument. Justice Louis Brandeis resided here for many years.

■ **18** The **Westmoreland**, 2122 California Street (1905, Kennedy & Blake, archi-tects), is a fine example of Washington's "apartment-house Baroque" architec-ture and now is a co-op apartment.

■ **19** **Equestrian statue of Maj. Gen. George B. McClellan**, Connecticut Avenue and Columbia Road. The bronze statue—completely lacking in personality—of the commander of the Army of the Potomac was designed by Frederick MacMonnies in 1907 and rests on a base designed by James Crocroft. MacMonnies had attracted worldwide attention and praise with his sculpture for the World's Columbian Exposition in 1893.

From the vantage point of the Lothrop House site (this tour, no. 21), one can imagine the wonderful view that the early houses on Kalorama Heights must have had. The commanding view was possible until the development of the Washington Hilton Hotel site across Columbia Road from the Lothrop mansion.

20 The **Washington Hilton Hotel**, 1919 Connecticut Avenue (1965, William B. Tabler, architect), and the **Universal Buildings** south of it dramatically changed the character of Kalorama east of Connecticut Avenue from primarily residential to significantly commercial. In 1981 the attempted assassination of President Ronald Reagan took place at the entrance to the hotel. The hotel is a rounded "M" in plan, providing views of the city to the south. In 2016, a slick glass tower, in contrast to the original concrete building, was constructed in the vacant space of half of the M. The new condominium building provides spectacular views of the city while obstructing views from that half of the hotel.

The large tract of land occupied by the hotel and office buildings was known as Oak Lawn, after the huge and ancient oak tree that stood there. In the 1920s the site was proposed to accommodate a national Masonic memorial, which resulted in the submission of an interesting scheme by Frank Lloyd Wright referred to as "Temple Heights." Sadly, it was never realized.

21 The **Alvin Mason Lothrop House**, 2001 Connecticut Avenue (1908, Hornblower & Marshall, architects), is a forty-room, Italianate limestone mansion that was commissioned by Lothrop, one of the two founding partners of the dry-goods firm of Woodward & Lothrop, which eventually grew into Washington's largest department store.

Alvin Mason Lothrop House

■ **22 2101 Connecticut Avenue** (1928, George T. Santmyers, architect) was built by the same firm that built the Shoreham Hotel. One of the two largest apartment buildings in Kalorama—the other is the Wyoming at 2202 Columbia Road—it has only sixty-six apartments. All have at least seven rooms with three baths and three exposures. Of special interest are the sculpted parrot gargoyles and lion's-head medallions above the entrance portals. Some of Washington's most prominent people have lived here. In its art deco flair and in its excess of elegant spaciousness, the building might be considered the last of the truly lavish grand apartment houses constructed in Washington before the Great Depression.

■ **23** The **Chinese Residence**, 2300 & 2310 Connecticut Avenue (2019, Esocoff & Weinstein, architects, and Stern & Tomlinson, architects, 1922). The new residence for the staff of the Chinese Chancery, two miles north on Connecticut Avenue at the Van Ness International Center (2009, I. M. Pei, architect), replaces a late 1940s yellow brick apartment building of pedestrian design. The new building, which incorporates the facade of an older apartment building and subtly reflects traditional Chinese ornamental elements, is a welcome improvement over the building that preceded it.

■ **24** The **William Howard Taft Bridge**, constructed 1897–1907, was designed by engineer George S. Morison and architect Edward Pearce Casey. It was one of the first and largest concrete bridges in the world. It is ornamented by two lions, designed by Roland Hinton Perry, at both ends of the bridge and twenty-four lamp posts, designed by Ernest Bairstow, along its span. Its completion, at a time when the city was rapidly outgrowing the original L'Enfant Plan—which ended at Boundary Street, now Florida Avenue—opened the city north of Rock Creek Park to rapid development. Until that time, Connecticut Avenue was carried over a lower and narrower iron truss bridge, slightly to the west of the current location. Constructed at a cost of $846,331, it was known as the Million Dollar Bridge. In 1931, it was renamed in honor of William Howard Taft, US president 1909–13, who died in 1930. As a resident of Kalorama, Taft often walked the bridge. The Red Line of the Metro was slated to run across the bridge but, instead, it runs under Rock Creek Park, in one of the deepest portions of the Metro. In 2003, the bridge was added to the National Register of Historic Sites.

■ **25** The **Mortimer J. Lawrence House**, 2131 Wyoming Avenue NW, was built for Mortimer J. Lawrence, the publisher of the *Ohio Farmer,* the *Michigan Farmer,* and the *Pennsylvania Farmer.* He was a Cleveland bank president as well. The house was Lawrence's wedding gift to his bride, Carrie Snyder. Both were infatuated with Italy and had their architect, Waddy Butler Wood, model the 1907 house after a Tuscan villa. Throughout, there is fine marble and mosaic work; barely any surface, interior or exterior, is wood. Note the beautiful soffiting.

■ **26** The **William Howard Taft House**, 2215 Wyoming Avenue (1908, Appleton P. Clarke, architect). Taft moved here in 1921 when he became chief justice of the United States. He purchased the large Georgian-revival house from Massachusetts congressman Alvin Fuller. After Taft's death, Mrs. Taft remained in the house until her death in 1944. It is now the **Embassy of Syria**.

■ **27** The **B. F. Saul House**, 2224 Wyoming Avenue (1923, George Ray, architect), was commissioned by Saul, the founder of Washington's first mortgage bank. He was responsible for financing many of Washington's most successful developers, including Harry Wardman. Unfortunately, Saul lived in the house only eight years, dying at the age of fifty-nine. It is now the **Polish Embassy**.

■ **28** The **Anthony Francis Lucas Residence**, 2300 Wyoming Avenue (1913, Waggaman & Ray, architects). One of the largest and most pretentious houses in the city, it was commissioned by Capt. A. F. Lucas, an oil explorer. Waggaman, during his short career, specialized in large suburban homes for the wealthy. Undoubtedly, this house is one of the most unusual in the city, so closely is it tied to the products of Italian mannerism, particularly the work of an architect like Giulio Romano. The most important space in the building is the two-story room behind the loggia on 23rd Street. The roof groin is vaulted and splendidly articulated. The dining room is noteworthy for its richly carved oak paneling. It is now the **Zambian Embassy.**

■ **29** The **Warren G. Harding Residence**, 2314 Wyoming Avenue (1915, George Ray, architect), is where Harding lived as Ohio senator from 1917 until becoming president in 1921. The house is more important for its historical than for its architectural values. However, the use of a side entry is unusual in Washington, while the use of classical elements and overall sculptural quality make the building more intriguing than a first glance might acknowledge. Most recently, it was the **Embassy of Monaco**.

■ **30** The **Anne M. Lawrence House**, 2125 Kalorama Road (1904, Jules Henri de Sibour). This Jacobean-revival mansion was purchased by Portugal in 1945 and served as its embassy until 2002. The **Portuguese Embassy** is now located at 2012 Massachusetts Avenue NW.

■ **31** The **W. W. Lawrence House**, 2221 Kalorama Road (1911, Jules Henri de Sibour, architect), occupies the largest lot in Sheridan-Kalorama and is the largest house in the District. The Tudor-revival manor house commands a view high above Rock Creek. Lawrence made a fortune in mining; however, the imposition of income tax in the early twentieth century made it difficult for millionaires to maintain their mansions. Many in Sheridan-Kalorama were sold to foreign countries to serve as embassies. The government of France purchased the house in January 1936 for about $400,000, including furnishings and household equipment. It has served as the **French Embassy** ever since. (The French Chancery is a large, twenty-first-century complex on Reservoir Road in Georgetown.) De Sibour, who was born in France in 1872 but grew up in the United States, studied architecture at the Ecole des Beaux-Arts. He had an extremely successful career in Washington, designing numerous mansions on 16th Street NW and Massachusetts Avenue. He worked most often in eclectic borrowings from French classicism.

■ **32** The **Royal Thai Consular Office**, 2300 Kalorama Road (1920, James Rush Marshall, architects) is one of the few Kalorama buildings built for a foreign mission. It was commissioned by the Siamese (now Thai) government. Note the Eastern symbolism incorporated into the concrete that was executed by concrete craftsman John J. Earley—for example, the garudas (a mythological bird that was the vehicle of Vishnu) atop the pilasters on the facade. The building terminates Kalorama Road at that spot and, since it faces west, at the right time of day, the sunset can be seen through the windows.

■ **33** **Sheridan-Kalorama** west of Kalorama Circle dates entirely from the period since 1925. The circle is unusual in that it is a rare instance in Washington of a site constructed for private development rather than as a public space. The superb views across Rock Creek Park and its seclusion create a quiet character that results in one of the city's most expensive and prestigious neighborhoods. Of special note are the two all-stone Tudor houses at 29 and 33 Kalorama Circle (1926, Horace W. Peaslee, architect).

■ **34** The **Lindens**, 2401 Kalorama Road. In this neighborhood of recreated historical styles, the Lindens is an example of the real thing—almost. The Georgian house was built in 1754 in Danvers, Massachusetts, for Marblehead merchant Robert Hooper. The Lindens served as the summer home of Thomas Gage, the last royal governor of Massachusetts, and for this reason is sometimes known as the Gage House. The Robert Hooper mansion was moved to Washington by Mr. and Mrs. George Maurice Morris in 1936. At the time, they were searching for a suitable home for their antiques, and by acquiring the Lindens, the Morrises spared the house from planned destruction. Walter Macomber, resident architect of Williamsburg, directed the disassembly of the building, which was carried out by Williamsburg workmen.

■ **35/36** The **Devore and Stewart Residences**, 2000 and 2030 24th Street, were built for two sisters whose father, Canadian-born Wisconsin lumber magnate Alexander Stewart, had in 1909 built the family's first Washington home at 2200 Massachusetts Avenue NW on the site of the Kalorama estate cemetery. In 1931, 2000 24th Street was built. The architect was New Yorker William L. Bottomley, who has been described as the "master of the old new house," and the Devore residence justifies his reputation. It is a limestone demi-palace in the style of a French hotel of the Louis XV period. In 1961, G. Howland Chase offered 2000 24th Street NW to the US government as a permanent home for the chief justice of the United States, along with an endowment to maintain it. The government refused the gift. A minor scandal erupted in 1982 when

The Lindens

the public learned that the Roman Catholic diocese of Washington planned to buy the home for its bishop. The building was subsequently purchased as a conference reception center for a Christian businessmen's organization. In 1938–39 the other sister built 2030 24th Street NW next door. The architect was Philadelphian Paul Cret. Again, France is the source of the design, although in the Stewart house there is something of a country house inspiration. The stonework and detailing are exquisite throughout.

36 Proceed south on 24th Street and take note of the many embassies along the way. When you reach S Street, you will see to your right the **Robert Emmet statue**, located at the corner of 24th and S Streets near Massachusetts Avenue. Emmet was an Irish revolutionary who looked to America as a guide to his country's independence. The Hon. Victor J. Dowling, chairman of the Emmet Statue Committee, presented this statue by Jerome Connor to the Smithsonian Institution on June 28, 1917, in the presence of President Wilson. It was erected on this site on April 22, 1966, fifty years after the proclamation of Irish independence. The quote on the back of the statue reads: "I wished to procure for my country the guarantee which Washington procured for America. I have parted from everything that was dear to me in this life for country's cause. When my country takes her place among the nations of the earth, then, and not until then, let my epitaph be written."

Woodrow Wilson House

■ **37** The **Woodrow Wilson House**, 2340 S Street (1915, Waddy Wood, architect), was commissioned by Henry B. Fairbanks, who died only three years later. Wilson and his wife Edith purchased the house in 1921 at the end of his presidency. He lived there until his death in 1924. Edith remained in the house until her death in 1961. She had bequeathed the house to the National Trust for Historic Preservation, which, in accordance with Edith's wishes, has been operating it as a house museum since 1964.

■ **38 2310 S Street** (John Russell Pope, architect, 1912) was commissioned by George H. Myers, heir to the Bristol-Myers pharmaceutical fortune. The house at **2320 S Street** (1908, Waddy Wood, architect) was commissioned by Martha S. Tucker. In 1924, Myers founded the **Textile Museum**, which was eventually housed in his mansion and the one next door. In 2011, the museum moved to George Washington University. In 2016, Jeff Bezos purchased both houses for his private use. In 2020, a superb renovation of the former museum was completed by the Washington architectural firm of BarnesVanze.

Adams Morgan

(Grand apartment houses, lively commercial area, ethnically diverse neighborhood)

Anthony Hacsi and Susan Harlem, updated by Stephen O. Santos

Distance: 1¾ miles

Time: 1½ hours

Bus: 42, 43, 96, L2, and the DC Circulator

Metro: Woodley Park-Zoo/Adams Morgan and Dupont Circle (Red Line)

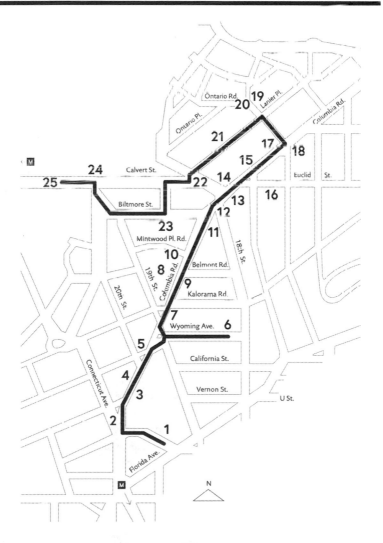

Adams Morgan, an ethnically and economically diverse neighborhood, started as a community for the wealthy. In the 1800s the area was mostly rural. With cool breezes and good views of the city, its location on a hill made it attractive, but before the extension of streetcar service in the 1890s, it was not practical for many to live so far from the city. In about 1900, construction began on large apartment houses and roomy row houses, and most of the buildings now in the area were in place by 1920. What in the 1950s would come to be called Adams Morgan then consisted of handsome subdivisions known as Washington Heights, Lanier Heights, Meridian Hill, and Cliffbourne. For the first half of the twentieth century the area was known for its elegance and its many politically or socially prominent residents.

With the Great Depression and later the World War II housing shortage, the area began to decline. Townhouses were converted to rooming houses, and large apartments were split into smaller units. In the postwar years, middle-class flight to the suburbs was coupled with an increase in lower-income residents. The new people found the area a good place to live but, along with longtime residents, they became concerned about further decline. Although local citizens' organizations had been active since before the turn of the century, cooperation between the racially segregated groups failed, and a new integrated organization was formed in 1955. Taking the names of two elementary schools in the area, the all-white Adams and all-Black Morgan, it was called the Adams-Morgan Better Neighborhood Conference. It marked the beginning of an era of increased neighborhood activism, and it created a new name for the area. An urban-renewal plan that evolved from the citizens' concerns was debated through the early 1960s but was never adopted. It was rejected largely because of fear of the displacement that had resulted from other urban-renewal projects, particularly in Southwest Washington.

During the 1960s Adams Morgan became known as the Hispanic center of Washington. Unlike Latino enclaves in other American cities, Washington's is heterogeneous, with representation from the Caribbean, Mexico, Central America, and South America. At one time a plan was proposed to develop a highly commercial "Latin Quarter" here.

The 1970s saw the arrival of another group of "immigrants"—young, middle-class whites. In a pattern repeated in inner cities across America, they found the close-in, low-cost housing very attractive. With higher demand, widespread renovation, and real estate speculation, prices soared. The displacement of the poor, feared in the 1960s as part of organized urban renewal, has become a reality because of the gentrification that began in the 1970s.

In the 1980s, Hazel Williams operated Hazel's, which featured live blues and jazz, and its soul food offerings made it a favorite of American jazz musician John "Dizzy" Gillespie and American professional boxer and activist Muhammad Ali.

Throughout the 2000s, several developers, including Douglas Development and PN Hoffman, converted warehouse buildings into loft-style condominium units. In 2012, 18th Street NW, one of the neighborhood's main commercial corridors, was reconstructed into a pedestrian-friendly thoroughfare. In 2014, the American Planning Association named Adams Morgan one of the nation's "great neighborhoods," citing its intact row houses, murals, international diversity, and pedestrian and cyclist-friendly streetscape.

■ **1** The **Hepburn**, at 1901 Connecticut Avenue NW, is a twelve-story, 195-unit luxury apartment building designed by architecture firm Beyer Blinder Belle (BBB). The building consists of studio, one-, two-, and three-bedroom apartments. In 2007 developer Lowe Enterprises acquired the Washington Hilton Hotel, one of DC's most important examples of the sculptural expressionist mode of midcentury modern architecture. The developer sought not only to complete a $150 million renovation of the existing hotel designed by William B. Tabler and built in 1965, but it also envisioned adding a new residential condominium tower to the hotel's site in a manner that also responded to the sensitive historic context. The sloped site's irregular shape called for an addition that carefully harmonizes with the geometric quality of the hotel and respects its height and scale. The glass facade is an intentional contrast to the concrete grid-work of the existing structure, while its semicircular form responds to the hotel's double arc, creating two primary open spaces: the interior hotel courtyard to the north and the residential terrace to the south. Rooftop amenities include multiple outdoor terraces and a pool with expansive views, from the Washington Monument to the Rosslyn skyline to the Washington National Cathedral.

The Hepburn sits on the former site of the Oak Lawn estate (1820–1948). This property was owned and greatly expanded in 1873 by Thomas P. Morgan, one half of the eponym of the Adams Morgan neighborhood. Oak Lawn was sought after by developers because of its expansive views of the city. In 1922, the property was sold to a Masonic group with plans to construct a temple complex. However, the project was canceled because of the lack of funds and the Great Depression. In 1940, Frank Lloyd Wright designed a massive, mixed-use project dubbed Crystal Heights, which would have included fourteen towers and a hotel. Wright's design was rejected by the National Capital Planning Commission. The Oak Lawn property was sold in 1945, and there were several unsuccessful plans pitched for the site. It was not until 1962 that developer Percy Uris was approved to build what is now the Washington Hilton Hotel. In 1981, an attempted assassination of President Ronald Reagan took place outside the hotel's front doors.

When developer Lowe Enterprises had finalized the design mimicking the trademark curve of the Washington Hilton's exterior, the 2008 recession hit. The Hepburn was put on hold. In 2010, the project resurfaced, but Lowe

The Hepburn

reassessed the market and concluded that there was no longer a demand for luxury condominiums units, especially since the proposed building would house 195 units. BBB successfully advocated for the hotel's designation as a historic landmark because of the site's history and evolution. The project broke ground in 2014 and was completed in 2016. The Hepburn has achieved rental rates well above any other luxury rental building within the Washington, DC, submarket.

■ **2 Columbia Road** was an Indian footpath before the District of Columbia was established and then an early post road between Georgetown and Baltimore. In the early nineteenth century it was known as Tayloe's Lane, when it led to a popular race track near 14th Street, where Gen. John Tayloe (for whom the Octagon House was built—see Tour 7, Foggy Bottom, no. 21) and others ran their horses. It has always been Adams Morgan's main thoroughfare and has become a major commercial street for the area. As you walk up Columbia Road, to your left is Kalorama Triangle (its other two sides are Connecticut Avenue and Calvert Street—see Tour 15, Kalorama), Adams Morgan's wealthiest section and one that has remained largely white.

■ **3** The **Wyoming**, 2022 Columbia Road NW (1905, 1909, 1911, B. Stanley Simmons). Dwight and Mamie Eisenhower and their son John lived here in apartment 210, and then in 302, from 1927 to 1935. This was their longest stay anywhere except the White House and their farm in Gettysburg. Twenty-four members of Congress and seventy high-ranking military officers have also lived at the Wyoming, and four countries have maintained their legations here. This large apartment house was constructed in three parts: the southern portion in 1905, the northern part and entrance pavilion in 1909 (you can see where the original entrance has been bricked up), and a rear addition in 1911. The monumental entrance pavilion has Corinthian columns and limestone ornamentation (note the lion's head). The original revolving doors were replaced long ago, but the pavilion retains its iron marquee. The lobby features white Italian marble walls and stairways, a tobacco leaf motif in the ceiling moldings, and mosaic tiled floors designed to simulate oriental carpets. The largest of the 106 apartments includes five bedrooms, a parlor, a library, a reception hall, and a trunk room.

Until the Washington Hilton Hotel was constructed in the early 1960s, the Wyoming enjoyed an exceptional view of the city. In 1980 this building and two adjacent apartment houses were threatened by a proposed expansion of the Hilton, but neighborhood groups protested, and the plan was disapproved by the city zoning commission. The Wyoming was converted into condominiums in 1982.

■ **4 2009 Columbia Road NW** (1889, William L. Conley). The oldest building on this tour was designed as a single-family home and used as such until 1947. It was split into apartments and has also been used as a dance studio, an art gallery, and the home for the Greek legation. It has been extensively renovated.

2009 Columbia Road NW

The eclectic design combines classical elements with a homey front porch and Victorian hooded windows. Notice how the first-floor columns and pediment are imitated on the third floor. These classic elements are mixed with Victorian hooded windows.

■ 5   The **Altamont**, 1901 Wyoming Avenue NW (1915–16, Arthur B. Heaton). Col. George Truesdell, a commissioner of the District of Columbia from 1894 to 1897, lived on this property for many years in his mansion, Managasset, before he had the Altamont built. It was designed in the Italian Renaissance style and has a tile roof with twin towers, a loggia, vaulted frescoed ceilings in the entrance halls, an Italian carved stone mantel and fireplace in the reception room, and patterned tile floors in the public hallways. The original tenants were offered an exceptional array of amenities: fireplaces, wallpapered bedrooms, copper cooking utensils, garbage incinerators, sitz baths, some oval and circular rooms, and sweepers in each apartment connected to the vacuum-cleaning plant in the basement. The upper floors contained only three apartments each: one with three rooms plus bath, and two with twelve to thirteen rooms plus five baths and a sleeping porch. Many of the large apartments were divided into smaller and less expensive units during the Great Depression. The seventh floor originally had the Palm Room, a café opening onto the loggia, and additional kitchens for entertaining. These spaces, along with the former billiard room in the basement, have been converted into apartments. The Altamont has been a cooperative since 1949.

The **Adams Elementary School**, the source of half of the name of this community, is located south on 19th Street at California Street. It was named for John Quincy Adams. The former **Morgan Elementary School**, now the Marie Reed School, is at 2200 Champlain Street NW. Thomas P. Morgan was a commissioner of the District of Columbia from 1879 to 1883.

■ 6   **Admiral Peary Residence**, 1831 Wyoming Avenue NW (1913, George N. Ray). Adm. Robert E. Peary, who led the first expedition to reach the North Pole in 1909, bought this house in 1914 and died here on February 20, 1920.

■ 7   The **Kalorama**, 1882 Columbia Road NW (1910, Merrill T. Vaughn; 1913, northern addition, Appleton P. Clark Jr.). To the casual observer it may not be apparent that this building was designed in two stages by two different architects. This is because Appleton Clark's addition has the same scale, wall surface, and roof style as the original. But while Merrill Vaughn's portion has squared corners and many oval and circular windows, Clark's has a rounded corner and only squared windows. Clark also added wrought-iron balconies, decorative carving, and a corner tower. The letter K on the tower refers to the 1913 owner, William Pitt Kellogg, a US representative, senator, and governor of Louisiana. A somewhat incompatible penthouse structure was added in the early 1990s.

■ **8 Kalorama Park**, with its fine old oak trees, is all that remains of the woods and farms that once covered the entire area from Florida Avenue to Rock Creek. In 1828 Anna Maria Thornton, wife of Capitol architect William Thornton, sold two large farms to Christian Hines and his brother, Matthew. They planned to cultivate silkworms on the property and planted a grove of mulberry trees for this purpose. The venture was not successful, however, and the mulberry trees were eventually removed. Members of the Hines family were buried in a plot in an oak grove in the northern section of their land, now the rear of stores at 2440–44 18th Street. The Hines brothers sold their property to John Little in 1836. "Little's Woods," as the area was known, became smaller and smaller as parcels were sold during the next hundred years. This last remaining section was considered for development in the 1940s, but citizen pressure to make it a public park prevailed.

■ **9** The **Norwood**, 1868 Columbia Road NW (1917, Hunter and Bell), was known only by its address until 1974, when the residents voted to name it in honor of longtime resident manager Kathryn M. Norwood. Actress Tallulah Bankhead lived here from 1918 to 1921, when she was a teenager. Her father, William B. Bankhead, was a US representative at the time and later became Speaker of the House. Her grandfather was a US senator while he lived there, from 1918 to 1922. William Edmund Barrett, author of *Lilies of the Field*, lived here in the 1970s. The Norwood's facade is extremely elaborate, with extensive white terra-cotta decoration and an ornate classical portico with flanking entrance lanterns. Above the front columns are ram's heads. Note also the swan's-neck pediment above the third floor, and the brickwork above the fifth floor.

■ **10** The **Woodley**, 1851 Columbia Road NW (1903, Thomas Franklin Schneider). This was the first apartment house on Columbia Road. It was designed and built by Thomas Franklin Schneider, architect of the Cairo (see Tour 14, 16th Street/Meridian Hill, no. 15). Schneider used light brick extensively, to simulate stone. This gives the building a heavy, solid look, reinforced by the massive porte-cochere. There is less stone simulation on the upper floors, where a lighter look was desired. Note the two-story gallery and the highly decorated frieze. On the roof is a cupola, although it is difficult to see from most vantage points. The original six apartments on each floor have been broken up into efficiencies and one-bedroom units and in 1976 were converted into condominiums.

■ **11 Southwest corner, 18th Street and Columbia Road** (Perpetual American Federal Savings and Loan; 1979, Seymour Auerbach). This is the site of the worst natural disaster in Washington's history. On this corner stood the Knickerbocker, an elegant movie palace built by Harry M. Crandall in 1915 as part of his prestigious chain of theaters. The Knickerbocker had a full orchestra,

The Woodley

which played during intermissions, and patrons often attended in formal dress. On the evening of January 28, 1922, during the city's heaviest recorded snowfall, the roof of the Knickerbocker collapsed onto a full house, under the weight of fifty tons of snow. Rescue operations involving the fire and police departments, the Marines, and the Walter Reed Hospital Corps continued through the night, greatly hampered by the snowstorm. The final toll was ninety-seven dead and 127 injured. Although investigations determined that the building contractor had failed to follow the design specifications, architect Reginald Geare, his career ruined, committed suicide five years after the accident. Harry Crandall hired Thomas Lamb to redesign the ruined building, and the Ambassador, another fine movie theater, opened in 1923. It was demolished in 1969 after several years of diminishing business.

The site remained vacant for the next decade. During the 1970s, community groups were successful in preventing the construction of a gas station on this prominent corner. The Perpetual American Federal Savings and Loan was constructed after months of negotiations with citizen groups, who fought for and won the right to community involvement in the bank's loan policies. The building eventually housed a SunTrust Bank and the Latino Liaison Unit of the Metropolitan Police Department. In 2016, the building and plaza area were sold to local developer PN Hoffman, who plans to construct a condominium building on the site.

■ **12** The **intersection of Columbia Road with 18th Street** is considered the heart of Adams Morgan. The community's commercial section began here in the early twentieth century; the 18th and Columbia Road Business Association's businesses opened their first stores near here, including Ridgewells Catering, Dart Drug, Toys R-Us, and the General Store. Eighteenth Street is now a colorful shopping strip, with restaurants, cafes, and shops representing many cultures—Salvadoran, French, Mexican, West African, Jamaican, Italian, Ethiopian. There are also galleries, picture-framing shops, and antiques and second-hand stores. Angle parking has replaced parallel parking here to make room for more cars and to create a more informal atmosphere.

■ **13** **Southeast corner, 18th Street and Columbia Road** (1899 [original structure], Waddy Butler Wood). The architect of the Department of the Interior Building and many large homes in the Kalorama neighborhood, including the Woodrow Wilson house (see Tour 15, Kalorama, no. 37), Waddy Wood designed this building as a single-family residence. Within four years after it was constructed, the commercial potential of this site was exploited by conversion of the first floor into a pharmacy. It continued as a pharmacy until 1969 (from 1922 to 1969 it was a People's Drugstore), and since then it has been a McDonald's. Note the steeply pitched roof with shed dormers.

■ **14** **Northeast corner, Columbia and Adams Mill Roads** (1915, B. Stanley Simmons; 1920 addition, B. Stanley Simmons and Charles S. Holloway). You should have no difficulty here in differentiating between the original building and its addition. The older tapestry-brick section was built to house shops on the ground floor and apartments on the upper floors. The newer section, with its classical facade of limestone and granite, was added as the home of the Northwest Savings Bank. From 1949 to 1969 Gartenhaus Furs was located here. The original bank vault is still in the building and has been used as a tiny auditorium for theatrical productions.

■ **15** **1777 Columbia Road NW** (1928, Frederic B. Pyle). When this neighborhood was a home for wealthy people who entertained, several catering and confectionery establishments in the area served their needs. Avignon Frères, in business since 1918 and at this location beginning in 1928, was the most famous. Although the name implied that the establishment was French, the founders and subsequent owners were from Italy. They catered events for the White House, and the quality of the ice cream attracted the children of presidents to the shop—Margaret Truman and Caroline Kennedy were two. After the riots in 1968, the restaurant part of the operation was closed. Its reopening

The Line DC Hotel

in 1978 was an indication of the area's commercial health, but Avignon Frères closed its doors for good in the 1990s.

■ **16**   The **Line DC Hotel**, at 1770 Euclid Street NW, was originally designed in 1911 by Marsh and Peter with E. D. Ryerson to house the first congregation of the First Church of Christ, Scientist in Washington, DC. The church is perched on a corner site and is a striking example of the City Beautiful Movement. When the congregation outgrew the building, they sought to find a buyer who would preserve the imposing Roman neoclassical building and provide an economic driver for the Adams Morgan neighborhood. From 2011 to 2018, New York–based architecture firm INC Architecture & Design was tasked with transforming a landmark Washington church into a luxury hotel. INC preserved the sixty-foot vaulted sanctuary with massive Diocletian stained-glass windows while providing dynamic spaces offering an all-hours social hub for locals and travelers. The mezzanine overhang creates an intimate space on the ground floor off the lobby, housing an all-day café. A more formal restaurant and bar experience upstairs overlooks the lobby area. The restaurant's open kitchen concept is tucked into a center vault, where the church's pipe organ used to reside. The organ's brass pipes were welded into a magnificent chandelier that hangs centrally from the vaulted ceiling. The Line DC Hotel has become a favorite spot for locals and political figures, including President and First Lady Barack and Michelle Obama, who have been spotted dining at the Line DC Hotel.

■ **17**   **1743–51 Columbia Road NW**. In 1906–7 Harry L. Wardman, the most prolific Washington developer of his time, built six small apartment buildings on this site. They were designed by his chief architect, Albert H. Beers. Wardman named them the Derbyshire, the Hampshire, the Cheshire, the Wilkshire, the

Yorkshire, and the Devonshire. In 1950 they were replaced by a Safeway and a Giant grocery store, side by side. They competed until the Giant closed in 1987.

■ **18 Beverly Court**, 1736 Columbia Road NW (1914–15, Hunter and Bell). For many years artists have lived and worked in this building, with its large and unusual spaces well suited for studios. After the death of Beverly Court's owner in 1977, the tenants formed an association to purchase the building. They became the first tenants group in Washington to finance the rental-to-cooperative conversion through private lending institutions.

■ **19 2809 Ontario Road NW** (1909). Paul Pelz, architect with John L. Smithmeyer of the original Library of Congress building, designed this house for Henry Parker Willis, a secretary of the Federal Reserve Board and a framer of the Federal Reserve Act of 1914. Note the unusual, rounded end walls, the arched dormers and entrance, and the lion's-head rainspout.

■ **20** The **Ontario**, 2853 Ontario Road NW (1903–4 and 1905–6, James G. Hill). Archibald M. McLachlen, founder of Washington's McLachlen National Bank, gave up his home on this property to build the Ontario. Although designed as a whole, it was constructed in two stages: the western portion in 1903–4 and the eastern, larger portion, in 1905–6. The smaller of the two entrance porticoes served as the original entrance. Constructed in a part of Washington that was at the time quite rural, the building had an unobstructed view of nearby Rock Creek Park and the new National Zoological Park.

Some of the Ontario's special features are the decorative keystones above the windows, cast-iron entrance doors and balconies, and a turret crowned by a cupola. Inside, there are brass mailboxes, tile-bordered floors in the lobby and hallways, and rare cast iron staircases with marble stairs. The twenty apartments on each floor range from two to nine rooms, with ten-foot ceilings, gas-burning fireplaces, and extensive wood trim.

Architect Hill, former supervising architect of the Treasury Department, lived here from the time the building opened until he died in 1913. Other notable residents have included Gen. Douglas MacArthur, Sen. Robert LaFollette, Adm. Chester Nimitz, and, more recently, author Nora Ephron and Watergate journalist Carl Bernstein.

■ **21 Engine Company No. 21**, 1763 Lanier Place NW (1908, Appleton P. Clark Jr.). When this site for the firehouse was announced in 1906, some in the neighborhood objected to it, not only because it was on a narrow street in a residential neighborhood, but also because it was not centrally located for its area of service. The justification given was that the only nonresidential street, 18th Street, was on a hill (difficult for the horses), and the price of land there exceeded the appropriation. Another factor in favor of siting the facility here may have been that, from this northern high ground, the horses could run downhill to fires. This stuccoed-brick building looks more like a Spanish mission than a firehouse. The tower was needed for drying hoses, but in this context it looks as if it should house bells. Notice how the design incorporates the rainspouts.

In 1925 the *Washington Evening Star* began an annual competition among fire stations to see which could most quickly get its fire engine out of a station. Engine Company No. 21 set a "world record" of six seconds the following year. Architect Clark lived on this block at no. 1778 from 1905 until his death in 1955. His home has been replaced by condominiums. Al Jolson's parents also lived on Lanier Place, at no. 1787, and the Stafford (1911, Hunter and Bell), at no. 1789, was one of the first two cooperatives in the city.   •

Engine Company No. 21

22 Calvert Street. From Lanier Place you reach Calvert Street (called Cincinnati Street until 1905) where it intersects Adams Mill Road (so-named because it once led to a flour mill owned by John Quincy Adams). The **Beacon**, on the northwest corner of Calvert Street and Adams Mill Road at 1801 Calvert Street NW (1911, J. J. Moebs), makes maximum use of its triangular lot. The **mirror-image duplex** at nos. 1847–49 was designed by Arthur Heaton. Notice how the right facade has been simply painted and the left has fallen into disrepair. At no. 1855, the **Cliffbourne** (1905, N. R. Grimm) has an unusual variety of window heads, while next door at no. 1915, the **Sterling** (1906, Appleton Clark Jr.) has Palladian windows and a loggia on the fourth floor. On the southwest corner of Calvert Street and Cliffbourne Place, **2516 Cliffbourne Place NW** (1901, Waddy Butler Wood) is a charming house with a tile roof, shed dormers, two open porches, and a second-floor balcony.

■ **23 Biltmore Street** is one of Adams Morgan's loveliest residential streets. Named Baltimore Street until 1905, it was once known informally as General's Row because of the many military officers who lived here. Coming from Cliffbourne Place, your first view is of four large row houses, nos. 1848–50–52–54, each with its own distinctive facade. Down to the left is the duplex, nos. 1822–24 (1906, Albert H. Beers). When its building permit application was filed, the question, "Will the roof be flat, pitch, or mansard?" was answered "All kinds." Toward the other end of Biltmore Street, at no. 1940, is the tapestry-brick **Biltmore** (1913, Claughton West) with its balustraded roof and overhanging Italian cornice. Each floor has only four apartments, and each apartment has its own fireplace. The hearths are arranged so that when one pulls a slide, the ashes drop through a metal chute to a bin in the cellar.

Biltmore Street

■ **24 Trolley turnaround.** On this site was a trolley turnaround known for many years as the Rock Creek Loop. Streetcar service, which spurred the development of what is now Adams Morgan, came to the area in September 1892. The first line ran north on 18th Street, then west on Calvert, across the bridge, and north on Connecticut Avenue to Chevy Chase Lake, Maryland. In 1935 the section of the run from here to Chevy Chase was replaced by bus service, and Rock Creek Loop became the end point of the streetcar line. Streetcar service continued here until Washington's last trolleys were replaced by buses on January 28, 1962. Buses now use this loop to turn around, and a small structure from the streetcar days remains.

Another streetcar line began to serve the area in 1897, coming up Columbia Road as far as 18th Street. In 1900 that line was extended east on Columbia, then north on what is now Mt. Pleasant Street to Park Road. It was replaced by bus service in December 1961.

■ **25 Duke Ellington Memorial Bridge** (1934–35, Paul Cret). As a requirement of its streetcar charter, the Rock Creek Railway built a 125-foot-high steel trestle bridge on this site in 1891. In 1911 it became shaky and had to be reinforced and narrowed. Finally, in 1934, construction of a replacement bridge was begun. Traffic here was too important to interrupt, so the old bridge was moved eighty feet downstream to be used as a detour until the new one was completed. To do this, the bridge's footings were put on rollers on top of parallel rails. The bridge was then moved by horse-powered machinery. Auto traffic resumed the same day, and streetcar traffic was interrupted for less than forty-eight hours. The new Calvert Street Bridge, as it was called for many years, was constructed of concrete faced with Indiana limestone. It was renamed in the 1970s for Washington native Edward Kennedy ("Duke") Ellington. The abutments are embellished by Leon Hermant's relief panels representing four modes of travel: ship, train, automobile, and airplane. This bridge has a reputation as the favorite Washington bridge for people seeking to leap to their death. It underwent extensive renovation in the 1980S with the addition of a security fence and railings to discourage suicides.

A pleasant way to end this tour is to stop in for some Middle Eastern food at the nearby Mama Ayesha's Restaurant, 1967 Calvert Street NW, in business here since 1960. On its west exterior wall is a sixty-foot mural depicting the late owner with every president from Dwight Eisenhower to Barack Obama. The work was completed by Karla Rodas ("Karlisima") in 2009.

Woodley Park and the National Zoological Park

(Early twentieth-century apartments, National Zoo, prestigious residential areas, and convention hotel area)

Christopher J. Alleva, updated by Stephen O. Santos

Distance: ½ mile
Time: ¾ hour
Bus: 96 and L2
Metro: Woodley Park-Zoo/Adams Morgan (Red Line)

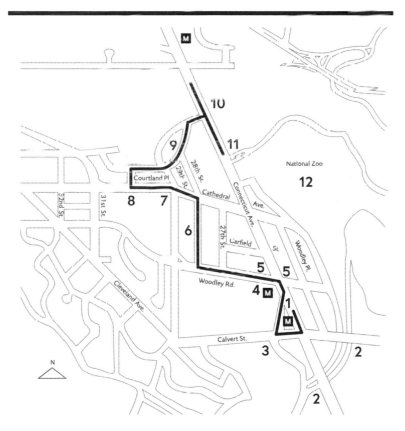

Woodley Park was originally part of a one-thousand-acre tract of hilly, wooded land purchased by Gen. Uriah Forrest shortly after the American Revolution. Around 1800 the general transferred 250 acres to a wealthy Georgetown lawyer named Philip Barton Key, uncle of Francis Scott Key. The house that Key built was known as Woodley House, named after the old bachelor hall in Elizabeth Gaskell's novel, *Cranford*.

Natural topographical borders locate Woodley Park on the peak of land that rises from the valley of Rock Creek, extends northward for a mile, and then slopes downward to a spring branch of the creek. The altitude and cooler summer temperatures made the area a desirable summer retreat from the city during the nineteenth century.

In the 1890s Sen. Francis G. Newlands of Nevada, owner of the Chevy Chase Land Company, purchased Woodley Park. Newlands was also principal owner of the newly chartered Rock Creek Railway of the District of Columbia, a line that would connect Chevy Chase with downtown Washington. Put into operation in 1892, the streetcar route opened the area to suburban development.

This area has two of the largest convention hotels (the Omni Shoreham and the Marriott Wardman Park) in the District of Columbia.

■ 1 As you exit the Woodley Park/Zoo/Adams Morgan Metro station, proceed south along Connecticut Avenue. Reflective of the eclectic residential character of Woodley Park, the shops and restaurants along Connecticut Avenue include everything from the neighborhood drugstore to international haute cuisine. Numerous **sidewalk cafés** provide congenial resting places.

■ 2 The original steel-deck truss bridge crossing Rock Creek Valley at Calvert Street has long since been replaced by the existing concrete structure, now known as the **Duke Ellington Memorial Bridg**e (see Tour 18, Adams Morgan, no. 24). The "million-dollar" **Connecticut Avenue Bridge** opened in 1907. At that time, it was the largest concrete bridge in the world, and its name and presence highlighted the appeal of Woodley Park.

■ 3 Proceed west along Calvert Street. The **Shoreham Hotel**, constructed in 1930 by Harry Bralove, proved a worthy rival to the Wardman Park. It has been said that the Shoreham attracted so many prominent Washingtonians that you could ring a bell there anytime and summon a quorum of senators. Jimi Hendrix stayed at the Shoreham, and he wrote some of the lyrics to his songs on Shoreham stationery during a tour stop in 1968 at the Washington Hilton Ballroom, just south on Connecticut Avenue. Omni Hotels have managed the property since 1980.

West of the hotel is a good example of the reuse of a public school site. The complex includes a public elementary school for the District of Columbia school system and upscale rental apartments, developed by the LCOR, a national mixed-use developer.

■ 4 Proceed north along 24th Street back to Connecticut Avenue. At the corner of Connecticut Avenue and Woodley Road stands the **Wardman Tower**. Harry L. Wardman, the master builder of Woodley Park, constructed the 1,500-room luxury hotel in 1918. Washingtonians called it "Wardman's Folly," little realizing that a hotel in the suburbs could prove so popular. Now primar-

Wardman Tower

ily a residential wing of the larger complex, the tower has served as home to many of the nation's vice presidents and other VIPs. Mihran Mesrobian built the tower portion of the hotel in 1928, now a Category 1 historic landmark The original crescent-shaped main building was demolished in the late 1970s and replaced with the present structure.

5 The **apartment buildings** at 2700 and 2701 Connecticut Avenue NW and the extensive Cathedral Mansions at 3000 Connecticut Avenue NW are also Wardman's work. By constructing reasonably priced houses and apartments along the streetcar line, Wardman converted rural property into comfortable town living.

6 The **Woodley** is an eight-story, 212-unit luxury rental apartment building adjacent to the former Marriott Wardman Park Hotel. The building was developed by JBG and designed by Washington, DC, firm David M. Schwarz Architects in 2014 on the vacant acreage of the Marriott Wardman Park Hotel property purchased by JBG in 2005. The red brick and limestone facade echoes the historic Wardman Tower's architecture as well as the grand apartment buildings along Connecticut Avenue. The building employs a symmetry and reveals eccentricities reminiscent of many traditional apartment buildings where the interior spaces inform window groupings and their arrangement on the facade. Most units include inset balconies or spacious terraces. An exclusive penthouse level defined by symmetrical pavilions and a colonnade expands the available space for entertaining. Upon the building's completion and prior to its lease availability, JBG sold the Woodley for $195 million, or $920,000 per unit, to the Teachers Insurance and Annuity Association of America—College Retirement Equities Fund (TIAA-CREF), which set a record for the highest price-per-unit ever paid for a multifamily project in the Washington, DC, metropolitan area.

The Woodley

■ **7** Turn right onto 28th Street. The **neo-Georgian brick townhouses**, many of which have been modernized to contemporary standards, are characteristic of the Wardman subdivision south of Cathedral Avenue, known as Woodley Park. No longer a suburb, the area is desirable now to old and young alike, offering a variety of lifestyles.

■ **8** Turn left on Cathedral Avenue. Proceeding down Cathedral Avenue away from Connecticut Avenue, you pass **Single Oak**, built in the mid-1920s by Senator Newlands as a residence for a married daughter.

■ **9** High on a hill behind a row of stately oaks stands the elegant **Woodley Mansion**. The white stucco Georgian house served as the summer home of four nineteenth-century presidents, including Van Buren, Tyler, Buchanan, and Cleveland. Henry L. Stimson lived there while serving as secretary of state for President Herbert Hoover and secretary of war for Franklin D. Roosevelt. The building is now owned and operated by the private Maret School.

■ **10** Turn right at the alley and cut through to Courtland Place. Take another right on Courtland Place and proceed past the playground that joins Klingle Valley Park to Devonshire Place. Many of the homes in this mixed residential neighborhood were part of the exclusive Wardman subdivision north of Cathedral Avenue known as **English Village**. The crescent-shaped streets give a picturesque effect.

At the intersection of Connecticut Avenue and Devonshire Place, decide whether you want to see the National Zoo (see this tour, no. 11), to the south. To the north is Cleveland Park (and the nearest Metro station). Or take the Cleveland Park and Washington Cathedral Tour (Tour 20) in reverse.

■ **11** Notice the **Kennedy-Warren** apartment building, 3133 Connecticut Avenue NW, at the east side of Connecticut Avenue where it intersects Devonshire

Kennedy-Warren Apartments

Place. It was built in the early 1930s in art deco style. Notice also the bridge of the same era and style, including eight **bridge lights** that were illuminated until a reconstruction in the late 1970s. An addition to the building's south wing was completed in 2004, adding many new apartments to the complex. Prior to the construction of the convention hotels in the area, this complex hosted many events in its glorious ballroom.

■ 12. At the crest of the hill is the entrance to the **National Zoological Park**, a Smithsonian facility. Designed by the famous landscape architect Frederick Law Olmsted, the world-renowned, 175-acre zoo exhibits over three thousand animals of more than eight hundred species and subspecies, many of them rare and not exhibited elsewhere in the country. The Smithsonian's National Zoo is open every day of the year except December 25. Exhibits and most concessions are open daily, 10:00 a.m.–6:00 p.m., April to October, and daily 10:00 a.m.–4:30 p.m. November to March. Admission to the National Zoo is free. More information can be found at www.nationalzoo.si.edu or by calling 202-633-4888.

Cleveland Park and Washington National Cathedral

(Turn-of-the-century residences; Gothic cathedral)

Charity Vanderbilt Davidson, updated by John J. Protopappas and Stephen O. Santos

Distance: 2 miles
Time: 2¼ hours
Bus: 31, 32, 96, and H4
Metro: Cleveland Park (Red Line)

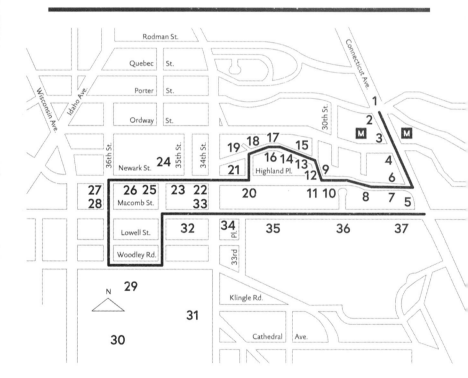

Cleveland Park is significant as a neighborhood with a strong sense of community and distinctive architecture. With its tree-lined streets, brick sidewalks, and large frame houses, it has successfully retained much of its late nineteenth- and early twentieth-century atmosphere. Many of the architectural styles that gained popularity in the late nineteenth century are represented in Cleveland Park's houses.

Cleveland Park and the close of the Washington National Cathedral (officially known as the Cathedral Church of Saint Peter and Saint Paul) were originally part of about twelve thousand acres purchased around 1790 by Georgetown merchants Benjamin Stoddert (who was also the first secretary of the navy) and Gen. Uriah Forrest (former mayor of Georgetown, friend of George Washington, and representative from Maryland to the US Congress). Forrest bought Stoddert's share in the property and in 1794 moved with his family to the house he built and named Rosedale after his ancestral home in England. The area remained rural until the late 1880s, when it became a fashionable retreat from Washington's hot, humid summers. Wealthy Washingtonians, including President Grover Cleveland (from whom the area derived its name after he established his summer White House at Oak View in 1886), built large, rambling summer "cottages," of which Twin Oaks is the sole surviving example.

In 1892 streetcar service began on Connecticut Avenue, connecting Chevy Chase to the city center. Cleveland Park was one of the chief beneficiaries and quickly became a desirable area for year-round residence. Housing starts mushroomed in the years between 1894 and 1920. The Cleveland Park Company, formed in the early 1890s with John Sherman as its president, was responsible for the most varied and interesting houses in this "streetcar suburb." Sherman was an enlightened developer who hired local architects to design his houses and provided certain amenities (a streetcar waiting lodge, stables, and a fire station), to make Cleveland Park life more attractive to his prospective residents. The residential development of Cleveland Park was virtually complete by 1920. At that time, residential and commercial development along Connecticut and Wisconsin Avenues intensified to provide services for the residents, who previously had ridden the streetcar into the city to purchase all their provisions.

Cleveland Park has remained a popular in-town residential area with a touch of rural atmosphere because of the preserved open space. Its residents consistently have been professionals including lawyers, high-level government officials, academicians, and journalists.

▪ **1 Cleveland Park Metro station** opened in December 1981. Accessible from both sides of Connecticut Avenue NW, it is among the deepest stations in the Metrorail system. After ascending the long escalator, walk north to Porter Street NW.

▪ **2 Firehouse No. 28** is on the west side of Connecticut Avenue. It opened December 1, 1916, making it the second building on this strip of Connecticut Avenue. Snowden Ashford, who was appointed the first municipal architect in 1909, designed it. This was a progressive fire station when it opened, with motorized equipment replacing the less-efficient horse-drawn engines. Notice the handsome stone arches and angle quoins as well as the red brick with white trim, especially the central swan's-neck pediment with a pineapple as a centerpiece. All are details of the Georgian-revival style, recalling the early plantation houses along the James River. After viewing the fire station, walk south on Connecticut Avenue. The renovated shopping center on the east side of Connecticut Avenue was one of the first shopping centers in Washington built to accommodate the automobile.

■ **3 3520 Connecticut Avenue NW** (apartment building, 1919); **3500–18 Connecticut Avenue NW** (unified series of townhouses, 1920). These were the first residences to be built along this stretch of Connecticut Avenue. Harry L. Wardman built them before he built the Wardman Tower in Woodley Park. The first and second floors of many of the townhouses along this street have been converted to restaurants and retail shops.

■ **4** The **Uptown Theater** joined the commercial strip in 1936, providing a new kind of entertainment. Notice the art deco details: decorative features in stone and brick, etched glass, and the marquee with its decorative use of lights and color. It hosted the world premieres of such movies as *2001: A Space Odyssey* and *Jurassic Park*. The theater closed permanently in March 2020. The theater's screen was the largest commercial movie theater screen in the Washington metropolitan area. Negotiations with Landmark Theaters to lease and reopen the theater are in the works.

■ **5 Cleveland Park Public Library** (3310 Connecticut Ave. NW) is a strikingly stylish public building designed in 2018 by Perkins Eastman. This site was designated in 1898 by John Sherman to be the location of an architect-designed stone-and-stucco lodge in which early residents could wait for the streetcar in warmth and comfort; it was also used for community meetings and activities. The lodge was largely destroyed by fire in about 1910 and was not rebuilt.

A limestone tower marks the building's entry as well as a civic gateway at the southern edge of the neighborhood. Large bay windows along the main commercial street on Connecticut Avenue provide views of active, vibrant spaces to draw patrons into the library. The interior layout is fitted out with spaces large and small that provide framed views of the historic community. The Cleveland Park Library ranks in the top three heaviest trafficked and circulating libraries in the district. The library provides a civic presence and embraces the character of its location serving as a focal point for the community. Turn west and walk up Newark Street.

■ **6 2941 Newark Street NW** (1898, Robert Head). A local architect, Robert Head designed at least seventeen houses that were built in Cleveland Park from 1897 to 1901 in styles ranging from the informal Queen Anne, which this house represents, to the more formal Georgian-revival. Notice the turret, the tall, ribbed chimney that joins the two distinct parts of the house, the variety of roof forms and window shapes, and the first use by Head of the rope-dipped-in-plaster motif on a gable on the west side of the house.

■ **7** **2940 Newark Street NW** (1903, John Sherman, architect-developer) This was one of the first houses built by the Cleveland Park Company after John Sherman had ceased employing architects. The change probably was the result of the imminent bankruptcy of Thomas Waggaman, who appears to have been the primary landholder and financial backer. This house was at one time home to the famous Arctic explorer Adm. Robert E. Peary.

■ **8** **2960 Newark Street** NW (1899, Robert Head). This Georgian-revival house was the residence of Oscar T. Crosby, who founded PEPCO, the local electrical power company in the District of Columbia and Maryland, in 1896. Notice that the house serves as a visual focal point as you ascend the hill. Also note the classical details.

■ **9** **3035 Newark Street NW** (1898, Robert Head). This magnificent Queen Anne–style house has a commanding view of the city. Notice the twisted columns and sun ray motif on the porch, the swags in the frieze area, the varied roof forms (including a central, bell-shaped turret), and the window forms (including leaded and stained-glass windows).

■ **10** **3038 and 3042 Newark Street** (1903, John Sherman). Notice the use of rope dipped in plaster and applied over the entrance of no. 3042 as a decorative motif.

■ **11** **3100 Newark Street NW** (1897, Waddy Butler Wood). Notice the varied windows, including an eyebrow window in the roof, and the decorative effects achieved by the cut shingles and the rope dipped in plaster in the arched shape above one window.

■ **12** **3121 Newark Street NW** (1903, Ella Bennett Sherman). Notice the two oriel windows on the east side of the house, the rope-dipped-in-plaster motif, and the handsome brackets supporting the central third-story balcony. The designer was the wife of John Sherman, the developer of Cleveland Park. Turn around and retrace your steps to Highland Place, where you turn left.

■ **13** **3100 Highland Place NW** (1896, Frederic Bennett Pyle). Notice the Palladian window in the dormer, the elliptical oculus window by the front door, and the varied shape of the porch, including a porte cochere.

■ **14** **3138 and 3140 Highland Place NW** (1901, Robert Head). These are two of the last houses designed by Head. They exhibit a Japanese influence in the sticklike brackets under the overhanging eaves and in the gentle upward flare of the roof on the central dormer of no. 3140.

■ **15** **3141 and 3155 Highland Place NW** (1895–96, Robert I. Fleming). These "twin houses" were the first to appear on Highland Place. They were built on the unsubdivided portion of Cleveland Park, which was still considered to

3100 Highland Place NW

be agricultural land. The irregular course of Highland Place seems to derive from a property line. No. 3155 is significant as the home and first office for the brothers W. C. and A. N. Miller, who formed their real estate company as very young men just after their father died. W. C. & A. N. Miller is still an active real estate development firm in Washington today.

16 3154 Highland Place NW (remodeled 1905, William H. Dyer). This early house has received its distinctive appearance through successive renovations. Early photographs show it as a simple frame house until the shingled pagoda-style porch was added in 1906, and then it was further modified in 1916, when the red tiles you see today replaced the shingles.

17 3209 Highland Place NW (1906, Hunter and Bell). This was the first brick house built in Cleveland Park. Notice the formality and symmetry of this Georgian-revival house and the use of darkly glazed bricks similar to those found in Williamsburg.

18 3225 Highland Place NW (1898, Robert Head). This represents Head's first attempt at a Georgian-revival house, with the Ionic columns on the porch and the Palladian window motif on the side. Once again, the house has a commanding presence on the street.

19 3301 Highland Place NW (1912, B. F. Meyers for W. C. and A. N. Miller). This is one of the earliest houses constructed by W. C. and A. N. Miller. They employed B. F. Meyers to design many of their early Cleveland Park houses. They are representative of the second wave of developers active in Cleveland Park after the demise of the Cleveland Park Company in 1909. Turn left at 33rd Place and walk to Newark Street.

■ **20 3300 Newark Street NW**. This house was built in 1920 on the site originally occupied by a frame building that housed the chemical fire engine and
the police office. The Cleveland Park Company provided these in 1901 for the
comfort and safety of the early residents.

■ **21 3301 Newark Street NW** (1895, Pelz and Carlyle). This modified Italian
villa–style residence was the first house built on the east side of 34th Street.
Pelz (one of the architects of the Library of Congress) and his partner, Carlyle,
were the first architects hired by John Sherman. The site of this house marks
the beginning of the subdivided area of Cleveland Park, which was laid out in
1894 in a regular grid pattern from Wisconsin Avenue to 33rd Place on Newark
Street. The area you have just walked through was unsubdivided agricultural
land; consequently, the developer or prospective owners determined the large,
irregularly shaped lots, and the curvilinear streets owe their charming character to property lines and the natural contours of the land. You will notice
the increased regularity of lot sizes during the remainder of your tour. Cross
34th Street with extreme caution and continue on Newark Street.

■ **22 3410 Newark Street NW** (1895, Pelz and Carlyle). Notice the tower rising
out of the west side of the house as you walk by. Look back to catch a glimpse
of the Palladian window beside the tower, which lights the landing on the
stairs.

■ **23 3418 Newark Street NW** (1982, Sam Dunn). This house is sensitively
designed of wood to match the traditional building materials of the neighborhood. Architect Sam Dunn said he wanted to create a "1982 Cleveland Park
house" with a creative flair of its own.

■ **24 Rosedale, 3501 Newark Street NW** (1794). This eight-acre tract is all that
remains of the large acreage Gen. Uriah Forrest originally owned in the 1790s.
It can be entered from the drive near the corner of Newark and 36th Streets. A
stone building on the property (referred to as the "old kitchen") is believed to
have been built in 1740; Forrest built the weatherboard farmhouse, typical of
the eighteenth century, about 1794. The Forrests made this their permanent
residence, and George Washington is believed to have been a guest at Rosedale
while the new capital city was being built. Pierre L'Enfant, also a personal
friend, is rumored to have helped design the original gardens.

In 1796–97 Forrest mortgaged Rosedale (420 acres and the house) to obtain
a loan from Maryland so that the new government could complete construction of the Capitol. Forrest then lost most of his money when the Greenleaf
real estate syndicate collapsed in 1797. His brother-in-law, Philip Barton Key,
who built the Woodley Mansion, bailed him out by buying all of this land at
auction, paying off the mortgage, and then dividing the land into generous
parcels, which he sold. He conveyed the farmhouse and 126 acres to Mrs. Uriah
Forrest, who was the sister of Key's wife.

Rosedale remained in the family until 1920, when Avery Coonley, a Chicago philanthropist, and his wife purchased it. Frank Lloyd Wright visited his former clients at Rosedale and is reported to have proclaimed it "honest architecture."

In 1959 the Coonleys' daughter and her husband, Waldron Faulkner, sold the house and eight acres to the National Cathedral School for Girls. The brick buildings that now surround the farmhouse (1968, Waldron Faulkner) were intended as dormitories and faculty housing for the school. The Rosedale Conservancy uses the modern buildings for its offices and classrooms while preserving and restoring the nineteenth-century farmhouse. Architect Winthrop Faulkner designed the three white brick townhouses on 36th Street at the entrance to Rosedale.

■ **25 3512 Newark Street NW** (1895, Pelz and Carlyle). Notice the Palladian window on the side of the house as you approach it, and then look back as you walk by to see the oriel on the west side of the house, which rises and has its own terminating roof form.

■ **26** The **stone wall** that you encounter just after passing 3518 Newark Street NW, with its distinctive Hugh Newell Jacobsen renovation, is all that remains of Grover Cleveland's summer home, Oak View. In 1886 President Cleveland purchased an 1868 stone farmhouse and hired architect William M. Poindexter to wrap fanciful wooden Victorian porches around it, giving it a totally new appearance. This was to become the summer White House for the president and his new bride, the handsome young Frances Folsom, who was the daughter of his former law partner. This set a precedent for the area; prominent Washingtonians followed his example and established summer homes nearby. Cleveland's home deteriorated and was razed in 1927 to make way for the present brick house, built the same year for a descendant of Robert E. Lee. The stones from Cleveland's house were used to build this wall.

■ **27 3320 36th Street NW**, stable for 3601 Macomb Street (1900, Sherman and Sonneman). You will pass on your right a most interesting Palladian window motif, which replaced the large opening in the upper story of the stable that had provided easy access for the storage of hay for the horses. The former stable, built out of Rock Creek granite, makes a very attractive little house.

■ **28** At this point you can continue south on 36th Street to reach the Washington National Cathedral (see no. 29), or you can turn west on Macomb Street to reach Wisconsin Avenue, where you will find restaurants and public transportation. To continue the walking tour of Cleveland Park, turn west on Macomb Street and begin to descend the hill. Most of the **houses in the next two blocks** were not built until the second decade of the twentieth century, when developer Charles Taylor was at work with architect R. G. Moore.

Washington National Cathedral

■ **29** The **Washington National Cathedral**. Late in 1891, a group of Washingtonians interested in planning a cathedral in the city met at the home of Charles Carroll Glover, a prominent local banker and the prime mover in an effort to establish Rock Creek Park. Two years later, in 1893, Congress chartered the Protestant Episcopal Cathedral Foundation to oversee the construction and operation of such a cathedral and to carry out an educational program. Mount Saint Alban, rising above the flatlands of the city, was selected as the site, and in 1906 Bishop Henry Yates Satterlee and the Cathedral Foundation decided on the Gothic design submitted by George Frederick Bodley, England's leading Anglican church architect. Henry Vaughan, a prominent American proponent of the neo-Gothic style, was selected as the supervising architect. More than twenty thousand people attended the laying of the foundation stone in 1907. The Bethlehem Chapel, opened in 1912, was the first section completed. Construction was halted during World War I and was resumed in 1922, under the supervision of Philip Hubert Frohman, of Frohman, Robb and Little.

Frohman, the cathedral architect for more than fifty years, modified the original design of the nave and the central tower. The choir, apse, and north transept were opened in 1932, the south transept in 1962, and the 301-foot Gloria in Excelsis tower (with its magnificent carillon and ring of bells) in 1964. The west front (Frederick Hart, sculptor) was dedicated in 1982. The west tower was completed in 1990. It is the sixth largest cathedral in the world, offering worship, concerts, tours, gardens, views from the towers, magnificent stained glass, carvings, dramatic architecture, a gift shop, and more. The cathedral sustained damage to several pinnacles and flying buttresses in the Virginia earthquake of August 2011. It reopened to the public in November 2011, at which time the full building repair was estimated to take ten years.

The Pilgrim Observation Gallery, high above the west facade, is open Monday through Saturday from 10:00 a.m. to 3:15 p.m. (admission charged) and offers a panoramic view of the city and suburbs. The cathedral itself can be entered from the north or south transepts or from the west end.

The Cathedral Foundation conducts guided tours of the interior. Call 202-537-6200 or go to www.nationalcathedral.org for information.

Leave the cathedral by the south transept or the west front and follow the stone wall to the entrance to the Bishop's Garden.

■ 30 The **Bishop's Garden** (1928–32, landscape design, Mrs. G. C. F. Bratenahl). Turn right through the Norman arch. The Bishop's Garden consists of several gardens, including a rose garden and a medieval herb garden, connected by boxwood-lined, stone-paved walkways. With its pools and ivy-covered gazebo, it is among the city's most pleasant and peaceful places.

Return to the main roadway and continue east to the Pilgrim Steps and the equestrian statue of George Washington (Herbert Haseltine, sculptor). Those wishing to explore the woodland path should descend the steps and cross Pilgrim Road.

■ 31 **Woodland Path**. This curvilinear walk, maintained by local garden clubs, leads to Saint Alban's School or to a lower section of Pilgrim Road. The branch to Pilgrim Road includes a large wooden footbridge (1961, Walter Dodd Ramberg); the bridge is noteworthy for its composition, the size of its members, and its overall character. Cross the footbridge to Pilgrim Road and then walk south on Pilgrim Road to Garfield Street, adjacent to the Saint Alban's soccer and tennis facilities.

The low, modern building (1964, Faulkner, Kingsbury & Stenhouse) is Beauvoir, the cathedral elementary school (founded in 1933). Other structures on the western end of the close include buildings for administration, the College of Preachers, the Cathedral Library, and canons' housing (all 1924–29, Frohman, Robb & Little).

Retrace your steps past the south transept entrance and Pilgrim Steps and walk west toward Wisconsin Avenue. The Herb Cottage on your left, one of the earliest buildings on the close, was originally built to house the cathedral's baptistery; it is now closed. Continue around to the left and notice the panorama of Washington stretching before you from the Peace Cross (dedicated in 1898). The buildings in this section of the close house the Saint Alban's

School for Boys (founded in 1903) and Saint Alban's Parish (consecrated in 1855; substantially altered in the early 1920s).

You can leave the close via Wisconsin Avenue or Massachusetts Avenue, both of which are served by major bus routes, or return to the Cleveland Park tour, using the entrance at 36th Street.

■ **32 3426 Macomb Street NW** (1897, Samuel Arthur Swindells). This little house, set so far back from the street, is the oldest house on Macomb Street and represents the cottage style popularized by Andrew Jackson Downing. Notice the change in the sidewalk at this point as you leave the early subdivision of Oak View and enter Cleveland Heights (Macomb and Lowell Streets from this point to 33rd Place). This house stood alone for almost twenty years before W. C. and A. N. Miller and George Small built some neighboring houses in Cleveland Heights.

■ **33 Macomb Playground** appeared on the real estate maps as early as 1937. In 1954 the neighborhood mothers raised $1,000 in one week to pay for trees and sod to beautify the playground.

■ **34 John Eaton School** (1911, west wing, Appleton P. Clark Jr.; 1923, east wing, Arthur B. Heaton) As you cross 34th Street, you are looking at the rear of the school, which opened in 1911. From here you can see the oldest wing, with the entry from the playground marked for boys and the tall chimney designed by Heaton. The school and the community particularly appreciate the landscaped playground. In 2021, the school underwent a major renovation by razing the 1930s and 1980s buildings to accommodate a three-story addition between the east and west wings designed by Cox Graae and Spack Architects.

■ **35 Twin Oaks** (1888, Francis Richmond Allen). 3200 Macomb Street NW (rear entrance); 3225 Woodley Road NW (main entrance). This is the only remaining example of a house designed to be a summer home located in the Cleveland Park area. Twin Oaks is an extremely early example of a Colonial-(Georgian-) revival house—perhaps the earliest one surviving in the United States. It bears a close resemblance to McKim, Mead and White's H. A. C. Taylor House of Newport, Rhode Island, of 1886 (demolished in 1952). Gardiner Greene Hubbard, a Bostonian, hired architect Francis Richmond Allen from his native city to design his summer home, which resembles the large, rambling New England frame seaside summer houses. Hubbard was the founder of the National Geographic Society and also was the chief financial backer for Alexander Graham Bell, a partnership that made possible the establishment of worldwide telephone service.

Twin Oaks remained in the possession of this family until it was sold in 1947 to the Republic of China. It then became the residence of the Chinese ambassador. In 1978, with the US recognition of the People's Republic of China, Twin

Oaks became the property of the Friends of Free China. Today it serves as the Taipei economic and cultural representative's residence. It is private property and therefore not open to the public, but the house, its wooded site, and the rolling lawns are visible from the lower ends of both driveways.

■ **36 Tregaron (formerly the Causeway)**, 3100 Macomb Street NW (original rear entrance); 3029 Klingle Road NW (original main entrance). The entire estate, including buildings and grounds, is a Category 3 landmark. This twenty-acre portion of Gardiner Greene Hubbard's fifty-acre estate was sold in 1911 by Alexander Graham Bell to James Parmelee, an Ohio financier. Charles Adams Platt, who was then the nation's foremost country house architect, designed the estate in 1912. Landscape architect Ellen Biddle Shipman assisted him. Platt's brick neo-Georgian mansion sits on the crest of the hill, surrounded by sloping meadows and landscaped rustic woodland areas, including bridle paths. The property was acquired by Joseph E. Davies (ambassador to the Soviet Union from 1934 to 1938) and his wife, Marjorie Merriweather Post. It was renamed Tregaron after the ancestral home of Davies's mother in Wales. Davies, who occupied the house until his death in 1958, added the Russian dacha (cottage).

In 1980 the property was sold and divided into two parcels. The six acres at the top of the hill, which include all the present buildings, belong to the Washington International School, which has established its middle and upper schools on the site. The remaining fourteen acres were purchased by the Tregaron Limited Partnership, which applied for permission to construct 120 townhouses that would have wrapped around the existing mansion on three sides. In 2006 the partnership agreed to donate thirteen of their fourteen acres to the new Tregaron Conservancy, which maintains them as open green space. The property is open all days of the week from 8:00 a.m. to 8:00 p.m.

Tregaron Estate

■ **37** As you complete your tour of Cleveland Park by walking down Macomb Street to Connecticut Avenue, you will be passing through the final phase of development completed by the Cleveland Park Company between the years 1905 and 1909. Notice **3031 Macomb Street NW**, at the corner of Ross Place, with its Palladian window decorated with a fan shape in the arch and motif of rope dipped in plaster. This house, with its large arch set in the main gable of the house, is repeated at **2929 Macomb Street NW**. You may also enter it from Newark Street. As you approach Connecticut Avenue you can probably pick out the other Sherman frame houses with their expansive porches, flaring roof eaves, and commanding positions above the street. You will also walk past the location of the **Cleveland Park Stable** (2932 Macomb Street NW). If you turn north, you can return to the Cleveland Park Metro station.

LeDroit Park

(Historic African American residential area, Howard University,
Howard Theater)

Maybelle Taylor Bennett, updated by William J. Bonstra

Distance: 1½ miles
Time: 1½ hours
Bus: 90, 92, G2 and G8
Metro: Shaw/Howard University (Green Line)
See also: LeDroit Park | Bloomingdale Heritage Trail

LeDroit Park is a Category 2 landmark of the District of Columbia and is listed
on the National Register of Historic Places. It is a small, unified subdivision
built during the 1870s that has been, since its inception, inextricably linked
with Howard University. Upon the resignation of his trusteeship at Howard
University, Amzi L. Barber purchased forty acres of land owned by the university (later to become known as LeDroit Park, named for Barber's father-
in-law and realtor, LeDroit Langdon) on a $115,000 promissory note without
a down payment between 1872 and 1873. The new subdivision first appeared
on the map in 1873, and in 1874 the university accepted $95,000 in full pay-
ment of the note. By 1877, forty-one new houses had been erected, all of them
designed by well-known architect James McGill. In time, more than sixty

detached and semidetached homes were designed by McGill in the Calvert Vaux cottage tradition. The area, which was adjacent to the boundaries of Washington when built, was advertised as offering the advantages of city living with the open space of the country. No fences were erected between the homes, although the entire area changed in the 1880s and 1890s as developers sold the remaining land within the district for the erection of row houses. An additional change occurred near the turn of the century as the area became a predominantly African American community, upon the removal of racially restrictive covenants.

For many years the area has been the home of prominent Black citizens. Located adjacent to Howard University and the Howard Theatre, two nationally significant Black educational and cultural centers, the neighborhood has served as an important cultural and political center for the entire District of Columbia. Indeed, it was once considered the area's hub for the Black intelligentsia and boasted renowned Black poets, statesmen, attorneys, jurists, educators, artists, politicians, clergy, scientists, and medical professionals.

Today, LeDroit Park retains much of the same scale and character and most of the architecture that it had at the turn of the century. Many of the original detached houses scattered among the slightly later brick-and-frame row houses are still standing. The row houses, constructed in the late 1880s and 1890s, are primarily low-rise brick structures with fine terra-cotta and decorative brickwork. They have roof lines frequently accented with turrets, towers, pedimented gables, and iron cresting that combine to provide a varied and rhythmic pattern to the streets. Many of the detached and row houses retain decorative ironwork fences and balustrades. Unique in the District of Columbia are the twisted porch columns found in the row houses on 3rd Street near the Anna J. Cooper Circle.

More important, the area has undergone a renaissance catalyzed largely by substantial investments by Howard University, Fannie Mae, and the Fannie Mae Foundation in the rehabilitation of existing row houses, the infill new construction of single-family row homes, and the upgraded infrastructure. This revitalization effort was part of a larger redevelopment scheme called the "LeDroit Park Initiative," which involved extensive housing, infrastructure, commercial, and cultural district improvements as well.

Together with other nonprofit housing developers and private property owners, the area is experiencing an increase in units being upgraded and occupied after decades of decline that began in the 1960s and continued through the 1970s and 1980s. New households include families of Howard University employees, community members who are returning to the city from the Washington suburbs, and first-time homebuyers in the area. The income diversity of the existing neighborhood has been supported through the purposeful efforts of Howard University, Fannie Mae, and the District of Columbia, whose partnership has resulted in moderated prices for new and rehabilitated housing, below-market mortgage interest financing, down payment and closing cost assistance, and substantial housing counseling efforts. To complement the new housing development and rehabilitation activities, the District of Columbia Department of Public Works and the US Department of Transportation provided support for ongoing infrastructure upgrades that are evident throughout the neighborhood. Note the improved brick sidewalks, trees, streetlights, and the resurfaced streets and alleys.

No visit to LeDroit Park would be complete without a walk through the campus of Howard University, which is located to the immediate north of the LeDroit Park neighborhood. Georgia Avenue runs almost through the center of the university and is the commercial hub of the campus.

Howard University is a private research university comprising fourteen schools and colleges. The university provides educational services and training to over fifteen thousand students from across the nation and approximately 109 countries and territories. Their varied customs, cultures, and dress give the university an international character. It is a research-oriented university founded in 1867 by members of the First Congregational Society of Washington and named for Gen. Oliver Otis Howard, head of the Freedmen's Bureau. Its mission was to provide an institution that would welcome all students, including freed men and women, and today it provides an educational experience of exceptional quality to students of high academic potential, with a particular emphasis on providing educational opportunities to promising Black students. Howard produces more on-campus African American PhD recipients than any other university in the United States. The university's eighty-nine-acre main campus contains dormitories, administrative offices, classroom buildings, the athletic complex, libraries, the Howard Hospital complex, radio and television broadcasting facilities, a chapel, theater, art gallery, and several auditoriums.

Many of the buildings are historic landmarks, and two of them represent the university's signature architectural style. Douglass Hall, built in 1936, and Founders Library, built in 1937, were designed by renowned architect Albert Cassell. The university's campus was planned by Cassell as well, with extensive terracing and landscaping designed circa 1935 by a prominent African American landscape architect, David Williston.

The Shaw/Howard University Metro station is at 7th and T Streets NW, approximately three blocks from the LeDroit Park neighborhood. Exit from the station's north entrance and walk north to Florida Avenue; turn right and walk one block north to T Street NW; walk east to 2nd Street. You may also take a Metro bus along Georgia Avenue to the Howard University campus. Enter the campus "quad" and walk two blocks south to T Street; proceed east to 2nd Street. The tour begins at the intersection of 2nd and T Streets NW. Visitors will walk west along T Street, which is LeDroit Park's main street. Second Street was formerly known as LeDroit Avenue, and T Street was formerly called Maple Avenue. Former street names are posted on all of the street signs.

■ **1 201 T Street NW**. This was the home of Dr. Anna J. Cooper, who was born enslaved, graduated from Oberlin College in 1884, and came to Washington to teach in the public high school for Blacks on M Street NW. She received an honorary master's degree from Oberlin and served as principal for the M Street High School from 1901 to 1906, where she became involved in the now-classic controversy between Booker T. Washington and W. E. B. DuBois as it related to the appropriate educational curriculum necessary to uplift the Negro race. She believed "colored" children needed a classical academic education and manual arts education, both of which were offered in the high school. This viewpoint got her in trouble with Booker T. Washington, a champion of the manual arts education for "colored children," and the white school board in Washington, DC, whose members were alleged to have used their influence to dismiss her from her post. She later returned to the high school to teach, and she earned her doctorate from the Sorbonne in Paris in 1925 at the age of sixty-seven, where, in the French language, she examined French attitudes toward slavery during the French Revolution. In 1906, Anna J. Cooper and Dr. Jesse Lawson founded the Frelinghuysen University to provide evening education classes for employed Blacks. When the university needed a permanent home, Dr. Cooper donated her house, which remained the location of the school until it closed in the early 1960s. Dr. Cooper lived to be 105 years of age.

■ **2 200 block of T Street NW** In this block of T Street lived A. Kiger Savoy, assistant superintendent of colored schools; Dan Monroe, an auditor at the Government Accounting Office; and Geneva Perry, a community activist, a musician who played at the Howard Theater, and the editor of a LeDroit Park community newspaper.

■ **3 Anna J. Cooper Circle, at 3rd (formerly known as Harewood Avenue) and T Streets NW**. In many ways, this circle is the spiritual heart of the LeDroit Park community. The developers of LeDroit Park were responsible not only for the architecture and the landscaping of the subdivision but also for designing the streets and sidewalks (which remained in private hands until 1901). The circle was part of the original street pattern, although the rationale for it is not entirely clear. The circle has been redesigned and landscaped to resemble its original appearance.

One of the early advertisements for the park referred to Harewood Avenue as a projected main thoroughfare for trolleys from the city out to the Soldiers' Home farther north. Early maps, however, show that this throughway did not develop, and that 3rd Street terminated just above Elm Street. It may be that the designers wished to imitate the L'Enfant plan with its monumental circles. Indeed, we know that the houses envisioned for Harewood Avenue were to be the most lavish and the most expensive in the park. The original vista of 3rd Street was quite different from the present view since most of the McGill

houses have disappeared. Despite this change, the circle remains a strong iden-
tification and orientation point for LeDroit Park and has been the focal point
of neighborhood celebrations and Christmas caroling. Although the street has
retained its relatively low scale, the openness and sense of "refined elegance"
envisioned by the developers has been compromised by later construction and
the disappearance of the bucolic setting with large open lawns surrounding
McGill mansions. The dormitory and apartment house on the east, the row
houses on the west, and the elementary school at the end of the street create
a more urban streetscape as one looks north along 3rd Street from the circle.

■ **4 1901–1903 3rd Street NW, at the northeast corner of 3rd and T**. The large
white-and-gray house on the northeast corner of the circle is a McGill-designed
house and belonged to Gen. William M. Birney and Arthur Birney. It is virtually unchanged from its original state. Continue walking west on T Street
beyond the circle.

1901–1903 3rd Street NW

■ **5 326 T Street NW**. This house, also referred to by some as the "half-house,"
was once the home of Mary Church Terrell and Judge Robert Terrell. The other
half of the house, which was burned in a fire and demolished, once belonged
to Mrs. Terrell's brother, Robert Church. Their father, Robert Reed Church, a
wealthy Tennessee native, purchased the two homes for his son and daughter.
He was once thought to be the first Black millionaire in the United States. This
house at 326 T Street is the only building in the LeDroit Park neighborhood
that is listed on the National Register of Historic Places. Mary Church Terrell
was a woman of great importance to the Black community, active in both the

women's suffrage movement and the Civil Rights movement. She was the first Black woman appointed to the District of Columbia Board of Education. In 1953, at the age of eighty-nine, Mrs. Terrell participated in lunch counter sit-ins that helped to desegregate public facilities in the District of Columbia. Her husband, Judge Robert Terrell, a Harvard-educated attorney, was the first Black municipal judge in Washington and served for a time as the principal of the M Street School. This house is being restored by architect Ronnie McGhee and Monarc Construction through the African American Civil Rights Grant Program.

■ **6 330 T Street NW**. This was once the home of Fountain Peyton, one of the first sixteen Black attorneys listed in the 1894 Union League directory as practicing in Washington, DC. Peyton was a graduate of Howard University Law School. This residence is the home of Frank and Windy Carson Smith. Frank Smith was a civil rights activist, former council member for Ward 1 in the District of Columbia, and founder of the African American Civil War Memorial and Museum.

■ **7 Vista, 4th Street (formerly known as Linden Street) NW**. The only north–south thoroughfare in LeDroit Park that was aligned with the street pattern to the north, 4th Street was the first area to be subdivided. For years, 4th Street accommodated rush hour traffic by permitting two lanes of traffic to flow south to employment centers in Washington in the morning, and two lanes to flow north away from those centers to residential neighborhoods and the suburbs in the evenings. With the revitalization that was taking place in LeDroit Park, area residents prevailed upon the Department of Public Works to reduce the volume of traffic that flowed along this street through the elimination of the reversible lane that accommodated rush-hour traffic. Continue walking west on T Street across 4th Street to the 400 block of T Street.

■ **8 400 T Street NW**. This was the home of the family of civil rights activist and former presidential candidate Jesse Jackson.

■ **9 405 T Street NW**. Professor Alonzo Brown, a professor of mathematics at Howard University, once lived at this location.

■ **10 408–410 T Street NW**. Washington's first elected mayor, Walter Washington, lived here until his death in October 2003. Washington was a graduate of Howard University, was active in the New Negro Alliance, and became the head of the National Capital Housing Authority. Mayor Washington helped to set the stage for the development of Metrorail in the nation's capital, championed housing for lower-income residents of the District of Columbia, and ushered the city through the difficult years after riots had devastated many city neighborhoods. The home was the former family home of Washington's first wife, Bennetta Bullock Washington, daughter of the Rev.

George O. Bullock, a prominent minister, pastor of Third Baptist Church, and social worker. Bennetta Bullock was educated at Dunbar High School and Howard University and later became principal of Cardozo High School and the director of the US Women's Job Corps. At the time of this writing, a renovation of the home was in process.

■ 11 **412 T Street NW**. This was the former home of Dr. Ernest E. Just, professor of zoology at Howard University for over thirty years, renowned biologist, and author of a classic biology text, *The Biology of the Cell Surface*. Dr. Just's portrait was placed on a Black Heritage US postage stamp.

■ 12 **418 Street NW**. Dr. Hattie Riggs, a Black educator from Calais, Maine, who taught at the M Street High School, lived at this location. Although Dr. Riggs earned her medical degree, she never practiced medicine.

■ 13 **420 T Street NW**. Professor Nelson Weatherless, early advocate of equal rights, educator, and activist, once lived at this location. Dr. Bernard Richardson, dean of the Howard University Chapel, also lived there with his family.

Continue walking west along T Street, crossing 5th Street (formerly known as Larch Street) to the 500 block of T Street NW.

■ 14 **504 T Street NW**. The first Black officer to die in World War I, Maj. James E. Walker, lived at this address, as did the principal of Armstrong High School, Capt. Arthur Newman. Captain Newman's wife, Jennie, and Major Walker's wife were sisters.

■ 15 **506 T Street NW**. This was the home of Roscoe I. Vaughn, who was an architect and head of the Manual Training Department of the District of Columbia schools.

■ 16 **517 T Street NW**. Another good example of McGill's work, this finely detailed home has been well preserved.

■ 17 **525 T Street NW**. McGill also designed this home, complete with stable, and it is one of the finest remaining homes in the historic district.

■ 18 The **Howard Theater**, just across Florida Avenue from the neighborhood at 620 T Street, was built in 1910. It was the first theater built exclusively for African American entertainers and audiences, who, because public facilities were segregated, were unable to go to theaters patronized by whites.

The Howard Theatre anchored the eastern end of what was then known as the "Old Black Broadway," a stretch of theaters, lounges, restaurants, and other social and entertainment venues patronized by both Blacks and whites. The LeDroit Park community provided accommodation for many of the entertainers who performed at the theater, which, along with the Apollo in New York,

517 T Street NW

the Uptown in Philadelphia, the Royal in Baltimore, and the Regal in Chicago, was the stage on which many of the more prominent Black entertainers in the past half century made their debuts. The Howard Theatre played a very important role in the development and promotion of Black talent. It not only hosted famous singers, big bands, dancers, and comedians but also introduced new talent through its amateur-night contests.

Winners of these contests included Ella Fitzgerald, Billy Eckstein, and Bill "Ink Spots" Kenny. The Howard was host to stars such as Pearl Bailey, Sarah Vaughan, Lena Horne, Sammy Davis Jr., Billie Holiday, and Dick Gregory. In the 1950s and 1960s, it showcased rock and roll music and the Motown sound. The Platters, Gladys Knight and the Pips, Smokey Robinson and the Miracles, James Brown, the Temptations, and the Supremes (who made their first stage appearance at the Howard) all appeared at this theater.

Early alterations stripped the building of its classical detailing and brick facade. Windows were covered with a layer of stucco, and the portico was replaced with a streamlined marquee. The building was further altered in 1941 and 1974 and closed in the early 1980s. Renovation efforts include an adaptive reuse as a six-hundred-seat multipurpose, contemporary performing arts facility that accommodates patrons in a mixture of fixed and flexible seating.

To make the theater more versatile and economically sustainable, the architects excavated a 10,300-square-foot basement to house a new 2,700-square-foot kitchen to cater to the theater's full-service dining menu and events such as weekly gospel brunches with the Harlem Gospel Choir and other special functions geared to the needs of entertainment that will be performing at the venue.

Turn north on 6th Street (formerly known as Juniper Street): Dr. Eva B. Dykes was one of the first Black women to receive a PhD. She lived on 6th Street NW.

Walk north one block on 6th Street to the 500 and 600 blocks of U Street (formerly known as Spruce Street).

To the west along the U Street corridor are examples of the redevelopment that is redefining the area and making it one of the city's most desirable neighborhoods. Although a tour is not included in this publication, the ten-block area is easy to negotiate on foot and is highly recommended if time for a tour permits. The corridor has attracted new residential condominiums and retail shops as well as extensive restoration. Near the easternmost entrance to the U Street/Cardozo Metro station, at U Street and Vermont Avenue NW, is a memorial park dedicated to African Americans who served in the Civil War. A four-story office building, with retail uses at street level, surrounds the westernmost entrance to the station at 13th and U Streets NW. To the north of the station are the historic Ben's Chili Bowl Restaurant, the restored Lincoln Theatre, along with a number of recently constructed apartment buildings and condominiums housing bars and restaurants.

■ **19 600 and 500 blocks of U Street NW**. Howard University and LeDroit Park have traditionally had a close relationship. Amzi L. Barber, one of LeDroit Park's developers, came to Washington to head the Normal Department at Howard, later serving as trustee and acting president of the university. Faculty members, administrators, and students have always lived and worked in the area. The renaissance taking place in the area has continued this tradition. The twelve newly constructed and nine rehabilitated homes on the north side of U Street were completed during the first phase of the LeDroit Park Initiative. Two-thirds of these homes were sold to and occupied by Howard University employees, with the other one-third occupied by municipal employees and area residents. The backdrop of the hospital serves as a visual reminder of the town-gown interface and the importance of developing harmonious relationships between the university and the community.

■ **20 621–607 and 529 U Street NW.** These are homes that have been renovated as part of the LeDroit Park Initiative. All have been sold to Howard University employees. Distinctive address plates identify these homes as part of the LeDroit Park Initiative.

■ **21 605, 603, 601 U Street NW; 535, 527, 525, 523, 521, 519, 517, 515, and 515½ U Street NW.** These newer homes were designed by a number of talented architects and constructed on lots owned by the university and were sold to community residents and Howard University employees. Distinctive address plates identify these homes as part of the original LeDroit Park Initiative.

■ **22 512 U Street NW.** Willis Richardson, dramatist of the Harlem Renaissance and the first African American to have a serious play produced on a Broadway stage, lived in a house once sited here. Richardson was educated at the M Street High School. The Ethiopian Art Players in Chicago, Washington, and New York performed his *Chip Woman's Fortune*. *The Broken Banjo* (1925) and *Bootblack Lover* (1926) were awarded the Amy Spingarn Prize.

Walk east on U Street to 5th Street.

At the northern terminus of 5th Street and visible from the intersection of 5th and U Streets is the historic **Freedmen's Hospital building**, which is now Howard University's John H. Johnson School of Communications building.

Continue to walk east along U Street to the 400 block.

■ **23 400 block of U Street NW.** This is the only remaining block in LeDroit Park that is original to the 1870s development and contains no intrusions. James McGill designed all of the houses in this block.

400 block of U Street

■ **24 419 U Street NW.** Oscar De Priest lived here while serving in Congress. When elected in 1928, De Priest was the first Black to serve in Congress since 1901.

■ **25 417 U Street NW**. This was the home of Percy A. Roy, craftsman, artisan, and manual arts instructor at the District of Columbia's Armstrong High School. His flower garden was highly acclaimed and photographed in the now-defunct *Evening Star* newspaper.

■ **26 414 U Street NW**. Clara Taliaferro, a pharmacist and daughter of John Henry Smyth, lived at this address. Smyth was an attorney and graduate of Howard University's first law school class in 1871. In 1878, President Rutherford B. Hayes called upon Smyth to serve as minister and consul to Liberia in recognition of his work for the Republican Party in the 1876 election. He served in this capacity until 1885.

■ **27 406 U Street NW**. This was once the home of Garnet C. Wilkinson, who was a graduate of the M Street High School, Oberlin College, and Howard University Law School. Wilkinson served as assistant superintendent of colored schools for thirty years until 1954 and then as assistant superintendent of the District of Columbia's integrated school system.

■ **28 402 U Street NW**. James M. Carter, professor of English at Howard University, and his family lived at this location.
      Continue walking east along U Street, crossing 4th Street to the 300 block of U Street.

■ **29 300 block of U Street**. The northern side of this block was redeveloped in the late 1990s by Manna, a nonprofit housing developer, with single-family row houses for first-time homebuyers. One of the founders of the first Black citizens' association, William Cochran, lived at 315 U Street. Next door at 317 U Street is the former residence of Theresa Brown, the first African American founder of a historic preservation society in Washington, DC, the LeDroit Park Preservation Society. She was instrumental in securing local and national historic designation for LeDroit Park and participated in the review of plans for the renewal of the area.

■ **30 338 U Street NW**. This was the home of Octavius Williams, a barber at the US Capitol, who bought this home in 1893 and was one of the first Blacks to buy a home in the area once the racially restrictive covenants were removed.

■ **31 321 U Street NW**. While the current 321 U Street address is part of the redevelopment sponsored by Manna in 1996–97, the original home with that address is where the renowned poet Paul Laurence Dunbar moved with his wife, Alice (also a poet), after their marriage.

■ **32 320 U Street NW**. Julia West Hamilton, civic leader and president of the Phillis Wheatley YWCA for twenty-eight years, lived at this location. She was the first woman president of the board of trustees of the Metropolitan AME Church, where she served for twenty-eight years, and she served as treasurer of the predominantly white Women's Relief Corps Auxiliary of the Grand Army of the Republic. She was also a member of the National Association of Colored Women and the National Council of Negro Women.

■ **33 319 U Street NW**. Maj. Christian A. Fleetwood and wife Sara lived at this location. Fleetwood was a Civil War hero and Medal of Honor soldier. His wife was the first Black superintendent of nurses at Freedmen's Hospital.

At the end of the 300 Block of U Street, turn north onto 3rd Street and walk to north Elm Street. Note the straight-on view of Slowe Hall Apartments, formerly Howard University's Slowe Hall Dormitory.

■ **34 Vista looking east on Elm Street**. See the Gage Eckington Elementary School, built in 1977 at the northern end of 3rd Street, and the Former Gage School at the end of Elm on 2nd Street. Also, in view on the north side of Elm Streets is Carver Hall Apartments, a former Howard University dormitory located at 211 Elm Street NW. This building was built in 1942 to house male Black government workers and was acquired in 1948 by Howard University to provide off-campus housing for male students. The former dormitory is named after George Washington Carver. The building was sold to a private developer in 2018 and renovated as market rate apartments by Bonstra | Haresign Architects in 2020.

■ **35 1915 3rd Street NW**. The former site of the Lucy Diggs Slowe Hall, a Howard University dormitory, named after the first dean of women at Howard University. The present building was constructed in 1942 to house single female Black government workers and was acquired by Howard University in 1948 to provide off-campus housing for female students. Along with Carver Hall, the Slowe building was sold to a private developer and renovated as market rate apartments by Bonstra | Haresign Architects in 2020.

The Slowe Hall site was originally the location of James McGill's home. McGill enjoyed a brief but prolific architectural career. At the age of nineteen, he joined the office of Henry R. Searle, a Washington architect, and during the next six years he rose from draftsman to architect. He opened his own office in 1872 and was soon associated with Amzi L. Barber, former trustee and acting president of Howard University in the development of LeDroit Park. In addition to the homes in LeDroit Park, he designed sixty other homes, five churches, two markets, a roller-skating rink, and four major office buildings, including the LeDroit Building, still a downtown Washington landmark. He moved out of the LeDroit Building in 1881, advertising both as an architect and a building supply salesman. He left architecture altogether the next year, and for the next twenty-five years ran a prosperous building supply business.

■ **36 1915 3rd Street NW**. Also, at the site where Slowe Hall Apartments now stands was once the residence of one of the best-known Black surgeons of the day, Dr. Simeon Carson. Dr. Carson had a private hospital in the 1800 block of 4th Street.

Also on 3rd Street was the house (now demolished) of Amzi L. Barber, the builder of most of the McGill-designed houses in LeDroit Park. Amzi L. Barber, like his father, was trained for the ministry at Oberlin College. He came to Washington in 1868 to head the Normal Department at Howard University. He was later elected to a professorship of natural history and, at age twenty-nine, was appointed acting president of Howard University. He left the university to spend full time developing the LeDroit community. His business interests included the building and management of the LeDroit Building in the 900 block of F Street NW and other real estate interests. During the 1880s, he developed homes in Columbia Heights, north and west of LeDroit Park, constructing Belmont, which he rented to Melville Fuller, chief justice of the United States. Barber's major interest changed in the mid-1880s to the Barber Asphalt Paving Company, which made him a wealthy man.

■ **37 1938 3rd Street NW**. This house was the boyhood home of Edward W. Brooke, who was educated at Dunbar High School, Howard University, and Boston University Law School. He was the first African American elected to statewide office in Massachusetts (attorney general, 1962). In 1963 Brooke was elected to the US Senate and served in that capacity until 1979. Brooke grew up in this house, and his family moved to Brookland while he was a student at Howard. His father, Edward Brooke II, was an attorney with the Veterans Administration for fifty years.

■ **38 1910 3rd Street NW**. A McGill-designed house, this is the former residence of J. J. Albright, a prominent Washington businessman and a dealer in coal.

Walk north again to Elm Street, turn west on Elm Street, and walk through the 300 block of Elm Street to the intersection of 4th and Elm. Look to the south on 4th Street.

■ **39 1934 4th Street NW**. This was the bachelor home of Paul Laurence Dunbar, where he stayed when he was working at the Library of Congress. Look to the north on 4th Street.

■ **40 2030, 2034, 2038 4th Street NW**. These homes were completely renovated and sold to Howard University employees as part of the LeDroit Park Initiative. The distinctive address plates identify these homes. Since the rehabilitation of these homes, all of the older homes on the west side of this block have been upgraded.

Walk west on Elm Street to 5th, turn north on 5th Street, and walk one block to the 400 block of Oakdale Place. Walk east on Oakdale Place for one block to 4th Street.

■ **41 2035 2nd Street NW, Parker Flats at Gage School**. The Gage School was dedicated on February 15, 1903, in honor of Nathaniel Parker Gage, a former supervising principal. Designed by architect Lemuel Norris and built in 1904, Gage School served the surrounding community as it grew. The historic landmark, abandoned for more than thirty years, was owned by Howard University and sold to a local developer in 2004. The historic school was converted into unique market-rate residential condominiums along with the addition of two new residential buildings with underground parking, all designed by Bonstra | Haresign Architects. Howard University professors and staff were given preferred pricing as part of the sale arrangement.

■ **42 422 Oakdale Place NW.** Lillie Robinson, a baker and longtime resident of Oakdale Place, lived at this location with her husband, Thomas Boyd Robinson. The two moved to Oakdale Place in the 1950s, at first living in an apartment building that was demolished prior to the construction of the Howard-owned parking lot on the north side of Oakdale Place. The couple subsequently moved into 422 and lived there for several decades. Before he passed away, Thomas Boyd told Lillie not to move, no matter how much she was encouraged to do so as other neighbors sold their properties to the university. She resolved to stay in place long after all of the other homes on the block had been purchased and vacated. However, Robinson, who died in 2001 at the age of eighty-five, lived long enough to see the entire block rehabilitated and to greet her new neighbors. She declined the university's offer to have her own home rehabilitated at no cost to herself, because her husband had paneled their home throughout and she did not want that evidence of his hard work and love demolished.

Vista on 4th Street at Oakdale Place NW. Looking east into the 300 block of Oakdale at the intersection of 4th and Oakdale, you can see a three-story apartment building, part of the Kelly Miller Public Housing development.

The Kelly Miller Development, which extends two blocks behind this building toward the north and east, was named for Dr. Kelly Miller, a prominent professor at Howard University who introduced the first social work curriculum to the campus. He later became dean at the university and lived in a home along 4th Street that has been demolished.

Walk south along 4th Street to the 1800 block.

■ **43 1839 4th Street NW.** This McGill home built in 1837, still in excellent condition, is the home of the former president of the LeDroit Park Civic Association. Another former president of the civic association resides across the street from this home in one of the row houses that was later developed in the area. Both neighborhood leaders were instrumental in obtaining resident consensus around the nature and quality of the redevelopment that Howard University and Fannie Mae were implementing in the area.

At Florida Avenue and 4th Street NW, walk east on Florida Avenue for a few feet. See the vista to the north and east of the intersection along Rhode Island Avenue and the large building on the north side of the street.

■ **44 301 Rhode Island Avenue NW.** This expansive property was once the site of the residence of David McClelland, one of the original owners and developers of LeDroit Park. The Elks Lodge later used the site, which eventually became the location of a Safeway grocery store.

Turning back west and right to Florida Avenue, proceed west along Florida Avenue NW. Florida Avenue was once an arterial that housed numerous Black businesses and physicians' offices. Many of the physicians ran their practices out of their homes; they included Ralph Wright, Sidney Sumby, Edmund Wilson, Clarence Tignor, and Algernon Jackson. Dr. Leo Williams opened the first Black pharmacy on Florida Avenue NW.

■ **45 455 Florida Avenue NW.** This was once the location of the popular Harrison's Café, which was owned and operated by Robert Harrison.

■ **46 463 Florida Avenue NW.** Educator, dentist, artist, and author Dr. John E. Washington lived at this location. He wrote a book titled *They Knew Lincoln*. His wife, Virgie, was a pharmacist and social worker.

■ **47 511 Florida Avenue NW.** Dr. Ionia Whipper, who sheltered unwed girls here in her home, was a descendant of William Whipper, a newspaper editor and an early advocate of nonviolent resistance.

Old Anacostia

(Black residential area, late nineteenth-century buildings, Anacostia
Community Museum)

Ryan Harris and Alvin R. McNeal

Distance: 1½ miles
Time: ¾ hour
Bus: 92, B2, and V2
Metro: Anacostia (Green Line)

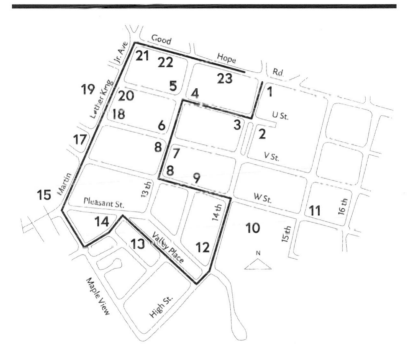

Incorporated in 1854 as one of Washington's earliest residential subdivisions,
Old Anacostia retains considerable historical, architectural, and environmental
appeal. The area had evolved from an ancient settlement of the Nacotchtank
("Nacostine") Indians into rich farmland. By the latter half of the nineteenth
century, a subdivision called Uniontown developed into a working-class neighborhood and encompassed other minor subdivisions. Though the composition
of its residents has changed over the years, many of its social and physical
resources endure and continue to influence the community. Old Anacostia
derives its distinctive sense of place from its rolling area, its views to downtown

Washington, the charm and human scale of its buildings, as well as an appealing neighborhood environment.

Old Anacostia has a positive and readily identifiable character. The cohesive quality is apparent in the physical evidence of a pleasant and remarkably intact low-density, late nineteenth-century neighborhood. Unfortunately, the neighborhood has become quite distressed over the years, and many boarded-up buildings and trash-strewn lots exist.

The Smithsonian's **Anacostia Community Museum** is located at 1901 Fort Place SE; it is a neighborhood landmark that should not be missed. The museum is open daily 11:00 a.m.–4:00 p.m. except December 25. Admission is free. More information can be found at www.anacostia.si.edu or by calling (202) 633-4820.

■ **1** The tour begins at **14th Street and Good Hope Road**. Old Anacostia first began to develop as a residential community after 1854, when John W. Van Hook and two other men purchased 240 acres of farmland from the Chichester Tract for development into a residential subdivision. The original grid of streets laid out by the Union Land Association has survived to the present day and is framed by Good Hope Road to the north, 15th Street to the east, W Street to the south, and Martin Luther King Jr. Avenue to the west. Known initially as Uniontown, the development was aimed at the middle-class employees of the nearby Washington Navy Yard across the Anacostia River.

■ **2** At 14th Street between U and V Streets is the striking **Old Market Square**, a block long and forty feet wide. It was part of the original layout for Uniontown and was the prime focal point of the community.

■ **3** The belfry of **Saint Philip the Evangelist Episcopal Church** provides an interesting visual reference along the square.

■ **4** The houses at **1312 and 1342 U Street SE** represent two of the early dwellings still remaining. No. 1312 features an elaborate bracket cornice, window pediments, and a handsome cubical cupola. This striking residence stands in pronounced contrast to the later houses around it.

■ **5** Though deteriorated, the houses at 1230–50 U Street SE, called **"Roses Row,"** are potentially handsome. Their form and detail are remarkably well integrated. The architectural character of Old Anacostia is in many ways unique when compared to that of other communities in the Washington area. Nowhere else does there exist such a homogeneous collection of late nineteenth-century small-scale frame and brick buildings. The pleasant environment of Old Anacostia is less the product of outstanding architecture than the result of average buildings working together with remarkable success to create a cohesive and expressive whole.

■ **6** The Victorian Gothic is represented by two churches at diagonally opposite corners of V and 13th Streets. **Saint Teresa of Avila Catholic Church** was designed by E. Francis Baldwin, partner in the Baltimore firm of Baldwin and Pennington, and was built by Isaac Beers in 1879. A stucco building of simple form, the church is embellished by a large rose window on the front facade, decorated with a simple circular tracery.

■ **7** **Delaware Avenue Baptist Church** (formerly Emmanuel Episcopal Church) is more irregular in form. Erected in 1891, the building employs rustic stonework with varied brown tones. Its highly picturesque massing adds considerably to the building. The massive corner belfry, with its tall spire and spreading eaves, makes the church one of the most prominent visual landmarks in Old Anacostia.

Delaware Avenue Baptist Church

■ **8** A walk along **13th Street between V and W Streets** shows an attractive streetscape with its canopy of trees, row of brick duplexes set off by white frame porches and iron fences, and picturesque churches and churchyards. The exteriors of the frame houses in Old Anacostia were embellished, often interchangeably, with varying degrees of cottage-style, Italianate, or mansard details of the period. The decoration of these buildings was simplified from that of the more elaborate brick townhouses built elsewhere in Washington at this time. Yet these small houses, with their repetitive rhythm of regularly spaced porches, windows, and doors, succeeded in achieving great expressiveness and neighborhood homogeneity. These buildings provided the setting for lively and interesting streetscapes and a community environment of great pride and appeal.

■ **9** The duplex at **1310–12 W Street SE** is an example of the prevalent worker's cottage built after the turn of the century. Notice the rooflines, which reinforce a strong geometrical appearance.

■ **10 Cedar Hill**, 14th and W Streets, built about 1855, was the home of Frederick Douglass, a runaway slave, abolitionist, orator, writer, civil servant, and diplomat, from 1877 until his death in 1895. The handsome brick house, with its commanding view of Washington, is listed in the National Register of Historic Places. The National Park Service restored the property in the 1970s and added a museum/visitors center. This earth-covered visitors center provides an unobtrusive architectural counterpoint to the commanding presence of the Cedar Hill mansion. Cedar Hill and the visitors center are open to the public, although the hours vary by season. Tickets are necessary to tour the mansion. More information can be found at www.nps.gov/frdo or by calling 202-426-5961.

Cedar Hill

■ **11** From the front of the Douglass home, notice the Queen Anne **house at 15th and W Streets**, built between 1887 and 1894.

■ **12** The house at **2217 14th Street SE** was remodeled with the assistance of the National Housing Services, as was the house at 1342 Valley Place SE.

■ **13/14/15** An interesting walk down **Valley Place and Mount View Place** will take you back to Martin Luther King Jr. Avenue.

16 If you are traveling by car, stop at Our Lady of Perpetual Help School, 1600 Morris Road SE. It offers one of the most sought-after **views of Washington** west of the Anacostia River. From 1854, what are now called Martin Luther King Jr. Avenue and Good Hope Road were earmarked for commercial development. The first establishments, which included the legendary Duvall's Tavern and George Pyle's grocery, were located at the intersection of these two streets. However, the two thoroughfares have not developed as envisioned. Today, many vacant structures abut the frontages.

17/18 Two later additions include an interesting **art deco building** at 2022 Martin Luther King Jr. Avenue SE and the colossal chair of the old Curtis Brothers furniture store. The chair is a neighborhood landmark.

19 The first home of the Anacostia Bank, **2021 Martin Luther King Jr. Avenue SE**, was built between 1903 and 1913 and is a marvelous expression of the Georgian-revival mode.

20 The monumental building at **Martin Luther King Jr. Avenue and U Street** is an example of neoclassical style and was built between 1913 and 1927 as the second home of the Anacostia Bank. This building presently houses a branch of PNC Bank.

21 Three storefronts at **1918–22 Martin Luther King Jr. Avenue SE** highlight a new treatment of commercial buildings that appeared between 1936 and 1943. Notice the pediments over each store. The unit at no. 1922 retains evidence of the original window-sash panels, revealing the richness of the initial composition.

22 Several two-story commercial buildings, such as **1227 Good Hope Road SE**, have been converted to residences. Though it was heavily modified on the first floor, the upper portion of the building remains substantially intact, revealing handsomely proportioned brick detailing in the corners and arches crowning the windows.

Notoriety was brought to Good Hope Road in 1865, when John Wilkes Booth used it as an escape route after he assassinated President Lincoln.

Although new structures have been built in Old Anacostia over the past decade, the commercial area has been subject to changes of varying scope, sometimes as minor as an addition of updated and often tasteless signs, at other times as major as the replacement of existing buildings with new ones. Many of the new buildings, unfortunately, are unarticulated structures that add nothing positive either to the streetscape or to the community. Some of them at least make an effort to maintain the scale and setback of the surrounding buildings.

23 The **Verizon Building**, one of the newer additions to the area, cuts a hole in the residential block of U Street.

Georgetown—West and Waterfront

(Historical residential district, new mixed-use infill developments, shops and restaurants, C&O Canal, Potomac River waterfront, Georgetown University)

James Troy, updated by Ralph Cunningham

Distance: 2½ miles

Time: 1½ hours

Bus: 31, 33, 38B, D2, D6, G2, and the DC Circulator

Metro: Foggy Bottom/GWU (Blue, Orange, and Silver Lines)

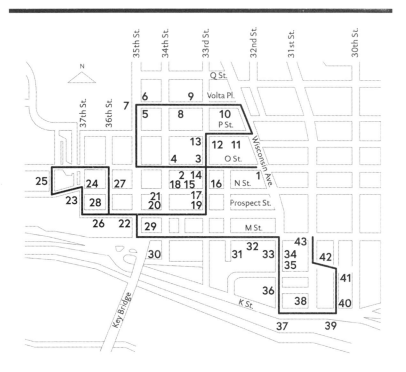

In 1751 the Maryland Assembly founded what it called Georgetown and drew up a plat for the land south of present-day N Street, to the river. However, there is evidence that a grant of land, comprising what is now known as Georgetown, was awarded much earlier to Ninian Beall in 1703. In the 1740s, tobacco from nearby Maryland growers was being inspected, crated, and shipped from warehouses along the Potomac River at Georgetown. Then, in 1791, Georgetown was included in the area selected by President Washington to be the seat of government. Work had already started on the Chesapeake and Ohio (C&O) Canal, much farther west, in 1785 even though this important artery was not completed through Georgetown itself until the 1830s.

By the beginning of the nineteenth century, the people who were successful in commerce and government were building their fine residences in the area north of N Street. (Dumbarton Oaks and Evermay were built in 1801, and more modest but handsome Federal houses still standing in the 3300 block, the 3100 block, and the 2800 block of N Street were built in the period between 1813 and 1820.)

Georgetown declined in importance as a major tobacco port in the early part of the nineteenth century, as steam navigation made deeper ports more desirable. In 1871 Georgetown was joined with the City of Washington and became part of the District of Columbia. For the next fifty years it was not the fashionable place to live that it is today, but speculators continued to add Victorian row houses next to formal Federal mansions, in their gardens or on subdivided land, and Georgetown took on its urban village character. Bounded by Georgetown University on the west; Rock Creek on the east; large houses along R and S Streets as well as Montrose Park, Dumbarton Oaks, and Oak Hill Cemetery on the north; and the Potomac River on the south, Georgetown today has grown within its "borders." Because of its proximity to downtown, its village and pedestrian scale, the beauty of its neighborhood streets filled with historic houses of all sizes, and its convenient shopping area, it is at the top of the list of desirable places in Washington in which to live.

Georgetown today is an urban, cosmopolitan neighborhood of contrasts. On relatively quiet, tree-shaded residential streets with brick sidewalks, fine old Federal homes with walled gardens are set next to Victorian workers' houses only twelve to fourteen feet wide. Entrances and setbacks vary; facades, doors, and trim are painted in subtle colors to blend with the architecture and neighboring houses. Montrose Park and Dumbarton Oaks on the north offer landscaped breathing space, as does the peaceful C&O Canal on the south, edged with a brick path for strollers and galleries, shops, and historic houses. Along the commercial streets of Wisconsin Avenue and M Street, on the other hand, there is continual bustling activity. Restaurants of all nationalities, shops, vendors, and movie theaters vie for attention from pedestrians on crowded sidewalks.

Within this historic neighborhood, the battle of preservation and compatible development is never ending. As new shops, hotels, townhouses, and apartments have been added on old parking lots, former gas station sites, and subdivided large lots, and as the waterfront has been developed, traffic congestion and citizen concern have become increasingly intense. There is no Metro stop in the area, although there is Metrobus service along the major thoroughfares.

The Old Georgetown Act, passed by Congress in 1950, defined the historic district, which was added to the National Register of Historic Places as a National Landmark in 1967. The Old Georgetown Act also calls for Commission of Fine Arts review of all new development and of exterior modifications to existing developments. In most cases, the review has helped to maintain a harmony of materials, architecture, and scale and has restrained commercialism.

With the redevelopment of the waterfront, the area below M Street is now densely developed with townhouses, apartments, restaurants, shops, and offices. It is as if a new community has been added to the old, yet Georgetown continues to hold its charm and to be one of the most fascinating parts of Washington.

Take the Foggy Bottom Metrorail and then walk west along Pennsylvania Avenue across Rock Creek Park or take the DC Circulator bus to Wisconsin Avenue and O Street.

■ **1** The tour of Georgetown begins at Wisconsin and O Streets NW, in the heart of the commercial area. Take a few steps down O Street to **Saint John's Episcopal Church** (1809) at the corner of O and Potomac Streets. This lovely old church is attributed to William Thornton, the original architect of the Capitol, and of Tudor Place in Georgetown and the Octagon House, headquarters for the American Architectural Foundation. Like the Capitol, this church has undergone many modifications. Thornton was a friend of Presidents Washington, Jefferson, Adams, Madison, and Monroe. Notice the old trolley tracks and brick street, a reminder of earlier days—and a way to slow the traffic moving through the neighborhood.

Saint John's Episcopal Church

■ **2** At 3322 O Street NW, the **Bodisco House** (1822) is a fine example of the Federal style of architecture. Notice the graceful wrought-iron stair rails, the elliptical fan-shaped window over the front door, and the slender sidelights. In the mid-nineteenth century, the house was the elegant home of the Russian minister to the United States. In the 1930s, in the midst of the Depression, it was converted into ten apartments. Now beautifully restored, it was home to Sen. John Heinz of Pennsylvania until his death in 1991.

■ **3/4** At **3325 O Street NW**, across the street from the Bodisco House, is a projecting-bay, conical-roofed Queen Anne row house. Built in the 1890s for about $3,500, it is one of many houses of this type in Georgetown and in other Washington neighborhoods. At **3331 O Street** is a Georgian-revival house with a mansard roof. Note the elaborate entry and the broken pediment.

■ **5** At 35th Street, turn right, noticing no. 1404, built about 1800. **1525 35th Street NW** was a home of Alexander Graham Bell's parents.

■ **6** On the opposite side of the street, across from the Georgetown Visitation School (1537 35th Street NW) is the **Volta Bureau** (1893). Alexander Graham Bell used his prize money for inventing the telephone to found the bureau to study the problems of the deaf.

■ **7** At 1500 35th Street NW is the **Georgetown Visitation Preparatory School and Monastery (Convent)**, the first Catholic school for girls in the original thirteen colonies. The white Gothic revival chapel was designed by a French chaplain and built in 1821. The corner red brick building on 35th Street was built in the 1830s, and the part facing P Street was built in the 1850s. The Academy Building, designed by Norris G. Starkweather and built in 1873, has Italianate features and a mansard roof. Notice the hood moldings around the tall windows and the elaborate molding over the front door. Much of the school burned down in early 2000 but has been nicely rebuilt. Here, you can turn right on Volta Place (no street signs are visible here, so it might get confusing—please refer to the map often) or take a short detour several blocks north on 35th Street to walk past the Cloisters, a residential development between Winfield Street and Reservoir Road. Built in the early 1980s, the row houses were designed to blend into Georgetown's brick vernacular architecture. At 35th and Reservoir is **Duke Ellington High School** (originally Western High School). Built in 1898 in classical-revival style, it is now a city-wide school for the arts. Theater groups for public performances use its modern theater, designed by Cox Graae + Spack Architects. Proceed back down to Volta Place for the next stop on the tour.

■ **8 Pomander Walk** (1885), on Volta Place between 33rd and 34th Streets. Once in sorry disrepair and called "Bedlam, DC," these ten small houses, first restored in 1950, are now choice places to live.

■ **9** Across the street on Volta Place, you will pass the **Volta Playground**. Its tennis courts, playground, and pool are actively used by nearby residents.

3230–16 Volta Place NW

■ **10** At **3230–16 Volta Place NW** you will see a former police station converted by Robert Bell Architects into an attractive residential enclave, with a rear communal courtyard. Turn right on Wisconsin Avenue, walking past the Georgetown Club at no. 1530. Its facade dates from the late 1790s. President Reagan dined here the night before he was shot and on his first night out after recovery. Turn west on P Street.

■ **11** The **Hyde-Addison Elementary School** project represents a campus modernization to current DC Public Schools standards in a historic urban neighborhood. It involved the renovation of a seventy-thousand-square-foot existing historic facility and an addition of almost thirty-thousand-square-feet of new space to the complex. The addition blends perfectly into historic Georgetown, while standing out as a distinguished contemporary building on its own.

■ **12** At **3264 P Street NW** you will see a surprisingly simple pink and tan frame house set in a country garden.

■ **13** At **1430 33rd Street NW**, the lovely yellow house on the southwest corner of 33rd and P was built in 1807 on the site of the oldest house in Georgetown, built in 1733. Turn left on 33rd Street.

■ **14** At **1316 33rd Street NW** is an unusual, former carriage house that combines Tudor-revival architecture in the back with its half-timbering, and Gothic-revival stained-glass windows in the front.

■ **15** You may have noticed that many of the mid-nineteenth-century houses in Georgetown retain on their facades **fire marks**, labels of the various fire assurance companies, which showed that the homeowner had sound credit with the company. Until 1871, volunteer firefighters served the community. Notice the symbols at **1312 and 1310 33rd Street NW**, for example.

■ **16** N Street, between 33rd and Potomac Streets, has a row of **six Federal houses** built by Walter and Clement Smith in 1815 that have remained essentially unchanged. Notice the wrought-iron stairway and graceful fan light over the door at no. 3259 and the Flemish bond pattern of the bricks (laid in alternating headers and stretchers).

■ **17 3307 N Street NW** (1811). John F. Kennedy and his wife lived here at the time he was elected president. William Marbury built this Federal house.

Cox's Row

■ **18 3327–39 N Street NW**. This group of five houses, known as **Cox's Row**, named after the owner-builder, a former mayor of Georgetown, was built in 1817. The handsome doorways, dormers, and garland decorations on the facade are characteristics of the Federal period.

■ **19 Wormley Row**, 3325 Prospect Street NW (Cunningham | Quill Architects). The Wormley School for the Colored was founded in 1885 by hotelier James Wormley, one of Washington, DC's first prominent African American businessmen. The school remained segregated until 1952 and was operated as a DC public school until 1994. The building was abandoned for ten years. In 2005, Encore Development purchased the property and hired Cunningham | Quill to spearhead design efforts, converting the existing school building into condominiums and constructing a new row of townhouses on the adjacent former schoolyard.

The original building contains seven new condominiums, and six new townhouses continue the rhythm of residences along Prospect Street.

■ **20 Halcyon House**, 3400 Prospect Street NW, was built in 1787 by Benjamin Stoddert, the first secretary of the Navy and a Revolutionary War hero. He

3334 N Street NW

modeled the Georgian design of the house after the elegant residential structures he had seen in Philadelphia while serving as secretary of the Revolutionary War Board from 1779 to 1781. In 1783 Stoddert became a partner in the prosperous Georgetown shipping firm of Forrest, Stoddert and Murdock. He acted as President Washington's confidential agent during the early negotiations for the establishment of the District of Columbia, and his home was the scene of frequent informal conferences important to the shaping of national as well as local history.

■ **21 3425 Prospect Street NW**. This handsome house is known as **Quality Hill** and was built in 1798 by a general in the Revolutionary War. Sen. Claiborne Pell lived here for many years.

■ **22 Prospect House**, 3508 Prospect Street NW. Erected in 1788, this house in the late 1940s was the home of James V. Forrestal, the first secretary of defense. The first two owners were friends of George Washington.

■ **23** At 37th and N Streets, the **Lauinger Memorial Library**, Georgetown University, was the subject of prolonged debate among the Fine Arts Commission, the Citizens Association of Georgetown, the National Capital Planning Commission, the university, and others. Designed by John Carl Warnecke & Associates, it was completed in 1970.

■ **24** A **housing complex** for 360 students on the right side of 37th Street, taking a half block between N and O, was designed by the internationally known architect Hugh Newell Jacobsen, a Georgetown resident. The U-shaped dormitory grouping surrounding an interior park resembles small townhouses, each with its own entrance. By following the natural slope and including English basements, the architect was able to maintain the scale and character of the nearby small residential buildings.

■ **25** At 37th and O Streets is the pedestrian entrance to **Georgetown University**, established in 1789 as Georgetown College. The university is the oldest Catholic and Jesuit institution of higher education in the United States. Straight ahead is the impressive Healy Hall, built in 1879 in the Flemish Romanesque style and designed by Smithmeyer and Pelz, who also designed the Library of Congress. Its central clock spire can be seen from many places around the city. Inside, Gaston Hall hosts concerts and lectures open to the public. Behind Healy Hall is Old North, which dates from 1795. Notice the mix of contemporary and traditional architecture on the campus.

■ **26** The **Georgetown Car Barn**, designed by noted Washington architect Waddy Butler Wood, was constructed between 1895 and 1897 as one of the first terminals of its kind not only in Washington, DC, but also in the country. As a "union" station serving four streetcar lines operating through DC, Maryland, and Virginia, the Car Barn represents a significant and dramatic shift from independent streetcar operations to a new paradigm of cooperation among private owners of public transportation concerns in the greater-Washington area. A pedestrian stairway located adjacent to the Car Barn was made famous for its association with the 1973 film *The Exorcist* and forms the oldest and best-known pedestrian link in the District.

The Car Barn is an excellent example of Romanesque revival architecture.

■ **27** Walk up O Street, turning right on 36th Street, where you will see the **Holy Trinity Church**, where President Kennedy worshiped. The church was originally built in 1851 and restored in 1979. The original church to the rear, entered at 3513 N Street NW, was dedicated in 1792 and remains the oldest standing church in the District of Columbia.

■ **28** Across 36th Street the **mix of shops and restaurants** is convenient for residents and students. Evening extension courses are offered to the community in classroom buildings on 36th Street. The 1789 Restaurant is a favorite watering hole for Georgetown students in the basement bar called the Tombs.

■ **29** At Prospect, walk to 35th Street. You are sure to see the high-rises of Rosslyn, Virginia, across the Potomac River. Without historic district protection, the character of Georgetown might have been threatened or destroyed by the intense development pressures that shaped Rosslyn. Just a few short steps from here is the steep staircase to M Street where *The Exorcist* was filmed. The **"Old Georgetown Falls Street,"** 35th Street from Prospect to

M Streets, has cobblestone paving. Its topography is similar to that of a San Francisco street.

■ **30** Notice across M Street the **Francis Scott Key Park** near the Key Bridge to Virginia. Francis Scott Key, author of the "The Star-Spangled Banner," was a resident of Georgetown for many years. His house (now torn down) overlooked the river at 3516–18 M Street NW.

At this point, you may wish to stop for a snack on M Street, continue another day, or continue along M Street and down to the waterfront.

■ **31** The **Market House** at 3276 M Street NW was restored in the late 1970s by Clark, Tribble, Harris & Li. Originally it was built as a public market in 1864 and used for that purpose.

■ **32** On M Street between the Market House and Wisconsin Avenue, where a tobacco warehouse once stood, is now **the Shops at Georgetown Park**. Part of the building that houses the shops was built in the 1800s; this historic site once accommodated horse-drawn omnibuses. Later it was used to service electric streetcars and trolleys. During the excavation process in transforming the site into its current Victorian-style, multilevel shopping center, archaeologists unearthed and cataloged thousands of artifacts that can be seen in the Georgetown Park Museum. The Georgetown Park mall was designed by Alan Lockman & Associates. The first part opened in 1981. It is an intriguing preservation project, which retains the exterior facades and scale of nineteenth-century buildings. The development includes apartments above the stores. As of this writing, the mall was expected to undergo substantial redevelopment.

Georgetown Park

33 Turn south on Wisconsin Avenue and cross the C&O Canal. Pause on the bridge in summer and you may see one of the mule-drawn barges, operated for tourists by the National Park Service, on the canal's towpath.

You may proceed down Wisconsin Avenue to the next sight, or you may want to wander a little around this area, taking a look down Cecil Place to Cherry Hill Lane, where you will find a group of well-restored townhouses. Across Cecil Place is the Peppermill, a large residential project that combines rehabilitation with newly constructed "mews houses"—and this is worth a look, too.

34 1055 High, 1055 Wisconsin Avenue NW (Beyer Blinder Belle Architects and Planners), is a luxury residential building located in the heart of the Georgetown National Historic District at the confluence of Wisconsin Avenue and the C&O Canal National Historic Trail. This seven-unit, fifty-thousand-square-foot building inhabits a site that was formerly a parking lot and remnant of the industrial era of the canal towpath and adjacent Potomac River. Today, this compelling building, built in 2014, provides a seamless transition in the urban fabric between old and new, historic and contemporary. The four-story building completes the canal edge and frames the forecourt of Grace Church, creating a beautiful urban space along Wisconsin Avenue.

The building's massing, articulation, and materiality directly respond to its historic context. The use of stone, steel, and brick evoke the former industrial character of the adjacent riverfront warehouses and rustic stone canal locks and walls. Similarly, its massing responds to Federal-style brick row houses to the north and the historic 1867 Gothic stone church to the south.

35 Walk down Wisconsin Avenue toward the river. On your left, you will notice **Grace Church**, set back from the street on its raised courtyard. Built about 1866 in the Gothic-revival style, it originally served as a mission church for boatmen plying the C&O Canal.

36 Waterfront Center. Near the corner of Wisconsin Avenue and K (Water) Street is the Waterfront Center, a ninety-foot-high office/retail building, designed by Hartman-Cox Architects. The rebuilding of the waterfront area has been the subject of bitter debate about height, density, and uses for several decades. The permit for this structure was obtained before new zoning took effect and reflects what the old industrial zoning would allow. Integral to its design is the preservation of the **Old Dodge Warehouse Company Buildings** (about 1813).

37 Whitehurst Freeway. The elevated Whitehurst Freeway, constructed in 1949 over K Street along the Potomac River, has been a cause for debate within the community for the past thirty years. When it was built, to relieve congestion on M Street and to serve as a commuter bypass, the waterfront area was

Waterfront Center

industrial, with a lumberyard, sand and gravel operation, a flour mill, and a rendering plant, as well as a rail line used to haul coal. As these activities disappeared and the waterfront began to be redeveloped, the freeway was seen by many as a visual barrier to the river. In the late 1980s, the District government studied alternatives to the elevated structure, including a ground-level parkway that would improve its relationship with its surroundings. The District government spent $48 million to rehabilitate the elevated freeway. The National Park Service developed a park with shade trees along the waterfront.

■ **38** The **Old Georgetown Incinerator** (about 1930) is a four-story art deco industrial structure with a towering smokestack. It sits on an acre of land that has been developed into a movie-theater complex, residential condominiums, and an eighty-six-room Ritz Carlton Hotel. A plaque on the side attests to its history. Suter's Tavern is believed to have stood here from 1783 to 1795. On March 30, 1791, George Washington is said to have met neighboring landowners in Suter's Tavern and negotiated the purchase of lands required for the Federal City, later called Washington. Pierre Charles L'Enfant, who reputedly completed the original plan for the capital city there in 1791, also used Suter's Tavern.

■ **39** Across K Street, between 31st and 29th Streets, is the **Washington Harbour**, a 1-million-square-foot office and residential development designed by Arthur Cotton Moore/Associates. The development includes a new east–west pedestrian boardwalk at the river's edge, as well as an adjacent small riverside park—public amenities that the city required the developer to provide. The design allows the river to be seen from all entrances, as well as from the restaurants and cafes that line the plaza. Although the scale and design of the major structures have been controversial, the plaza and boardwalk have created a lively public space that welcomes strollers, bikers, boaters, residents, workers, sunbathers, and restaurant patrons. To protect against flooding, a state-of-the-art system of adjustable floodgates around the project has eliminated the need for permanent barriers.

40 New red brick offices and residences: Leaving Washington Harbour through the main entrance, cross K Street and walk along (or through the courtyard of) **Jefferson Court**, 1025 Thomas Jefferson Street NW, an office building designed by Skidmore, Owings & Merrill and completed in 1984. It can be entered on Thomas Jefferson, K, and 30th Streets. As you walk up 30th Street, notice recent red brick residential developments at **1001 and 1111 30th Street NW (James Place)**.

41 1055 Thomas Jefferson Street NW. Designed by Arthur Cotton Moore, the **Foundry** combines its new red brick construction with the preservation and adaptation of a landmark structure (an old foundry) and is oriented to the C&O Canal. The landscaped areas on both sides of the canal, maintained by the National Park Service, offer pleasant sites for summer concerts and the terminal for canal boat tours.

42 1058 Thomas Jefferson Street NW. The current office use is an example of the continuing uses of old structures for changing purposes over a period of time. This little structure was built originally as a Masonic Hall in about 1810. Between Thomas Jefferson and 31st Streets, along the canal's towpath, is a **group of small houses** built on speculation in 1870. Artisans and workers originally used them. Since that time, they have been converted into shops, offices, and residences.

43 **Canal Square**, 1054 31st Street NW, is an innovative office and specialty shop complex that successfully incorporates some old warehouses along the C&O Canal into the project and is built around an inner court. It was designed by Arthur Cotton Moore and completed in 1971. Leave the complex and head for 31st Street, turn into the small courtyard, and then go up through the stairs into the alley ahead. Then turn east and notice Blues Alley on your left as you leave the alley. Blues Alley is a long-established place to hear fine jazz. Back on M Street, you can take any bus on the 32 or 36 routes to the George Washington University Hospital stop and walk down 23rd Street to the Foggy Bottom Metro station at I Street NW.

Georgetown—East

(Historic residential district, specialty shops, restaurants, C&O Canal)

James Troy, updated by Ralph Cunningham

Distance: 2 miles
Time: 1 hour
Bus: 31, 33, 38B, D2, D6, G2, and the DC Circulator
Metro: Foggy Bottom/GWU (Blue, Orange, and Silver Lines)

Start your tour on M Street, just west of the M Street Bridge over Rock Creek Park. This point corresponds to one of the eastern entrances to Georgetown. Take the Metrorail to the Foggy Bottom/GWU stop and walk west to M Street NW.

■ **1** On your right is a **mixed-used complex** that was created out of the old Corcoran School (facing 28th Street) and its former playground. The project, designed by Arthur Cotton Moore, is intended to reflect its gateway location by siting a four-story building (2715 M Street NW) containing a pointed tower at its east end and making a connection, by means of a three-story wing, with the smaller-scale existing structures on the west. The building contains retail and office space along M Street and apartments in the rear, looking into the courtyard. The carefully restored **Corcoran School Building** (now containing offices) and five townhouses complete this small-scale but interesting project.

2 Across M Street between 28th and 29th Streets is the **Four Seasons Hotel and office complex**, designed by the Washington office of Skidmore, Owings & Merrill. The rectangular brick structure includes hotel, office, and retail space. This contemporary building also celebrates its gateway location with a dramatic clock tower rising from its midst and facing Pennsylvania Avenue. The building wraps around the nineteenth-century row of shops at the corner of 29th Street known as Diamond Row, and its back doors connect to the C&O Canal and its towpath.

3 On the northern side of the intersection of 29th and M Streets are two successful infill office buildings. The **Embassy of Mongolia** is located on the east at 2833 M Street NW. Across the street, the whimsical Wells Fargo Bank, designed by Martin and Jones and built in 1981, is a good example of postmodern contextual architecture. Its multipaned windows with their round tops are similar to those on the building across 29th Street; its classical columns relate to the decorative columns of the art deco drug store next door to the east.

4 **2806, 2808, and 2812 N Street NW** make one of the most outstanding groups of fine Federal architecture in the Georgetown area. They were all built between about 1813 and 1817. Nos. 2806 and 2808 are almost identical, except that they are opposite handed. No. 2812 is larger and has symmetry. It is referred to as the Decatur House because it is said that Commodore Stephen Decatur's widow lived here after his death.

5 **1350 27th Street NW**, built in 1968, was designed by Hugh Newell Jacobsen. The house represents an excellent alternative to the "fake Federal" style found elsewhere throughout Georgetown as new infill houses were added in the 1950s and 1960s. Its scale and materials fit in well with the Victorian neighborhood.

6 **1411–19 27th Street NW.** These townhouses were built in 1954 after a revision to the zoning regulations required off-street parking at the rate of one parking space for each dwelling unit. Although parking space is required to be shown on building plans and the buildings then built accordingly, it is not ultimately required to be used for that purpose. (Note the subsequent conversions of the garages to other uses.)

2806 N Street NW: The Gannt-Williams House

■ **7** Across Q Street and located down an extension of 27th Street is **Mount Zion Cemetery**, a site rich in local history. For the burial of its members, both white and Black, the Dumbarton Street Methodist Church acquired the eastern half of the cemetery in 1808, although in 1816 the Black members of Dumbarton Church withdrew to form the Mount Zion AME Church (located at 1334 29th Street NW). The western half of the cemetery was purchased in 1842 by the Female Band Society, a cooperative benevolent society of free Black women, for the burial of free Blacks. With the opening of Oak Hill Cemetery in 1849, however, white members of Dumbarton Church began to favor that newly fashionable "garden cemetery," and eventually they leased the eastern half of Mount Zion Cemetery to Mount Zion Church.

In 1975 the cemetery was designated a National Historic Landmark and was recommended for nomination to the National Register of Historic Places. Also fortunate for the cemetery's future maintenance was its inclusion in 1988 in a Black History National Recreation Trail directed by the National Park Service.

■ **8 Dumbarton House**, at 2715 Q Street NW, now the headquarters of the National Society of the Colonial Dames of America, was built between 1799 and 1804. Though described as Federal architecture on the plaque set into the mansion's wall, it has decidedly Georgian characteristics (the central pedimented pavilion, which projects very slightly, and the keystone lintels). It was moved from its original location on what is now Q Street to its present location in 1915. The Dumbarton House is open Friday through

Sunday, 10:00 a.m.–3:00 p.m. The last admission to the museum is at 2:45 p.m. Admission is $10 for adults and free for children, youth, and students with ID. More information can be found at www.dumbartonhouse.org or by calling 202-337-2288.

■ **9 Mother & Child,** at 2727 Q Street NW (Cunningham | Quill Architects). This three-story brick residence is one of the earliest examples of the Colonial revival style in Washington, DC. Once a part of the adjacent Evermay estate, the three-story Colonial-revival residence was built in 1893 and renovated in 1900 and 1961.

The house is a thirty-eight-foot cube in plan and elevation, forming the basis for the twenty-five-foot cube brick and glass pavilion in the rear. The project restores the original design by returning the main entry to the front of the house and reestablishing the formal sequence of rooms back to a central hall, large living room, and grand staircase. The addition provides a modern, yet contextual, garden pavilion in the rear.

■ **10** At 2813 Q Street NW is a Victorian house that was redone and doubled in size by Hugh Jacobsen in 1959. It was one of the first attempts in Georgetown to renovate in a manner that combines contemporary ideas and materials with more traditional themes.

■ **11** Evermay, at 1623 28th Street NW, is one of the showplaces of Georgetown. It was built between 1792 and 1794, greatly modified over the years, and finally carefully restored to its original Georgian splendor. The original owner purchased the ground for this building with money he made from proceeds of sale of the land where the White House and Lafayette Square now stand.

■ **12** Inside Oak Hill Cemetery, at 29th and R Streets, stands the **Oak Hill Chapel**, designed by James Renwick. It was erected in 1850 and is one of only four structures designed by Renwick still standing in the District. This strong and dignified little Gothic revival building is based on much earlier rural English chapels of the thirteenth and fourteenth centuries, though the materials used were acquired locally: Potomac gneiss and red Seneca sandstone. The cemetery is approached through the handsome gates next to its fanciful gatehouse (1849). The cemetery's office and grounds are open 9:00 a.m.–4:30 p.m., Monday through Friday, and 1:00–4:00 p.m. on Sunday, weather permitting. The cemetery is closed on Saturdays and national holidays.

■ **13** Across the street at **2920 R Street NW** is the former home of the late Katharine Meyer Graham, the chairman of the board of the Washington Post Company.

■ **14 Dumbarton Oaks,** at R and 31st Streets, is worth an afternoon's visit all by itself. This magnificent, sixteen-acre estate is now owned by Harvard University but reflects the generosity and interests of its original benefactors,

Park Hill Chapel

Robert and Mildred Bliss. If you visit at the right time of the year, you can see extensive gardens by Beatrix Ferrand, ranging from a formal pebble mosaic pool to a romantic rustic pool shaded by lindens. Pre-Columbian works of art are now housed in a handsome museum designed by Philip Johnson. It is reached from the 32nd Street side of the property. Not to be overlooked is the great Georgian mansion, which was the original house at the Oaks and was built in 1801. Information about admission fees and hours of operation can be found at www.doaks.org or by calling 202-339-6401.

■ **15** The **Scott-Grant House**, at 3238 R Street NW, was built in 1858 and was once occupied by President Ulysses S. Grant as a summer White House. The property, quite large for Georgetown, has had some additional houses built on it, though the original mansion still has an appropriate setting.

■ **16** **Tudor Place**, which has its main entrance at 1644 31st Street NW, occupies nearly the entire large block created by Q, R, 31st, and 32nd Streets. It was built in 1815 and was designed by William Thornton, the winner of the original competition for the design of the US Capitol. This important building, its style unique in Georgetown, provides an interesting contrast between its severe Federal north facade and its south facade, with its generous and finely detailed windows and its classical, domed two-story Greek temple. Quite remarkably, this great house, until 1983, housed only one family, descending from Thomas Peter and his bride, a granddaughter of Martha Washington. Information about admission fees and hours of operation can be found at www.tudorplace .org or by calling 202-965-0400.

■ **17 Cooke's Row** consists of four double detached houses (3007–29 Q Street NW) built in 1868. These basically Victorian structures appear to derive from the design for an Italian villa, though their heavier sculptural effect and prominent mansard roofs (on the two end buildings) reflect a Second Empire French influence. The houses, set back from the street in little green parks and separate from each other, create a pleasant precinct that is unlike most of Georgetown.

■ **18** The house at **1527 30th Street NW** is one of two Italianate villas designed by Andrew Jackson Downing and Calvert Vaux in the 1850s. (The second villa, greatly altered, is located at 28th and Q Streets.) The house at 1527 30th Street NW (which has now been converted into condominiums) has been extensively added to on the south along 30th Street and on the east along Q Street. The original building at no. 1527, however, retains much of the flat-walled and asymmetrical massing of an Italianate villa.

1527 30th Street NW

■ **19** The central portion of the large house at **3014 N Street NW** was built in 1799, though obvious additions were added later. It is notable for its nicely detailed round-top windows on the first floor, and for that reason is thought to be the work of William Thornton. In 1915 it was acquired by Abraham Lincoln's son, Robert Todd Lincoln, who served as secretary of war and ambassador to England.

■ **20** The house at **3017 N Street NW** was acquired by Jacqueline Kennedy after the assassination of her husband in 1963. She didn't stay there very long, however, since hordes of sightseers caused her to complain of the invasion of her privacy. She subsequently moved to a high-rise apartment building in New York.

■ **21** The fine old Federal house at **3038 N Street NW** was built in 1816 and was occupied by W. Averell Harriman up to his death. It has typical Federal details: bull's-eye lintels over the windows and a modest but finely detailed fanlight over the door.

■ **22** Though the building at **1221 31st Street NW** now houses the Georgetown branch of the US Postal Service, this Renaissance-revival building, designed in the manner of an Italian palace, was originally a customs house for the bustling port of Georgetown. It was designed by Ammi B. Young and constructed in 1857–58.

■ **23** The **Old Stone House**, at 3051 M Street NW, is believed to date back to about 1766. In any event, it is generally accepted as the oldest unchanged building in the District of Columbia and is now the property of the National Park Service, which maintains it as a public museum. The ample grounds to the right and behind the house contain beautiful gardens and attract, in their own right, weary tourists and local office workers at lunchtime.

3001–3009 M Street NW

■ **24** The row of four houses at **3001–3009 M Street NW** (now with retail space on the ground floor) show the common three-bay facade typical of the Federal period. The two houses on the right are dated about 1790, the two on the left a little later. The group was carefully restored in 1955.

You are now in the heart of the retail section of Georgetown, so you may want to finish your tour at a local bar or step into any of the nearby specialty shops along M Street and Wisconsin Avenue.

About the Authors and Contributors

The following individuals contributed to this edition of Washington on Foot.

Sally Berk is a native Washingtonian who has lived in Sheridan-Kalorama for more than four decades. With an undergraduate degree in architecture and a graduate degree in historic preservation, she has been a preservation activist for the same four decades, volunteering with the DC Preservation League—for which she served as president—and the Committee of 100 on the Federal City.

José Castellanos is the marketing coordinator for Bonstra | Haresign Architects in Washington, DC. After diverse career beginnings in graphic design and hospitality, José received his master's in marketing from American University in 2021. He credits his international upbringing in several different countries for his love of architecture. José resides in Rockville, Maryland, with his family.

Ralph Cunningham, FAIA, is a native Washingtonian. He received his master of architecture degree from Columbia University, and is founding principal of Cunningham/Quill Architects, located in Georgetown, Washington DC.

Megan Davey is an architectural designer with a master's in architecture from the Catholic University of America. After researching Union Market as part of her graduate thesis, she is honored to contribute to the neighborhood's corresponding walking tour.

John DeFerrari was born and raised in Washington, DC, and is a trustee of the DC Preservation League. His latest book on DC history, coauthored with Peter Sefton, is *Sixteenth Street NW: Washington, DC's Avenue of Ambitions* (2022).

Edwin Fountain is general counsel of the American Battle Monuments Commission. As vice chair of the World War I Centennial Commission, he led the development of the National World War I Memorial featured in this book.

Executive Director of the DC History Center, **Laura Brower Hagood** has twenty years of experience as a nonprofit leader in Washington. She held development, communications, and audience-building roles at the National Building Museum and Cultural Tourism DC, known for its neighborhood heritage programs.

Christopher J. Howard is a practitioner and full-time professor at the Catholic University of America within the classical traditional concentration. Some of his research includes the documentation of heritage architecture in the Washington, DC, area, with a particular focus on Monuments and Memorials. He is the principal at his own firm, CJ Howard Architecture, LLC, where he is involved with historic restoration, monument, church, and urban design projects.

Frank Leone, a licensed DC attorney and tour guide is the cochair of the Foggy Bottom Association History Project, and author of its Funktown blog (https://www.foggybottomassociation.org/funkstown). He is active with the DC History Center and DC Preservation League and resides in the Foggy Bottom Historic District.

Andy Merlo, AIA, is an associate with Mushinsky Voelzke Associates. A graduate of Penn State, he has fifteen years of experience on mixed-use projects throughout the city. He serves as vice president of the Tiber Island Cooperative in Southwest.

Stephen O. Santos is a native Washingtonian and Project Designer at GTM Architects in Bethesda, Maryland, specializing in custom single-family residential architecture.

He holds a bachelor of science degree in architecture and a master of architecture with a concentration in real estate development.

Peter Sefton came to Washington to attend George Washington University and considers the area his adoptive home. His latest book, coauthored with John DeFerrari, is *Sixteenth Street NW: Washington, DC's Avenue of Ambitions* (2022).

Jim Voelzke, FAIA, LEED AP, is a pioneer and continues to lead a paradigm shift in the design of community-based, urban-mixed developments in Washington, DC. Jim received his bachelor of architecture degree from the Catholic University of America.

Denise Vogt lives in the row house in the Foggy Bottom Historic District that her parents occupied for over thirty years. She is a Foggy Bottom Association Board member, cochair of its History Project (https://www.foggybottomassociation.org/history-project), and a DC History Center Community Council representative.

The following individuals contributed to previous editions of Washington on Foot. *Their contributions range from writing and expanding, to rewriting and updating.*

Chris Alleva, Sharon Augustyn, Maybelle Taylor Bennett, Lin Brown, Pierre Paul Childs, Robert H. Cousins, Charity Vanderbilt Davidson, Paul Douglass, John Fondersmith, Peter Fuchs, Suzanne Ganschinietz, Anthony Hacsi, Susan Harlem, Ryan Harris, Dan Hessman, Alan A. Hodges, Carol Hodges, Marilyn (Mickey) Klein, Antoinette J. Lee, Alvin R. McNeal, Julia Pastor, Ruth Polan, Frederic Protopappas, John J. Protopappas, Stephanie Protopappas, Carol Truppi, Berry Steeves, Charles Szoradi, William Washburn, Lindsley Williams, James L. Wilson, and Kathleen Sinclair Wood.

Many artists have contributed to the artwork included in *Washington on Foot,* most notably Brian Barth, José Castellanos, Fred Greenberg, Coleman McLaurin, Reena Racki, Leo Schmittel, Ayse Elif Ozkan, Priyashi Galiawala, Prova Zaman-Haque, and Gelila Yoseph.